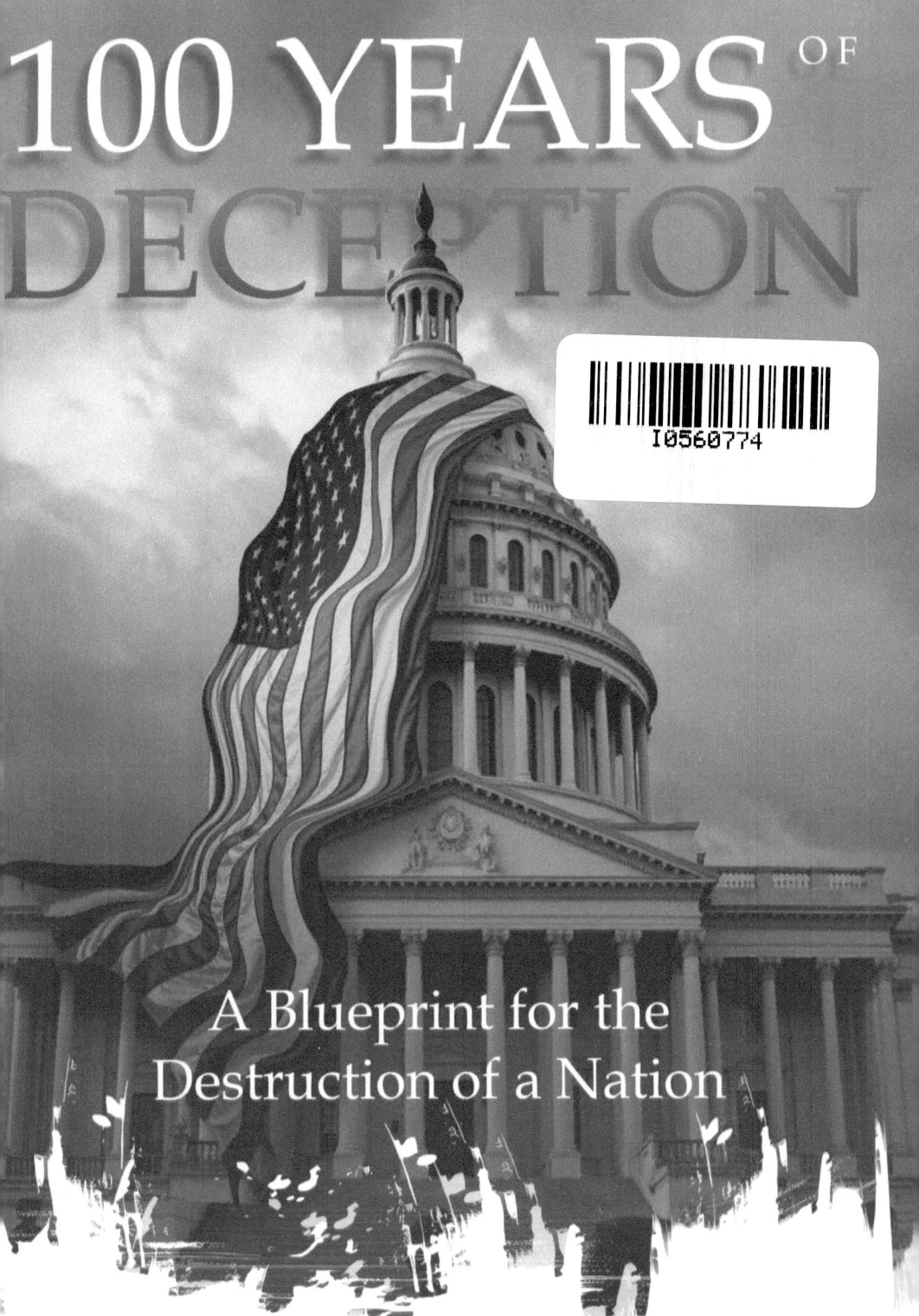

100 YEARS OF DECEPTION

A Blueprint for the
Destruction of a Nation

ALAN R. ADASCHIK

100 YEARS OF DECEPTION

A BLUEPRINT FOR THE DESTRUCTION OF A NATION

ALAN R. ADASCHIK

ISBN: 978-1-967375-72-1 (Paperback)
ISBN: 978-1-967375-73-8 (E-book)

Library of Congress Control Number: 2025917504

Printed in the United States of America

Published by:

info@thequippyquill.com
(302) 295-2278

DEDICATION

This book is dedicated to my father, Anthony, who left us for a better world on March 10, 2013, at the age of ninety-seven. Without his support and guidance, I would not be the person I am today. My loss is shared by all who knew him. He truly was a man of compassion, substance, and integrity. The world we live in has been diminished by his passing.

CONTENTS

INTRODUCTION

What if our government had been overthrown at the start of this past century? Surely, this question is absurd! If our government had been overthrown, wouldn't people know this? Furthermore, if people are not aware of an overthrow, how bad could it have been? This last question is not so absurd because not only do the vast majority of Americans have no clue our government was overthrown, but they also have no comprehension of the insane and exorbitant price we have paid as a result. Americans living today go about their lives oblivious to what has been done to us. They are content to live in denial because it is the easiest thing to do and because they prefer to feel good about our national government, irrespective of what it has done. To most Americans, the notion of our government having been overthrown is the fodder of conspiracy nuts or the province of people out of touch with reality.

This book will demonstrate that an overthrow of our government has occurred. It will also provide an accounting of the catastrophic consequences resulting from this overthrow. Among these are the senseless and needless squandering of trillions of dollars of money and resources, as well as destroying and ending the lives of hundreds of millions of people. Furthermore, the rule of law, justice under the law, and the inalienable rights of mankind are casualties of this overthrow. Indeed, the insanity that took control of our government in 1913 is presently enslaving the rest of the world. However, this is not the worst of it. The final result of what these amoral people have wrought is that life as we know it on this planet is at risk. Unless we wake up soon, the future is going to be a living hell for our progeny. We all share a measure of blame for this. Because of our ignorance and complacency, those who rule us are firmly entrenched within the power structures of the world. Thus, there is no end in sight to the waste, suffering, and madness they bring upon us.

Our government, the one we lost, was special and something to be proud of. For the first time in history, a group of men came

1

together, put their personal interests aside, and established a new government designed to best serve and protect all those fortunate enough to live under it. The government created by the founders embodied the loftiest of governing principles, and because of these principles, the United States of America became the greatest nation in all of history. Not only did our citizens enjoy the highest standard of living in the world, but we also opened our doors to others and became a beacon for the oppressed and downtrodden of other nations. Our government exemplified an ideal, and it was for this ideal that so many Americans made the ultimate sacrifice. Unfortunately, to our shame and dishonor, these sacrifices were made in vain.

America once truly was a land of freedom and opportunity. However, without our knowledge, everything changed upon the passage of the Federal Reserve Act in 1913. These changes were extensive in regard to how our government functioned, yet from a citizen's point of view, nothing major or important happened. This was no accident! Instead, it was an important aspect of their plan. The changes Americans would experience came slowly at first, so nobody noticed or became alarmed. Eventually, Americans were put on the roller-coaster ride we live with today. Almost all Americans know something is terribly wrong with our ship of state, but most of us have no idea what is wrong or how it can be fixed. As a result, we sit back and watch helplessly as the American dream crumbles and dies around us.

If this book achieves its intended purpose, it will leave you troubled and frightened because what you are about to read belies everything you have been taught or want to believe. Despite this, you owe it to yourself and everyone else to fight the impulse to reject this information out of hand. As a responsible citizen, you should strive to see our world and nation as it really is. As previously stated, there is something very wrong with our government. However, television, the news media, and entertainment industries posture that all is well and there is nothing happening that should be of concern. The fact that there is a contradiction between what we know and what we are being told should be of grave concern. The implications are that there is a lot going on in our government wants to keep hidden from us.

If you are a true American, you understand you have a responsibility to seek and stand up for the truth. This is why I wrote this book. During my life, I walked a path that brought me to where I am today. As a citizen, I cannot sit back and let what I have learned remain hidden. However, there is a risk in standing up for what I believe. This book will not be well received by those in positions of authority. Many people who read it will question my credibility, motives, and sanity. Worse than this, I run the risk of being labeled an atheist and anti-Semite, both of which couldn't be further from the truth. Among my detractors will be those who willingly shoot the messenger. They believe that if a revelation is too terrible to contemplate, then the problem lies with the messenger, who should be discredited and shouted down. However, this is a risk I have to take. I believe fear should never decide a person's course of action, and being a Navy veteran, I have sworn an oath to preserve and defend our Constitution.

This is a book about momentous events that have occurred over the past one hundred years. For each occurrence, there are a number of explanations for what happened. However, most people accept the official explanations at face value and automatically assume that what our government tells us is true. Furthermore, once an official explanation is accepted, alternatives become conspiracy theories, which lie within the realm of malcontents and screwballs. Under such circumstances, we refrain from asking government officials to prove what they say. In contrast, we demand this from everyone else. By reading this book, you will have an opportunity to learn the truth. By doing so, you will realize our government's versions of most major events are fabrications. The intent of these fabrications is to make us feel good and let responsible parties off the hook. If we feel good about something, we instinctively believe it is true. When this happens, our government has succeeded in keeping us ignorant and subjugated.

Be warned that what you are about to read is the mother of all conspiracy theories. I describe it this way because this book addresses what is behind the events that have shaped America and the world over the past one hundred years. More importantly, it makes sense out of what is happening to us now. A way of finding the truth is by focusing on what makes sense. When this becomes a habit, the events of our world weave together into a unified pattern, and the official explanations dissolve into a puddle like the Wicked Witch of the West in *The Wizard of Oz*.

CHAPTER 1:
The Overthrow of Our Government

The first event we will discuss is the granddaddy of them all, *the overthrow of our government*. Unlike other events in this book, this one will be demonstrated to be true. Of course, you are free to believe as you wish, but an overthrow did take place. Any intelligent person who is honest with himself will agree with this conclusion. People tend to hear what they want to hear and believe what they want to believe. To be sure, no American wants to believe we live in a nation ruled by conspirators who overthrew our government. However, wishful thinking is not a sound basis for what we believe. Understanding this, if you are going to profit from reading this book, you must give credence to the possibility that our government was overthrown and not dismiss any idea out of hand just because it is repugnant.

The United States of America is supposed to be a constitutional republic. This is easy to say, but what do these words mean? A *republic* is a form of government where all authority is exercised by the people through their elected representatives. A *constitutional republic* is a government where this state of affairs is formerly established by a written constitution. A *constitution* is an expression of the will of the people, and it defines the nature of the government they agree to live under. From a citizen's perspective, it is a contract between citizens that contains the laws and rules that control their agreed-upon government. The government in question had nothing to do with creating its constitution. Instead, it is a document created by citizens and imposed upon the government. The constitution, once established, is the wellspring of all other laws, rules, and regulations that govern a nation and its citizens.

Understanding all the above, it is obvious that the government bequeathed to us by the founders was a constitutional republic. The word *was* is used in this last sentence because it should also be obvious that this is no longer true. Our present government pays lip service to our Constitution and routinely ignores its most important provisions.[1] Furthermore, when government officials refer to this nation, they call us a *democracy* and never describe us as being a constitutional republic. This is not an oversight! Government officials know full well they no longer respect the provisions of our Constitution, so they call us a democracy, hoping that knowledge of our constitutional roots fades into oblivion. As citizens, we are no longer supposed to think *constitution*. Instead, we are continually reminded to think about *democracy*. This is done so that those who rule us will be free of our Constitution's constraints and limitations. With our Constitution neutered and forgotten, their goal has been realized.

If our government is no longer a constitutional republic, it is reasonable to conclude that somewhere along the way, a change took place. The key question is whether this change happened gradually over time or suddenly at one point in our history. The answer to this question is important. If our government changed gradually over time, it is reasonable to assume that nothing criminal or underhanded occurred. However, if the change occurred suddenly at one point in our history, then the implications are that the changes were the result of a plan. If a deliberate plan was behind how our government changed, and this plan was implemented without our knowledge or consent, then it follows that our government was overthrown. A hallmark of the American experiment in democracy is that our government rules by the consent of the governed. If major changes to how our government functions are made through stealth and subterfuge, then the government we are left with does not enjoy our consent and is not legitimate.

Unfortunately, the facts are clear. The evidence supports the conclusion that the government we have today is not the outcome of gradual changes that took place over time. Instead, it is the handiwork of a group of conspirators who met in secret to plot our government's demise. This was done so they would enjoy a government easier to control and better suited to their self-serving purposes. Who are these people? One name we call them is the Federal Reserve Bank or Fed, but they also call themselves the New World Order. This name is deceptive because the so-called New

World Order is really the *old-world order* with an upscale name. Whatever they call themselves, they are the rich and powerful old-line banking families who have pulled the strings that made the world dance through the centuries. Their plot was brought to fruition concurrent with the passage of the Federal Reserve Act in 1913. Most Americans think the Federal Reserve Act was a legitimate act of Congress. Nothing could be further from the truth.

In order to establish that our government was overthrown, four elements of this crime must be demonstrated to be true. These elements are as follows:

- identification of a group of conspirators
- establishment of the group's willful intent to commit the crime
- identification of actions taken to consummate the crime
- identification of what changed as a result of the actions taken

Before proceeding, it should be understood that the Federal Reserve Act is unconstitutional. Article 1, section 8 of our Constitution states that Congress shall have the power "to coin money and regulate the value thereof." This power is not so much a power but instead a responsibility of Congress. Nowhere in our Constitution is authority given to defer, subordinate, or transfer this responsibility to someone else, especially to a foreign banking cartel. The Federal Reserve Act is unconstitutional because it stands in flagrant violation of Article 1, Section 8 of our Constitution, but more so when one realizes the tremendous authority and power Congress wrongfully handed over to a group of private bankers. These men were voted the right to create our money with the stroke of a pen and then loan it back to us at interest. The problem is, upon doing so, the American people are on the hook to pay back the amount borrowed plus interest, with money not created out of thin air, but money earned through industry and hard work. What do Americans get for toiling to make these men rich beyond anyone's wildest dreams? Nothing! We get absolutely nothing but recessions, depressions, inflation, war, destruction, suffering, mayhem, and death!

At this point, it should be clear that we have identified our group of conspirators, and from this point forward we will call them

Banksters. This name works well because they are an international banking cartel that owns most of the central banks of the world. In any case, in 1910, representatives of these Banksters met secretly at Jekyll Island, Georgia,[1] to map out a strategy to hoodwink Congress into passing the Federal Reserve Act. This act of Congress made the Banksters' foreign banking cartel the Central Bank of the United States. As terrible and wrongful as this development is, taken at face value, it does not constitute a willful intent to commit a crime.

However, if one understands what really happened, the criminal nature of these doings becomes apparent. Mayer Amschel Rothschild, who was one of the most influential and powerful bankers of all time, said, "Permit me to issue and control the money of a nation and I care not who makes its laws." The legislative process, without question, is a prime function of government. If, as Mr. Rothschild explained, this prime function is trumped or overshadowed by those who issue and control money, then it follows that the Jekyll Island conspirators knew that by obtaining control of our money supply, they would also be taking control of our government.

It is one thing for a special interest group to induce Congress to pass legislation that will be of benefit to them. It is quite another thing to cajole, bribe, and hoodwink Congress into passing legislation that changes the nature and form of our government. Unfortunately, this is what happened. The Jekyll Island conspirators knew that passage of the Federal Reserve Act meant they would have the power to dominate and control our government. To argue, these men met in secret for some other purpose beneficial to the American people is ridiculous. Taking control in the manner and for the reasons they did was solely to their benefit and to the detriment of the American people. Thus, the conspirators' willful intent to commit a crime has been demonstrated.

In all likelihood, you are still not convinced that an overthrow of our government occurred. If all that happened in 1913 was the passage of the Federal Reserve Act, I would agree with you. However, the plot was far more extensive than the simple passage of an act of Congress. In 1913, Amendment XVI was also ratified.[3] The intent of this amendment was to create a new source of revenue by legalizing a tax on the wages earned by American workers. Prior to

1913, our government obtained all the money it needed from duties, tariffs, and other charges for services. A tax on the wages of working Americans is prohibited by article 1, section 9, clause 4, of our Constitution. This Clause provides that Congress cannot levy a direct tax on individual citizens. However, the Banksters knew that a new and significant revenue source would be needed to pay for the soon-to-be rapidly growing national debt. They also wanted to ensure that they owned a measure of every working American's time and labor. Therefore, they took steps to get this wrongful and misplaced power through the ratification of Amendment XVI. However, despite all their efforts and the strings they pulled to ensure its ratification, they never anticipated that the Supreme Court would throw a monkey wrench into their plans by ruling that Amendment XVI did not accomplish its intended purpose.

The Banksters believed the wording in Amendment XVI provided them with a new source of revenue: a direct tax on the earnings of every working American. However, in the case of *Stanton v. Baltic*,[4] the Supreme Court ruled that a tax on the income of working Americans was unconstitutional. This ruling applied to Amendment XVI, and as a result, a tax on the wages of working Americans remained unconstitutional. The Court reasoned that income referred only to returns from investments and profits realized by businesses. Wages paid to American workers, according to the Court, are not income. Instead, wages are a simple exchange of money for a person's time and labor. Such an exchange is akin to bartering or the exchange of things of equal value between people. No income is involved or derived from such an exchange. This ruling meant that the Banksters failed to constitutionally create the new revenue source they coveted. However, this setback presented no problem for them, and what happened next demonstrates that these doings are a step in a well-thought-out plan.

The Banksters simply ignored the Supreme Court ruling and implemented a tax on wages anyway, even though it was unconstitutional. Today, we dutifully pay our income taxes without realizing that paying them is not legally required. There is no basis for paying a tax on earnings under constitutional law. Taking this a step further, it can reasonably be argued that when our government insists, we obey the law and pay our income taxes, it is guilty of fraud.

Furthermore, if our government takes us to court and forces us to pay income taxes, it is guilty of robbery. If this state of affairs doesn't demonstrate the wrongful and misplaced power handed to the Banksters by Congress through the Federal Reserve Act, then nothing does. From 1913 forward, our newly created government was above the law and could ignore our Supreme Court when necessary. In case one fails to see the significance of this, it means that our Supreme Court is no longer supreme.

Amendment XVII[5] was also added to our Constitution in 1913, and this amendment provided for the direct election of senators by citizens instead of being appointed by state legislators as the founders intended. The Founding Fathers must have made a mistake when they decided on this matter. Amendment XVII is a wonderful step forward for democracy. Upon ratification, *we the people* had the right to vote for all our representatives in Congress instead of just those in the House of Representatives. Unfortunately, while this development appears to be beneficial, nothing is further from the truth. Instead, ratification of Amendment XVII was a diabolical step that completed the ignoble transformation of our government.

Prior to the ratification of Amendment XVII, the federal government was a federation of state governments. In keeping with this, the states exercised control over the federal government by appointing two representatives to the United States Senate. The Senate is the superior arm of Congress and serves as a check on the powers of the President. By changing this arrangement, the Banksters eliminated a crucial check and balance of our Constitution. However, far worse is that this also changed the fundamental nature of our government. Upon ratification of Amendment XVII, our federal government was no longer a federation of states answerable to the state legislatures. Instead, it became an all-powerful national government superior to and dominant over our state governments.

At this point, we have identified three major changes, all of which occurred in 1913, and were specifically designed to change the nature and form of our government. Furthermore, when these changes were implemented, most people had no clue as to what they really entailed. In other words, the nation was hoodwinked into accepting these changes. This is not the way such things are supposed to be done. Informed consent means that we the people are apprised of the implications or end results of what our government is trying to accomplish through legislation or the amendment process. In 1913, neither our government nor the media informed us about what was really being done to us.

To summarize, the Federal Reserve Act gave the Banksters control of our monetary system. This gave them enormous wealth, which enabled them to control and corrupt our government as well as other key institutions of our society. Amendment XVI was supposed to create a new revenue source by taxing the wages of American workers. When Amendment XVI failed to accomplish its intended purpose, the Banksters implemented an unconstitutional tax on wages anyway. Finally, Amendment XVII was added to our constitution, which severed the control the states had over our federal government. The coup was complete! The Banksters were in control, and we were a subjugated people. A summary of these changes follows:

Before 1913

- Our federal government obeyed the law and our Constitution.
- Our federal government was a federation of state governments and was limited in scope and power.
- Senators were appointed by state governments.
- The Supreme Court was supreme.
- Congress created our money and regulated its value.
- State governments had a measure of control over our federal government.
- No tax on income or wages was necessary.
- Americans were free to keep and enjoy the fruits of their labor.

After 1913

- Our federal government became a national government with unlimited power.
- Our Constitution was rendered dysfunctional and nonbinding upon our new national government.
- State governments no longer had any way of controlling our new national government and were subordinate to it.

- The Supreme Court was no longer supreme.
- The Fed controlled our money supply and regulated its value.
- An unconstitutional income tax on the wages of American workers was established.
- Senators were elected to office by popular vote.

In conclusion, in 1910, a group of conspirators met on Jekyll Island to plan an across-the-board takeover of our government. The nature of this takeover was complex and far-reaching. It changed Americans from being free and independent people into being the economic slaves of the Banksters. There may be many of us still reluctant to acknowledge the validity of these astounding conclusions. Fortunately, we have a high-level government official who will help us surmount this hurdle. President Woodrow Wilson was our president in 1913, and he championed the passage of the Federal Reserve Act. However, President Wilson was a man with a conscience. In his waning years, he came to realize the terrible mistake he had made and the horrible consequences of his mistake. To save his conscience, he issued the following statement:

> I am a most unhappy man. I have unwittingly ruined my country. A great industrial nation is now controlled by its system of credit. We are no longer a government by free opinion, no longer a government by conviction and the vote of the majority, but a government by the opinion and duress of a small group of dominant men.

President Wilson was not an ignorant man, nor was he delusional when he wrote the above words. He knew exactly what he was talking about. The passage of the Federal Reserve Act in 1913 meant the American people were no longer masters of their own fate. Instead, a group of super-rich bankers would call the shots and pull the strings that made us dance. The great irony in this is that the wealth we are talking about came from us. The Banksters did nothing to earn this money and had no justification for keeping it. However, keep it they did because Congress foolishly and wrongfully voted to allow them to do so.

For the record, the following is a list of the banks that own and control the Federal Reserve Bank:

- N. M. Rothschild of London
- Rothschild Bank of Berlin
- Warburg Bank of Hamburg
- Warburg Bank of Amsterdam
- Lehman Brothers of New York
- Lazard Brothers of Paris
- Kuhn Loeb Bank of New York
- Israel Moses Seif Bank of Italy
- Goldman Sachs of New York
- JPMorgan Chase Bank of New York

The N. M. Rothschild bank of London, is on the top of this list because the Rothschild family, which owns this bank, is beyond question the most powerful and influential banking family in the world. It is also the family that played a key and pivotal role in the creation of the State of Israel.[6]

Notes

1. "A Letter to Cousin Jerry," This Book - Appendix XX
2. The Creature from Jekyll Island .com
3. Amendment XVI of the United_States_Constitution
4. Stanton v. Baltic Mining Company, 240 US 103
5. Amendment XVII of the_United_States_Constitution
6. The Rothschilds and Israel (Lord Rothschild: My Family Created Israel - News Punch)

CHAPTER 2:
How a Private Banking System Works

In 1913, Congress made the Federal Reserve Bank (Fed) the central bank of the United States. This name is the epitome of deception. First of all, because of the passage of Amendment XVII, we no longer had a *federal* government. Amendment XVII transformed our federal government into a national government. Thus, there was nothing federal about the Federal Reserve Bank. Furthermore, it is not an agency or a part of our government. Instead, it is a privately owned banking cartel accountable to no one other than the people who own it. The Fed is not a reserve of any kind and has nothing to do with reserves. Finally, it is not even a bank because no one deposits money with the Fed.

The best description that applies to the Fed is that it is a money pump for those who own it, and this enables these people to harvest huge amounts of money from working Americans without giving them anything in return. In other words, the Federal Reserve Bank is a racket far worse than a Ponzi scheme or Mafia-created con game. However, the tragedy of our situation is that the Fed is a racket that Congress made legal by voting it into existence.

Money is a medium of exchange, and the study of its use is called economics. In days gone by, bartering was the order of the day. If you had corn and wanted wheat, and I had wheat and wanted corn, we would decide how much of one commodity was equivalent to the other and make an exchange on this basis. However, bartering is an awkward process because of the unwieldy items involved. Obviously, exchanges of goods would be facilitated if people used something less cumbersome as a medium of exchange, such as gold or silver. If I grow wheat, by exchanging my wheat for gold, this permits me to obtain other things conveniently when I want them. Thus, hard to find metals like gold and silver became a widely used mediums of exchange.

Once people started using precious metals to trade goods, the need to transform these metals into standardized amounts became necessary. This led to the development of rudimentary coins, whereby a ruling authority would weigh out various amounts of these precious metals and stamp them according to purity and weight. Once this practice became common, it was only a matter of time before coins took on their characteristic disc shape and were impressed with a mint date and the likeness of important officials. With the development of coinage, a person could exchange the fruits of their labor for coins and use them to obtain other things when convenient. During good times, some people ended up with more coins than they needed. Thus, they had to find a safe place to keep them. This brought the goldsmith into the picture.

Goldsmiths worked with precious metals and, as a result, needed a safe or strongbox within which they could keep their supplies. Having this capability, it made sense for people to take their excess coins to the goldsmith for safekeeping. Upon doing so, the goldsmith gave them a written receipt for the number of coins being stored. Soon, people realized that instead of trading coins for the things they needed, they could conveniently trade the receipts instead. Thus, paper currency was born and this blessing freed people from carrying bags of bulky coins when they went to market.

This rudimentary monetary system worked well in small agrarian economies, but as villages turned into towns and towns into cities, a need to borrow money developed. And who was better positioned to loan money than the goldsmith? Not only did he have his own money on hand, but he also held other people's money, which was sitting in his coffers doing nothing. Of course, if the goldsmith was going to loan other people's money, he needed to share some of the interest he earned with them. This was the start of modern banking. The goldsmiths were our first bankers.

People would entrust their money to the banker/goldsmith, and instead of paying for this service, he would pay them a share of the interest he received from loaning their money to other people. From a depositor's or borrower's perspective, this made sense, was beneficial, and appeared reasonable. However, appearances can be deceiving, and exactly how deceiving will soon be addressed.

If people were going to borrow money from a goldsmith, for obvious reasons, it would be far more convenient if the loan were made in paper demand notes instead of coins. However, the demand notes in circulation were for all the coins held by the goldsmith. How could the goldsmith issue demand notes on coins that he did not have? Being a clever fellow, the goldsmith solved his quandary by reasoning that *it was a rare occurrence when someone retrieved all the coins they deposited. Therefore, if I issued demand notes for more coins than I had, the chances are I would always have sufficient money on hand to cover the notes that were redeemed by one or even several of my depositors.* This line of reasoning made sense, so our enterprising goldsmith went out on the limb and adopted this practice. Upon so doing, fractional banking was born.

No one would be injured or hurt by this practice unless there was a run on the goldsmith's strongbox. Aside from this possibility, this development was a blessing to society. However, unknown to almost everyone, it was a far greater blessing to the goldsmith. In fact, it was so much greater that the goldsmiths became much wealthier than your average citizen. For every loan made by the goldsmith, the borrower had to pay the goldsmith not only the interest accrued by the loan but also the total amount originally borrowed, and this was true for every loan the goldsmith made. The borrower was happy because he was able to obtain something he wanted before he earned the money to buy it. The fact that this privilege also cost him the interest he agreed to pay did not dampen his enthusiasm. On the other hand, the goldsmith was much happier than the borrower. He was reaping huge returns from his loans, and he was loaning money to every borrower in town. This state of affairs made the goldsmith very wealthy, and it was this unconscionable wealth that positioned the goldsmith to hold sway over the institutions of society and, in time, even over governments.

It is not right for one person to reap huge returns from someone else's labor while doing virtually nothing themselves to earn the money they receive. This is why usury was a crime in many early societies. In some places, the punishment for usury was death. While it is true that the borrower benefited from his loan, it is also true that until the loan was paid off, the borrower was an indentured servant to the lender. The lender owned a piece of the borrower's time and efforts. In effect, this made the borrower a part-time slave to the lender. In the olden days, such a state of affairs was considered to be wrong and immoral.

Throughout history, knowledge about the nature of debt and its creation was a mystery to mostly everyone. The Banksters took great pains to keep things this way. They knew what a tremendously good thing they had going. Therefore, their first order of business was to ensure nothing upset their apple cart. This is why most governments have never addressed or come to grips with this extremely unfair situation. The bankers were always around and more than willing to use their great wealth to persuade those in positions of authority to help keep their secret. Thus, concurrent with the advent of modern banking, we also have the development of government corruption. These two things are symbiotic, and one goes hand in hand with the other. No one can honestly posture that central banking by a private bank is a good thing for the citizens of a nation. However, many people do, and because of this, it follows that either they are complete fools or feathering their nest by ingratiating themselves to the Banksters. There are no other possibilities.

Governments should own and operate their own central banking system. If a private company is chosen to provide this service, the government involved should set the interest rate used by this company. Furthermore, said company should only be allowed to keep the interest they earn from their loans. This interest will be a sufficient return on their investment to keep them in business and provide them with reasonable profits. The monies paid to retire the loan, which are windfall profits to the bank, should be surrendered to the government involved and placed in its general fund. If this arrangement had been in place for the United States over the past one hundred years, we would be blessed with everything we have today but would not have a huge national debt hanging over our heads. Furthermore, there would be no need for an income tax, and citizens would be able to keep and enjoy all the fruits of their labor. Instead, our elected leaders foolishly allowed the Federal Reserve to keep the windfall profits realized by creating credit. These windfall profits enabled the Fed to corrupt our government and many other key institutions of our society, including corporations, educational institutions, the media, our entertainment industries, state and local governments, and of course, our Federal Government.

The following is a list of changes that would be to our benefit had Congress not passed the Federal Reserve Act:

- A tax on income and wages would not be needed.
- The national debt would be negligible.
- The wealth garnered from establishing credit would finance government operations.
- Citizens would be able to keep the fruits of their labor.
- Inflation would be minimized.
- Depressions and major recessions would be eliminated.
- Only one member of a household would have to work.
- People would be able to buy things through savings.
- Credit card use would be less prevalent.
- The workweek would be shorter, and people would be able to take longer vacations.

The above-listed things are lost to us because Congress passed the Federal Reserve Act in 1913. Incredibly, the Fed has given us nothing in return for the sacrifices made by the people of this nation. In lieu of being a benefit to us, the Fed and its owners have brought us nothing but chaos, depression, and war. They used our money to corrupt the major institutions of our society, and now they are using our military, resources, and money to corrupt the entire world.

CHAPTER 3:
Zionism and the World Wars

World War I

Prior to WWI, the United States was an isolationist nation. As far as foreign policy was concerned, we heeded President George Washington's advice, offered in his farewell address, where he told the nation to have as little to do with foreign powers as possible, especially those in Europe. President Woodrow Wilson was elected to a second term of office in November 1916. His campaign slogan was "He kept us out of the war." Yet, five months later, Woodrow Wilson did an about-face and championed our entry into WWI on the side of the Allies. WWI was billed as being "the war to end all wars" and "the war to make the world safe for democracy." With publicity like this and the media furiously fanning the flames of war, no one bothered to ask why our president had changed his mind.

There was no good or valid reason for America's entry into WWI. While we view Great Britain and the other Allied nations as being one with us today, this was not the case in 1916. As far as we were concerned, the Central Powers, led by Germany, were no different from any of the other powers in Europe, including Great Britain. Furthermore, during WWI, without Adolf Hitler running the show, Germany was not the evil empire we came to know in WWII. Instead, Germany was one of the more sophisticated and advanced nations of the world in both science and the social arts.

Unlike most wars throughout history, WWI was not fought over territory, resources, or religion. The conflict arose because Europe was divided into two military alliances at odds with each other. This powder keg exploded on June 28, 1914, when a Serbian national assassinated the Archduke of Austria.

It has been argued that one reason the United States entered WWI was because of Germany's unrestricted submarine warfare, which resulted in the sinking of the HMS *Lusitania*, a British ocean liner, with the loss of 153 American lives. Another reason talked about was that Germany had approached Mexico in the hope that Mexico would become its ally if America entered the war against Germany. Supposedly, Germany promised to return Texas to Mexico after winning the war against us. These are not valid reasons for a nation to go to war. The war drums were definitely beating in the United States over these incidents, but the important question is who was beating those drums and why? In regard to those Americans who died on the *Lusitania*, this number of our citizens being killed is a serious matter. However, Germany was not an enemy of the United States and had declared the waters around England to be a war zone. Furthermore, the New York German community had taken out an ad warning Americans not to sail on the *Lusitania*. Despite this deplorable loss of life, Germany did not deliberately target Americans. The 153 Americans killed would not have died had they not foolishly sailed on a British liner known to be carrying munitions when Germany had declared unrestricted submarine warfare against England. None of the reasons proffered are adequate to justify our nation's entry into WWI. This is especially true in light of the fact that in December of 1916, Germany proposed a negotiated end to the fighting.[1] The United States had nothing to gain no matter which side won, and neither side was an evil empire that was a threat to the other nations of the world. Furthermore, had we not entered this war, there is a very good chance that Germany's offer of peace would have been accepted, bringing an early end to the war. Thus, our entry into WWI was a misguided and foolish blunder. It was misguided because we had no good reason for entering the war. It was a blunder because we entered a senseless war and fought on the wrong side.

As stated above, in 1916, Germany issued a peace proposal that could have brought WWI to an honorable conclusion. Also, to its credit, Germany made this proposal at a time when they were winning the war. Therefore, at this juncture, had the United States sided with Germany instead of England, the Allied powers would have had no choice but to accept Germany's offer of peace. This would have brought an immediate end to the hostilities. Unfortunately, the United States opted to side with pro-war England instead of pro-peace Germany. As a result, the war raged on for two more years. These two years turned out to be horrible, with the fighting being the worst of the war.

Because of our blunder, we sacrificed 137,000 American lives and needlessly spent $22 billion on the war. As bad as this is, it pales in comparison to the price paid by the other warring nations. From the time the United States entered WWI to its end, collectively, these nations lost an additional 5.5 million men and spent $100 billion. All this came to pass just to fight the most senseless and idiotic war in the history of mankind. At this point, you should be beginning to sense that there was a lot more behind our nation's entry into WWI than meets the eye, and you are right. Unfortunately, what doesn't meet the eye is sickening.

Where the worm turns on this is revealed by England's issuance of its Balfour Declaration.[2] This declaration was made in a letter written by British Foreign Secretary Arthur Balfour, who sent it to Baron Walter Rothschild for delivery to the Zionist Federation of Great Britain and Ireland. This declaration, dated November 2, 1917, issued seven months after America entered WWI, reads as follows:

> His Majesty's government views with favor the establishment in Palestine of a national home for the Jewish people and will use their best endeavors to facilitate the achievement of this object, it being clearly understood that nothing shall be done which may prejudice the civil and religious rights of existing non-Jewish communities in Palestine, or the rights and political status enjoyed by Jews in any other country.

The issuance of this declaration was an astounding development! In the midst of a world war having nothing whatsoever to do with the Jews, England issued a declaration that gave Palestine to them. Why would England do this? Great Britain had no authority or right to speak either for the Jews or the people of Palestine. Benjamin Freedman[3] provided us with the answer to this question, and his revelation about what happened has an undeniable ring of truth to it. According to Mr. Freedman, England issued its Balfour Declaration because the British had struck a deal with the Zionists, whereby England would support and assist them in their goal to establish the State of Israel at the war's end. In return, the Zionists would use their considerable influence in the United States to bring us into the war on the side of the Allies.

The Balfour Declaration was issued at the request of the Zionists because they wanted assurances from England that they would honor their side of the bargain when the war was over. Stop for a moment and imagine you are a German soldier in WWI. Early on, your side was winning and this was a source of pride for you. Then one day, the Americans enter the war and you ask yourself, how *could this happen?* For the next two years, you watch the tide of battle change and see your friends and fellow soldiers die under the enemy onslaught. Again and again, you ask yourself, how *did this happen? When we were winning, we offered our enemies peace with honor, and now America's entry into the war has ensured our defeat.* Eventually, at the war's end, England's Balfour Declaration was revealed to the world, and with this, the above question was answered.

America's entry into the war against Germany was engineered by the Zionists in exchange for a commitment from England to support the establishment of a homeland for the Jews in Palestine. Wouldn't such a development be enough to make a normal person angry? Wouldn't a development such as this be sufficient to drive a war-weary, unstable person to madness? How many Germans who fought in the trenches were enraged by this turn of events? The Jews were a respected and accepted element of German society prior to WWI. Now the talk in German beer halls turned to how the German Jews had used Germany and stabbed her in the back.

Unfortunately, this is not where this story ends. Getting the Western powers to sanction the creation of the State of Israel was easy. In order to establish a nation, you need people, and at the time, the Jews living in Germany were not willing to abandon their homes and leave what Europe had to offer to live in a desert. Something more had to be done to change this. Toward this end, the Zionists decided to fan the flames of hatred for Jews in Germany. Their hope was to make things so bad for the Jews that they would have no choice other than to flee Europe.

The Balfour Declaration had planted the seeds of anti-Semitism in the minds of the German people. Now, these seeds needed to be watered and made to grow. An opportunity for doing this presented itself in the Treaty of Versailles. What better way to foster hatred for the Jews than to force the Germans to accept responsibility for starting a war they did not start and then wrongfully punish them with the harsh and humiliating terms of the Versailles treaty?

The Treaty of Versailles had a devastating impact on the German people. This terrible situation was compounded further by the Great Depression that took hold in Germany following WWI. Is it any wonder that the German people looked for someone to save them from the horrible circumstances that had come to dominate their lives? Is it so hard to understand why the conditions they lived with made these intelligent and once-proud people susceptible to accepting an eloquent demigod as their leader? In his speeches, Hitler promised redemption, justice, prosperity, dignity, and to restore German honor and pride. In light of what the Zionists had done to Germany, far too many Germans gladly bought this message.

The Germans did not care that Hitler was a failed artist, a former wallpaper hanger, and a deranged anti-Semite. All they cared about was that Hitler offered them hope. Despite the appeal Adolf Hitler had to many Germans early on, most saw him for what he was and wanted nothing to do with him. Despite the treachery of the Zionists, most Germans were intelligent enough to realize that their Jewish friends and neighbors had nothing to do with the tribulations that had fallen upon them. This being true, it was clear to the Zionists that more had to be done if Israel was going to have the people it needed to become a nation.

No rational human being would deliberately foster hatred for their own people to accomplish what was believed to be a worthwhile goal. The fact of the matter is that Zionist leaders were not rational. They came from a long line of subversives who thought nothing of instigating wars so they could play both sides against the middle and get what they wanted. What Zionist leaders wanted were huge fortunes and the political power, which extreme wealth gave them.

The Zionists believe that as Jews, they are God's chosen people and that it is God's will for them to have a nation of their own. In keeping with this, they believe anything they do to achieve their goal is sanctioned by God. Therefore, a Zionist can do no wrong in the eyes of God. Anything they do to help the nation of Israel is blessed by God, even if it means hurting some of their own people. Zionists believe that *you have to break a few eggs to make an omelet.* As fantastic as all this sounds, it is the truth—but don't take my word for it. Following are the words of Zionist founder Theodor Herzl (1860–1904) taken from his diary:

> It is essential that the suffering of the Jews...becomes worse...this will assist in the realization of our plans...I have an excellent idea...I shall induce anti-Semites to liquidate Jewish wealth.... The anti-Semites will assist us thereby in that they will strengthen the persecution and oppression of the Jews. The anti-Semites shall be our best friends.

World War II

As fate would have it, along came a former German soldier who, before the war, was a failed artist and paperhanger. His name was Adolf Hitler, and he is the unstable person driven to madness by WWI, of which we spoke earlier. After WWI, Hitler became a member of the Nationalist Socialist Workers' Party, or Nazi Party, as it is more commonly known. Because of his charisma, speaking ability, and hatred for the Jews, Hitler rose rapidly to a position of leadership in this party.

In Adolf Hitler, the Zionists had found their man! If anyone was able to make the Jews flee Germany, surely Hitler and his Nazis would be up for the job. So, what is a good Zionist supposed to do? The answer to this question is mind-boggling! The Zionists contributed money to the Nazi Party and helped finance Hitler's rise to power.[4] Yes, you read this right! This is so astounding that I will repeat it. To foster hatred for the Jews in Germany prior to WWII, the Zionists helped finance the Nazi party's rise to power. Unfortunately, the Zionists were not done yet. Other than regaling against the Jews in his speeches, at this point, neither Hitler nor his followers did nothing to directly hurt Jews. However, this would soon change. One of the reasons it changed took place in 1933 when World Jewry held a conference in Amsterdam.[5] At this conference, it was decided by Jews to declare war on Germany with the stated goal of bringing about Germany's total defeat and destruction. On March 24, 1933, the *Daily Express* of London ran these headlines:[6]

Judea Declares War on Germany
Jews of All the World Unite in Action

Think about the effect this development had upon Adolf Hitler, and think about how this affected the German people. In their minds, the Jews were responsible for Germany's defeat in WWI, and now they wanted to destroy Germany a second time. Shortly thereafter, Hitler assumed dictatorship of Germany and, upon doing so, declared, "If the Jews want total war, they will have total war, and through it, I will rid this planet of them forever." Amazingly, no one in Germany dared to stand up and tell him he was crazy.

Beyond any doubt, Adolf Hitler was an insane megalomaniac. The fact that he rose to power in one of the most technologically advanced and sophisticated societies in the world is astounding. However, this happened, and because it did, WWII also happened. Clearly, Hitler's rise to power before WWII was a direct and inevitable result of Germany's loss in WWI and the way Germany was humiliated by the Treaty of Versailles. Contributing factors to these events were the Zionist financing of the Nazi's rise to power and the declaration of unconditional warfare against Germany by the World Jewish Congress. All the foregoing ensued because of Zionist meddling in world affairs, the purpose of which was to establish a homeland for the Jews in Palestine.

If the Zionists had not taken the actions they did, America would not have entered WWI, Hitler would never have come to power in Germany, and the European theater of WWII would not have happened. The total number killed in WWI and WWII as a result of Zionist meddling is sixty-three million people at a cost of approximately $2 trillion to the warring nations. Presently, the world is embroiled in a debilitating war on terror. This war is being fought so 8.2 million Jews can live in a desert that was forcibly taken from the Palestinians. Furthermore, with no end in sight to the injustice fueling this war, there is no end in sight to the destruction, mayhem, and murder. Is this price worth it? Apparently, it is if you are a Zionist.

The above conclusions are hard for the average American to accept because they are so contrary to what we have been taught to believe. Surely, the New World Order (NWO) Zionists are not as twisted and perverted as they have been portrayed so far. Neturei Karta International is a worldwide Jewish organization whose roots are in Jerusalem. In an article on their website[7] entitled "Why Orthodox Jews Are Opposed to a Zionist State," they offer the following assessment of what the Zionists have brought upon their own people:

> It is openly stated in books written by the founders of Zionism that the means by which they planned to establish a state was by instigating anti-Semitism, and undermining the security of the Jews in all lands of the world until they would be forced to flee to their state. And thus, they did—they intentionally infuriated the German people and fanned the flames of Nazi hatred, and they helped the Nazis, with trickery and deceit, to take whole Jewish communities off to concentration camps, and the Zionists themselves admit this (See the books Perfidy, Min Hameitzor, etc.).

Notes

1. The German 1916 Proposal for Peace – Total War and Peacemaking: (http://worldhistoryproject.org/1916/12/12/germany-makes-first-peace-proposal-toallied-nations)
2. The Balfour Declaration of 1917 - Wikipedia.org: (http://en.wikipedia.org/wiki/Balfour_Declaration_of_1917)
3. The designs and actions of the Zionists in our government – The Amazing Warnings of Benjamin Freedman; (http://www.biblebelievers.org.au/benjamin.htm)

4. The Americans who funded Hitler, Nazis, German economic miracle, and World War II (linkedin.com) by Nikolay Starikov.

5. http://www.wintersonnenwende.com/scriptorium/english /archives/articles/jdecwar.html.The Barnes Review, Jan. /Feb. 2001.

6. JewsDeclareWarOnGermany1933.pdf (archive.org).

7. Neturei Karta International (http://www.nkusa.org/ AboutUs/ Zionism/opposition.cfm)

CHAPTER 4:
The HMS Lusitania Incident

The United States never should have entered WWI because we had nothing to gain by fighting this war. However, having made a decision to go to war, we opted to fight for England, the aggressor nation, instead of Germany, the nation that wanted peace. In the October 13, 1972, issue of *Life* magazine, there appears a feature article by Colin Simpson, a British journalist, entitled *"LUSITANIA: New evidence on the 'unprovoked' sinking that dragged us toward war."*[1] This article supports the above conclusion. For thirty years, our government purposely withheld vital information about the sinking of the *Lusitania*. This act of omission led people to wrongfully believe that the *Lusitania* was an innocent passenger vessel carrying innocent cargo. She was not! Because of these erroneous impressions, Americans viewed the sinking of the *Lusitania* as an unprovoked and unjustified act of war against the citizens of the United States.

According to Colin Simpson, The British Admiralty financed the construction of the HMS *Lusitania* and as a result, the ship was fitted with twelve 6-inch guns. Also, in times of war, the ship would serve as an armed auxiliary cruiser under the command of the British Admiralty (navy). Cruiser rules, subscribed to at the time by maritime nations, specified that unarmed merchant vessels would be warned before being sunk; thus, allowing the crew time to abandon ship. Because the *Lusitania* was an armed vessel, these cruiser rules did not apply, and legally, she sailed under the rules of war. From October 1914 onward, the British Admiralty made it an offense for British merchant ships to obey a German U-boat's order to halt. They were also ordered to use their weapons to sink an approaching U-boat. If no weapons were available, then they should make every effort to ram the submarine. This meant that U-boats could no longer safely make surface attacks. As a result, the possibility of mistakenly sinking vessels of neutral nations was increased. To aggravate this situation further, the Admiralty ordered British ships to paint over their names and port of registry as well as to fly the flag of a neutral nation.

In retaliation for Germany's mining the entranceways to British ports in the North Sea, England mined wide areas of open sea lanes in the North Sea and declared the entire area to be a war zone. Germany soon followed suit and followed up with a declaration to the neutral powers, which said that due to British misuse of neutrality rules, no vessel was safe from attack in the North Sea and that neutral vessels and citizens should avoid the area. President Woodrow Wilson declined to pass this warning on to American citizens and responded to it by informing Germany that despite the circumstances, any sinking of an American ship or the loss of American lives on any foreign vessel would be considered an indefensible violation of America's neutrality rights. This message shocked the Germans because they had no way of knowing if Americans were present on any of the targets they encountered. Understandably, the British greeted President Wilson's message with jubilation.

On March 28, 1915, at the approach to the English Channel, German submarine *U-28* commanded the HMS *Falaba* to halt by firing across her bow. She refused, but eventually was forced to heave to, and her crew was ordered to abandon ship. The *Falaba's* crew stalled for time and secretly sent a wireless message for help. In response, an armed British trawler appeared on the horizon. With this development, the *U-28* fired a torpedo into the stern of the *Falaba*, setting off the thirteen tons of explosives she was carrying. Among those killed was Leon C. Thresher, an American citizen. The American press reacted with unbounded fury to this incident despite the fact that cruiser rules were properly followed, and the crew of the *U-28* had no knowledge of an American being on board. An American was killed, and the circumstances of how did not matter.

On her ill-fated return voyage to England, the *Lusitania's* cargo was primarily contraband: 1,639 ingot bars of copper, 1,248 cases of three-inch shells, 76 cases of brass rods, and 4,927 boxes of cartridges, each containing 1,000 rounds of ammunition. The weight of all these high explosives was 10½ tons. It was common knowledge that carrying such cargo was a routine undertaking for the *Lusitania*.

Because of the increasingly volatile situation, George Vierick, a representative of the New York German community, attempted to place ads in fifty American newspapers, warning Americans about the risk of embarking on a transatlantic voyage to England. In response, the State Department advised the newspapers that it would be highly dangerous to run the ad, so none did. Eventually, Mr. Vierick convinced the editor of the *New-York Tribune* to run his ad, which the *Tribune* did on the morning the *Lusitania* sailed. Apparently, no American sailing on the *Lusitania* elected to change their plans at this late point in time.

The *Lusitania* set sail on its final voyage shortly before noon on May 1, 1915. Her master, Captain William Turner, was under orders to steer the same course used on previous journeys. This known course would take the *Lusitania* south of Ireland, where she would be met by the British cruiser *Juno*. The *Juno* was under orders to escort the *Lusitania* for the rest of her journey. At this point in time, the *U-20* was patrolling the waters south of Ireland where the *Lusitania* was heading. By monitoring transmissions, the British Admiralty was able to pinpoint the locations of the *Juno*, *Lusitania*, and the *U-20*. By plotting these positions, it was apparent that if the *U-20* stayed where she was, the *Lusitania* would run into her the next morning. However, the *U-20* was not content to just sit and wait for the *Lusitania*. The afternoon before their meeting, the *U-20* sank both the HMS *Candidate* and HMS *Centurion*. There was no response from the British to these two tragic losses.

Normally, destroyer escorts are dispatched by the British Admiralty to the seas south of Ireland at the first hint of a U-boat's presence. Not this time! In light of this enemy action, Admiral Coke of the British Admiralty wanted to send a message to the *Lusitania* to warn them of the looming danger. He was ordered not to. Having a conscience, Admiral Coke disobeyed orders and sent his message anyway, which was picked up by the *Lusitania*. However, Captain Turner decided not to heed the warning because he felt his scheduled rendezvous with the cruiser *Juno* would be sufficient protection for his ship. Furthermore, he was sailing under Admiralty's authority and could not change course without getting permission. Meanwhile, back at Admiralty headquarters, Admiral Oliver advised Winston

Churchill that the *Juno* was unsuited for protecting the *Lusitania* and was also at risk of being sunk. This being the case, he recommended that elements of a nearby destroyer flotilla be dispatched to protect the *Lusitania*. What happened next is told in Colin Simpson's own words:

> At this juncture, the Admiralty War Diary stops short, perhaps understandably, as it was here that the decision was taken that was to be the direct cause of the disaster. No one alive today knows who took it, but shortly after noon on May 5, the Admiralty signaled Juno to abandon her mission and return to Queenstown. They did not dispatch any destroyers, and the *Lusitania* was not informed that she was now alone, and closing every minute with the U-20.

The rest is history! A German submarine, the *U-20*, sank an innocent passenger vessel, killing 1,198 people, 123 of whom were Americans. Obviously, the Germans are the bad guys, and to get even with them, this nation spent $22 billion and sacrificed the lives of 137,000 of our finest young men and women.

Who is to blame for the sinking of the HMS *Lusitania*? To be sure, the Germans loaded the gun and pulled the trigger. However, in contrast to what we have been told by our government, the Germans were justified in committing what was a legitimate act of war. On the other hand, it was the British Admiralty that made the HMS *Lusitania* a target by

- arming her with deck guns and loading her with munitions.
- insisting she maintains a course known to the Germans.
- removing an escort vessel that may have saved her.
- failing to provide readily available destroyer escorts.
- refusing to warn her of the impending danger.
- not ordering her to take a course north of Ireland instead of going south, where it was known that a German U-boat lay in wait for her arrival.

England wanted the United States to enter the war on her side. Toward this end, the British Admiralty set up the HMS *Lusitania* and two thousand people to be torpedo fodder for a German U-boat. But what was *our* government's role in this sordid affair? The Zionists had a special interest to see as many Americans as possible sail on the *Lusitania*. The more Americans killed, the louder Americans would scream for German blood. Could this be the reason why President Wilson failed to warn Americans to not sail on Allied ships heading into a war zone? Is this also why our State Department discouraged newspapers from running ads about the danger of sailing on British vessels? What other reasons are there for government officials to remain silent while Americans foolishly placed their lives in grave danger?

Are we really to believe that the governments of the United States and England would deliberately sacrifice the lives of thousands of innocent men, women, and children just to give the United States an excuse to go to war? Winston Churchill, in *The World Crisis*, his autobiography, said, "At the summit, true politics and strategy are one. The maneuver which brings an ally into the field is as serviceable as that which wins a great battle."

Notes

1. "LUSITANIA: New evidence on the 'unprovoked' sinking that dragged us toward war1." 1. Life Magazine, October 13, 1972, page 58.

CHAPTER 5:
The USS *Liberty* Incident

The Six-Day War between Arab nations and Israel was fought in June 1967. The USS *Liberty*, an American spy ship, was involved in this war. What happened to the *Liberty* is called the USS Liberty Incident. Most people have little recollection of this event, and there is a good reason for this. The Zionists want the story to fade and become a minor footnote in history. In 1917, our government used the unintended death of 153 Americans on the *Lusitania* as an excuse to enter WWI. Every newspaper in America carried this story as headline news. In contrast, when the *Liberty* Incident occurred, instead of being headline news as it should have been, the article about the event was hidden in plain view by relegating it to the back pages of most newspapers. In the USS *Liberty* Incident, 174 Americans were wounded, and 34 American servicemen were deliberately murdered. Ho-hum, who cares? Americans are no longer supposed to be concerned when those who defend us are slaughtered by a foreign power. After all, the members of our armed forces are paid to take such risks.

Our government was overthrown in 1913 by the rich banking families who had ruled the Western world for centuries. The house of Rothschild was the most influential and powerful banking family of them all. It was the house of Rothschild that championed the creation of the State of Israel. This state of affairs raises an important question: if the Zionists are in charge, whose interests come first, Israel's or ours? The answer to this question, while not obvious, upon examination becomes clear. The United States is a Christian nation where the separation of the church is supposed to be a bedrock principle. This being the case, we have no interest or business supporting a religious state anywhere in the world, and this includes the State of Israel. Despite this, it is apparent that those who lead us consider Israeli interests to be coincident with ours. However, our situation is far more compromised than this. Not only do the Zionists hold that Israel's interest coincides with ours, they also believe that when push comes to shove, Israel's interests take precedence over ours. The USS *Liberty* Incident clearly demonstrates this to be the case.

There are three sources for the information provided in this and the subsequent two chapters: a 2002 video documentary produced by the British Broadcasting Corporation entitled "Dead in the Water,"[1] a pamphlet distributed by the USS *Liberty* Veterans Association called "The USS *Liberty* Story,"[2] and an online website called the *Liberty* Incident Timeline.[3] The video can be viewed for free on YouTube, or a DVD copy may be purchased directly from the USS Liberty Veterans Association. The video is a must-see item for every American because the information provided is of grave importance to us all. To say the least, this video is shocking and a serious embarrassment to both our government and Israel. The USS *Liberty* Incident happened forty-eight years ago. The survivors of this incident, many of whom are still alive, lived through the years with the knowledge that our government not only let them down but also covered up its involvement in this sordid affair. However, the truth is far worse than the mere betrayal of America's defenders. By reading this and the next two chapters of this book, you will learn how much worse the truth really is.

What follows is unsettling, not only because of what happened, but also because of the associated implications. Our government deliberately covered up the USS *Liberty* Incident, and this cover-up is still in place today. A wealth of information about what happened is classified and still not available. Not only is key information wrongfully kept secret, but a plethora of available information is fabricated nonsense. Apparently, it was created to confuse things so much that interested parties would become frustrated and give up pursuing the matter. The BBC is a professional news organization with no ax to grind. Therefore, it is safe to assume that their documentary is an accurate portrayal of what really occurred.

In the summer of 1967, hostilities between the Arab world and Israel were escalating. Today, it is common knowledge that the armed forces of Israel are far superior to those of other Middle Eastern nations. This was not so apparent prior to the Six-Day War.

There had been a number of clashes and minor wars before 1967, but the coming June war was shaping up to be a major showdown. Lined up against tiny Israel were Egypt, Syria, Jordan, and Iraq. Israel's armed forces consisted of 264,000 troops, with 800 tanks and 300 combat aircraft. On the other side, the Arab forces mustered out 547,000 troops, with 2,504 tanks and 957 combat aircraft. From these statistics, one would assume that the Arab forces would be victorious over Israel. Back then, this possibility was of great concern to Israeli commanders. Furthermore, Israel's leaders understood that if the Arabs won, it would be the end of their nation. With the outcome of the war so critical and victory so heavily favored by Arabs, Israel sought an ace in the hole to change the balance of this equation. Unbeknownst to everyone, Israel had its ace in the hole in the guise of the United States. The situation in this nation was such that our leaders could not openly join the war in its early stages, but this would change if something happened that enraged the American public. Not only did the Israelis find a way of doing this, they gave it a code name: Operation Cyanide. Operation Cyanide was a highly secret and classified joint operation between Israel and the United States.

However, we are getting ahead of our story. We will talk more about Operation Cyanide in chapter 6 of this book.

The USS *Liberty* was a lightly armed United States spy ship. It was loaded with the most sophisticated and up-to-date electronic equipment for capturing and listening to radio communications over the entire spectrum of broadcast frequencies. The *Liberty* could travel to any hotspot in the world and intercept communications from both sides of the conflict. This would allow the ship to provide Washington with real-time information as to what was happening. On May 24, 1967, the *Liberty* was sailing off the coast of Africa. The ship received orders from the US Joint Chiefs of Staff to proceed to the Eastern Mediterranean Sea and take up station in international waters thirteen miles off the coast of Gaza, a tiny strip of land bordering both Egypt and Israel. All other United States naval vessels were ordered to remain a minimum of five hundred miles away from the war zone.

On June 5, 1967, hostilities broke out between the parties involved with the first blow being struck by Israel. The Israel defense forces launched a costly and devastating air attack against Egyptian airfields. With the war now raging and the USS *Liberty* heading into an active war zone, the captain of the Liberty, Captain William McGonagle, contacted Sixth Fleet headquarters and asked Vice Admiral William Martin to send a destroyer as an armed escort for the *Liberty*. Because of the nature of its mission, the *Liberty* only had four 50-caliber machine guns for protection. The following day, June 6, 1967, Vice Admiral Martin replied to Captain McGonagle's request with the following message, "Liberty is a clearly marked United States ship in international waters, not a participant in the conflict, and not a reasonable subject for attack by any nation...request denied."

On June 8, 1967, the *Liberty* was patrolling about thirteen miles off the coast of Gaza, and during the course of the morning, a message was sent to the *Liberty* from the Joint Chiefs of Staff, ordering the ship to move twenty miles away from the coast. About an hour later, a second message was sent, ordering the *Liberty* to move to a position at least one hundred miles from the coast of Gaza. Unfortunately, for various reasons, neither of these messages arrived in time to prevent the looming disaster. Throughout the morning of June 8, the *Liberty* was overflown several times and observed by a number of different Israeli aircraft. Some of these planes reported back to their ground controllers that the USS *Liberty* was an American ship. Pinchas Pinchasy, the naval liaison at Israeli Air Force headquarters, reported to Israeli naval headquarters that the ship cruising off El Arish was an electromagnetic audio-surveillance ship of the US Navy. The ship was named the *Liberty*, and its markings GTR-5, identified the *Liberty* as being an NSA intelligence vessel. During the course of the morning, the *Liberty*'s crew lounged on the ship's decks, secure in the knowledge that our friends the Israelis knew who they were, and therefore, they would be safe from attack.

At 11:20 a.m., three Israeli motor torpedo boats of MTB Division 19, left the port of Ashdod with orders to patrol between Ashdod and Ashkelon. Shortly thereafter, the *Liberty* was overflown by two unidentified aircraft for a final time. At 11:27 a.m., Israeli Defense forces received a report from its Southern Command that an unidentified ship was shelling the ammunition dump at El Arish.

Subsequently, the Israeli torpedo boats (MTBs) detected the *Liberty* on their radar and assumed that it was the target responsible for the shelling. At this point, the *Liberty* was patrolling at a speed of 5 knots. However, an MTB radar operator wrongfully calculated its speed to be 28 knots. This was a critical mistake for two reasons: only warships can reach speeds this fast, and if this speed was accurate, the MTBs would not be able to overtake the *Liberty* because their top speed was nearly the same as the target. As a result of this error, a flight of unmarked delta-winged Mirage jets was vectored toward the Liberty with orders to attack if the target was a warship.

At this point, it is important to know the following:

- When the *Liberty* was attacked, it was a sunny, clear day, and the ship had been properly identified and reported by several Israeli patrol craft during the course of the morning.
- The *Liberty* was a clearly marked United States vessel with its name and designation code written in large block letters on its hull.
- The *Liberty* was a former victory ship built in WWII to carry cargo to Europe, and its profile looked nothing like a warship.
- The *Liberty* was painted gray like most military vessels but was lightly armed and had no weapons on its decks to indicate it was capable of harming anyone.
- The *Liberty* was flying an easily seen United States flag, and the winds were such that said flag was fully unfurled in the stiff breeze.

Despite all of the above, the pilots of the Mirage jets maintained they could not identify the Liberty and, at approximately 2:00 p.m., commenced their attack with rockets and cannon fire. This attack was followed shortly thereafter by three unmarked Dassault Mystere 111C jets firing rockets, cannons, and napalm canisters. Both attacks taken together lasted about thirty minutes. During this time period, the *Liberty* tried to contact Sixth Fleet headquarters through fleet frequencies but failed because the six available channels were being jammed. However, during the course of the attacks, a radio operator braved the onslaught to string up a makeshift antenna. Despite the horror raging around him, this hero managed to get out a general distress call that was picked up by Sixth Fleet ships. This distress signal announced, "Under attack by unidentified aircraft, require immediate assistance!" The two Israeli jet aircraft attacks had killed nine of Liberty's crew, and approximately sixty men were wounded.

At 2:35 p.m., the three Israeli torpedo boats positioned nearby sped toward the *Liberty* in attack formation. Nearing the ship, they were fired upon by one of the *Liberty*'s 50-caliber cannons. To the Israelis, this was a sufficient provocation to launch five torpedoes at the *Liberty*. Fortunately, only one found its mark. Because this torpedo hit the edge of a structural bulkhead, it exploded external to the *Liberty*'s hull and not inside it. This saved the *Liberty* and was the reason she did not sink. However, the blast of the torpedo killed twenty-five more of the Liberty's crew, bringing the death toll to thirty-four men. The torpedo boats, with no torpedoes left to fire, circled the *Liberty* and machine-gunned the ship, deliberately targeting its life rafts both on the ship and in the water. The only possible reason for this was to render them useless, so there would be no survivors. Finally, the Israeli Defense Forces, mistakenly believing that American fighters were approaching, broke off their attack, approached the *Liberty*, and offered assistance. This offer was refused by Captain McGonagle.

The USS *Liberty* was under attack for one hour and fifteen minutes. For approximately an hour of this time, the Sixth Fleet was aware of the *Liberty*'s plight and launched several relief sorties to assist them. However, these rescue attempts were aborted. Because of this, the crew of the *Liberty* endured over one hour of pure hell, while the rest of our navy sat back and did nothing. As shocking as this is, what is even more shocking is that during this fiasco, a flight of nuclear-armed A-4 Skyhawk bombers was launched by the Sixth Fleet, with orders to drop their payloads on Cairo. You read this right! During the USS *Liberty* Incident, the United States was poised and only minutes away from vaporizing Cairo with all its inhabitants, including the staff of the American embassy. Apparently, the only reason this nuclear attack was called off was that the *Liberty* did not sink.

Notes

1. Dead In the Water; (http://www.youtube.com/watch?v=kjOH1XMAwZA)
2. The USS Liberty Veterans Organization Phamplet (www.usslibertyveterans.org)
3. The Liberty Incident Timeline: (www.thelibertyincident.com/docs/timeline.pdf)

CHAPTER 6:
The USS Liberty Analysis

The USS *Liberty* was attacked by Israeli Defense Forces, killing 34 and wounding 174 members of its crew. The issue at hand is whether or not the attack was a blunder on the part of the Israeli Defense Forces as they claim or a deliberate act executed for some sinister purpose. Answering this question is critical because evidence exists that indicates that the United States government may have been complicit in the Israeli attack. If this is true, then it follows that our government is guilty of participating in a false-flag attack on one of its own ships. An obvious purpose of this attack would be to justify the United States entering the war on the side of Israel.

If this is the case, then it is also true that our first act as Israel's ally would have been to incinerate Cairo in a nuclear explosion. As absurd as this possibility sounds, the facts are such that this scenario is the most plausible.

The Israeli side of the story is as follows; while it is true that they had positively identified the *Liberty* as being an American ship earlier in the day, by the time of the attack, it was thought that the *Liberty* had departed the area. As fate would have it, late in the morning, there were several explosions at the El Arish ammunition dump, and these were thought to be the result of shelling from an unknown offshore vessel. Three torpedo boats of MTB Division 19, which were patrolling in the area, were ordered to investigate. When the MTBs picked up the *Liberty* on their radar, they mistakenly calculated its speed to be 28 knots, a speed attainable only by combat vessels. Knowing they could not overtake a vessel that was capable of matching their speed, the MTBs called in a flight of Mirage jets to chase down the *Liberty* and investigate the situation.

Upon overtaking the *Liberty*, the pilots of the Mirage jets mistook it for the Egyptian vessel *El Quseir*. For this reason, they commenced an attack. This initial attack was immediately followed by a second flight of jets. After this second flight of jets had expended their ordinance and headed back to base, the MTBs moved in. Upon doing so, they could not identify the USS *Liberty* as an American ship because according to their group leader, the fires and smoke upon its decks obscured the ship and made a definitive identification impossible. As they approached the *Liberty*, they were greeted by machine-gun fire from one of its 50-caliber machine guns. It was this development that caused them to pull back and launch the torpedo attack that almost sank the *Liberty*. According to the MTB group leader, at no time during their attack did the MTBs fire upon or deliberately destroy lifeboats either on the *Liberty*'s decks or in the water around the ship.

The Israeli explanation appears to make sense, and it is easy to understand why someone sympathetic to the Israeli cause would accept this explanation at face value. However, upon further analysis, there are a number of weaknesses evident in the Israeli version of events, and collectively, they establish that the Israeli explanation for the attack on the USS *Liberty* is a fabrication. The key elements offered as an excuse for the air attacks are the following:

- The *Liberty* was thought to have left the area.
- The miscalculation of the USS *Liberty*'s speed to be 28 knots, indicating it was a combat vessel.
- The misidentification of the USS *Liberty* as an Egyptian ship, the *El Quseir*.

The first item above is absurd in light of the fact that the *Liberty* had been loitering in a random pattern at 5 knots all morning. The last known sighting of the *Liberty* by an aircraft was 11:45 a.m., and at that time, she was twelve to fifteen miles off the coast of Gaza. This being the case, at a speed of 5 knots, the distance the *Liberty* could cover in a little over two hours is twelve miles. This is how far the *Liberty* could travel in the time available, and this distance would only have been achieved had the *Liberty* traveled in a straight line. Israeli planes had been monitoring the *Liberty*'s position throughout the morning. Under these circumstances, for anyone to think that *Liberty* had sufficient time to be out of the area is ridiculous.

The truth is, almost every pilot in the Israeli Air Force knew the *Liberty* was in the area, and none of them had any valid reason to think that the situation had changed to any degree in just a little over two hours' time. Under such circumstances, caution demanded an attacking airplane or torpedo boat to assume that any possible naval target may be an American ship and not the enemy. Instead of operating under this assumption, the opposite was the case. Israeli defense forces assumed their unknown target was the enemy and attacked the *Liberty* under this wrong assumption. Doing so was unconscionable and indefensible.

In regard to the miscalculation of the *Liberty*'s speed, such determinations are a routine and straightforward procedure for any vessel at sea. To be sure, the accuracy of such a calculation is always in error to some degree. However, the Liberty's speed was only 5 knots in comparison to a calculated speed of 28 knots. This is an error in speed of 23 knots, or almost six times the Liberty's actual speed. No matter what the circumstances, an error of this magnitude is outside the realm of possibility, and this is especially true in consideration of the fact that this wrongful determination was made *twice*. According to MTB logs, the first calculation of the *Liberty*'s speed occurred when the MTBs were at an extreme range from the *Liberty*. The second calculation was made nine minutes later when the MTBs were seventeen miles from the *Liberty*. The situation was such that by simply observing an MTB radar screen for a few minutes, it would have been readily apparent that the MTBs were closing the *Liberty* at a significant rate. There is no need for a calculator to make this determination. Thus, the MTBs did not need assistance to close and identify their target. For this reason alone, it is reasonable to conclude that the Israeli version of events is an after-the-fact fabrication offered in the hope of evading responsibility for what occurred.

Because of a ridiculous error in the determination of the *Liberty*'s speed, a flight of armed Mirage jets was called in to investigate the situation and determine if the *Liberty* was an enemy vessel. If it was, they were under orders to attack. What happened? On a clear, balmy day, with identification markings clearly visible on the *Liberty* and a large American flag flying briskly from its mast, they mistakenly identified the *Liberty* as being the *El Quseir*. The *El Quseir* is an Egyptian military vessel one-half the size of the *Liberty* and having a profile that was somewhat like the *Liberty* but with clearly notable differences.

The USS *Liberty* is a retrofitted WWII victory ship that was previously used to ferry cargo and supplies to Europe. On any given day with reasonable visibility, even an untrained person could easily see that the *Liberty* was not a combat vessel. Incredibly, the flight of Mirage jets, with specific orders to identify the target before attacking, was unable to make this distinction. During the course of their attack, these jets made several low-level passes over the *Liberty*. To believe that while making these passes, none of the Israeli pilots saw the *Liberty*'s American flag or noticed that the *Liberty*'s decks had no offensive weapons on them, defies comprehension.

The first air attack on the USS *Liberty* was by cannon fire and rockets. This kind of ordinance would not cause the decks and bulkheads of a metal ship to burst into flames. This being the case, there was no obscuring smoke to block the view of the *Liberty* for the second wave of jet fighters. These planes pounded the *Liberty* with cannon fire, rockets, and napalm. It was the burning napalm that torched the ship and generated the obscuring smoke observed by the MTBs.

As circumstances had it, during this second air attack, one of the pilots recognized the *Liberty* as being an American ship. He called this information into his controllers on the ground. Upon doing so, this pilot was told *to continue his attack*. Not satisfied, the Israeli pilot questioned his orders a second time. Again, he was ordered to *proceed* with the attack. Unfortunately for the crew of the *Liberty*, the pilot's conscience did not overrule his sense of duty and loyalty to Israel. Left unexplained is why one pilot could identify the *Liberty* when the other pilots could not. According to the MTB group leader, his boats commenced their torpedo attack on the USS *Liberty* because smoke from the burning ship prevented him from making a positive identification of his target, and upon approaching, one of the *Liberty*'s 50-caliber machine guns opened fire on them. Granted, a 50-caliber machine gun being fired in their direction would have been of concern to the MTB crews. On the other side of the coin, the *Liberty* had just been strafed, rocketed, and napalmed by two sorties of unknown aircraft. This being the case, it certainly is understandable why one member of the Liberty's crew attempted to defend his ship. According to the MTB group leader, the Liberty was so shrouded in smoke that a positive identification was impossible. One has to wonder how much smoke it takes to make a WWII victory ship appear to be a modern-day warship. Smoke, being warmer than air, rises. In other words, despite the contention that the *Liberty*'s decks and superstructure were shrouded in smoke, this was not true for the ship's hull, which should have been clearly visible below the smoke.

From the profile of its hull alone, anyone familiar with ships would be able to readily discern that the *Liberty* was not a warship, and this is true even if its decks and superstructure were clouded in smoke. Therefore, the prudent thing for the MTB group leader to do, if he was not able to positively identify the ship he was dealing with, was to back off out of machine gun range and observe the situation. Clearly, the burning and stricken *Liberty* was a threat to no one. This being the case, to give an order to fire five torpedoes at an unknown and defenseless ship was an unconscionable act of villainy.

According to the crew members of the *Liberty*, after launching their torpedoes, the Israeli torpedo boats circled the *Liberty* and machine-gunned its life rafts, some of which had been lowered into the water in anticipation of abandoning the ship. It is understandable why the MTB captains would deny doing this. Such conduct is a war crime. To deliberately deny defenseless sailors a chance to save themselves from a sinking ship is murder. On the basis of the testimony that is readily available, such charges cry out for investigation. This has not happened because the testimony about this particular aspect of the USS *Liberty* Incident never appeared in the report issued by the official US Naval Court of Inquiry, the first group to investigate the incident.

The Israeli government has provided us with its version of what transpired during the USS *Liberty* Incident. However, their excuses and posturing are feeble and approach the theater of the absurd. The truth is that it is impossible for the dozen or so Israeli sailors and pilots to see the *Liberty* while she was being attacked and not realize that she was a defenseless ship and not a threat to anyone.

Furthermore, it was impossible for the attacking pilots and sailors to not see the *Liberty*'s markings, which identified it as being an American ship. Therefore, we are left with the conclusion that Israel deliberately attacked a United States ship with the intent of sending it to the bottom of the Mediterranean Sea, with all hands-on board. Why would they do such a thing?

CHAPTER 7:
Was Our Government Culpable

During the Six-Day War, why would Israel knowingly attack one of our ships with the intention of sinking it, with all hands on board? The answer to this question should be obvious. Israel attacked the USS *Liberty* with the intent of sinking it so Egypt would be blamed for the attack. This would surely bring the United States into the war on the side of Israel. Therefore, the attack on the USS *Liberty* was a war crime. However, to an Israeli, it was a justifiable war crime committed for a good cause—the survival of the State of Israel. Surely the death of a few hundred unsuspecting American sailors is a small price to pay to ensure "God's chosen people ", have a nation of their own. However, the situation is not this simple. Examination of the information available indicates that our government was complicit and played a role in this plot. If this is true, then not only is our government guilty of being a coconspirator of a war crime, it is also guilty of grave treason against the American people.

At the time of the attack on the USS *Liberty*, the Sixth Fleet in the Mediterranean Sea was comprised of two aircraft carriers: the USS Saratoga and the USS America. These two carriers were under the command of Vice Admiral William I. Martin (COMSIXTHFLT). The Sixth Fleet was split into two task force groups, each comprised of an aircraft carrier, a cruiser, and several destroyers. Carrier Task Force 60 was commanded by Rear Admiral Geis. Most of the time, the fleet concerned itself with operational readiness (practice and training) but was also there to show the American flag and make our presence known to the Mediterranean Sea nations. During times of crisis, the fleet enters an operational mode where its presence and the threat of intervention serve to temper the actions of contending parties.

During the Six-Day War, Sixth Fleet ships were ordered to stay at least five hundred miles from the Gaza coast. This restriction did not apply to the USS *Liberty* because it was not a Sixth Fleet ship.

However, with orders to proceed into the heart of a war zone twelve miles off the coast of Gaza, the USS *Liberty*'s skipper, Captain McGonagle, prudently requested that a Sixth Fleet destroyer be sent as an escort for the scantily armed *Liberty*. Vice Admiral Martin declined this request because the *Liberty* was a non-participating, clearly marked American ship in international waters and not subject to attack by any nation."

The above response from Admiral Martin is shocking. The *Liberty* was ordered to stay in international waters. However, international boundaries mean nothing during a war. Furthermore, providing an armed escort for a lightly armed ship on a real mission is standard military procedure.

Prudence and caution demanded that Admiral Martin honor Captain McGonagle's request. Furthermore, at the time of this incident, the Sixth Fleet was not involved in any real mission.

Therefore, Admiral Martin's destroyers were doing nothing of importance when the *Liberty* was attacked. For these reasons, Admiral Martin should have been censured for his decision and brought up on charges of dereliction of duty. His first responsibility as commander of the Sixth Fleet is to protect American lives and property. He failed fulfilling this responsibility, and because of his decision, 174 sailors were wounded and 34 lost their lives. Admiral Martin's wrongful decision was so questionable and out of line with standard military procedure, that it is reasonable to wonder if it was made for him by someone in Washington. When professionals in positions of authority fail to do their jobs properly, there is usually more going on than meets the eye.

Another extremely troubling aspect of the USS *Liberty* Incident is the recall of the aircraft launched to assist her. Upon learning that the *Liberty* was under attack, the Sixth Fleet launched several sorties of aircraft to assist and rescue the *Liberty*, but these rescue efforts were *called back*.

This was a horrendous development. The full story of what really occurred in regard to these aborted rescue attempts should be a matter of record and easily discernible. This is not the case. Everything associated with the launch of these airplanes is shrouded in mystery and confusion. It is difficult from the information made public to definitively discern how many rescue sorties were launched, which carrier launched them, how many planes were involved, what kinds of aircraft they were, and the time the launches occurred. It's as if someone deliberately clouded the facts to make the determination of what actually occurred impossible.

The implications apparent from the recalled rescue attempts are nothing short of mindboggling. They imply that a high-level official of our government did not want the crew of the *Liberty* to be rescued. This being the case, it follows that the government official in question was operating from a hidden agenda, more important to him than the lives of those innocent sailors. As Americans, we have a right to know what this agenda was and who made this decision. It has been demonstrated that Israel's intent was to sink the *Liberty* and thereby murder its crew. Therefore, it also must be true that the relief flights were called back to help Israel accomplish this goal. Voila! We now know the true colors of our mysterious government official. Either he was sympathetic to the Israeli cause to the extent that he was willing to facilitate murdering American servicemen, or he was in a position where he had no choice other than to cooperate with the Israelis. Either way, there is one thing that we can be absolutely certain of: the USS *Liberty* Incident proves that Israel's interests are more important than ours, the issue being who are the people that decided it should be this way?

We presently know a lot about the individual who called off the rescue attempt, but we still have not determined who this person was. We can rule out an officer of the Sixth Fleet because they were the ones who launched the rescue efforts in the first place. Furthermore, it is extremely doubtful that Admiral Martin would arbitrarily reverse a decision like this once it was made by him or one of his subordinates. Thus, the recall order had to come from Washington because there is no one senior to Admiral Martin in the Mediterranean Sea. Admiral Martin's immediate superior in Washington was Secretary of the Navy Paul Nitze. In turn, Secretary Nitze reported to General Earle Wheeler, chairman of the Joint Chiefs of Staff. General Wheeler's boss was Robert McNamara, the secretary of defense, who reported directly to President Johnson. It is hard to imagine that any of the people between Admiral Martin and President Johnson would take it upon themselves to recall the Liberty's rescue effort without President Johnson's approval. If the president had not agreed with this ignoble decision, it would have been the end of their career.

The decision to call back the rescue attempts for the Liberty rests squarely upon the shoulders of President Johnson. Reinforcing this conclusion is the fact that the flight of A-4 Skyhawks, armed with nuclear weapons, was launched and called back in almost the same time frame as the rescue aircraft. The only person who had the authority to order a nuclear strike was our president, and once ordered, the president was the only person who could call a halt to such a mission. Therefore, it is reasonable to conclude that President Johnson was a party to all these decisions. Confirmation of this is provided by Rear Admiral Larry Geis, commander of Sixth Fleet Task Force 60, who, immediately following the USS *Liberty* Incident, assembled his staff and informed them that it was President Johnson himself who had gotten on the circuit and told him that the reason for his recall order was, "We are not going to embarrass an ally (Israel)." Left unexplained is, how was it possible for President Johnson to know that the attacking aircraft were Israeli? At this point in time, no one provided President Johnson with this information, and not even the crew of the USS *Liberty* knew which nation was attacking them. Therefore, it is reasonable to conclude that President Johnson had knowledge of the attack before it occurred.

It is clear that our mysterious government official is none other than President Johnson. Such decisions could only be made by our president in his capacity as commander-in-chief. The buck stops clearly on the president's desk on this one. However, this puts us in an untenable and very disturbing situation. We must come to grips with two possible conclusions, both of which are profoundly sad and regrettable. The first is that President Johnson was sympathetic to the Israeli cause, to the point where he would sacrifice the lives of American servicemen to help the Israelis achieve their goals. This is the least likely possibility. President Johnson loved his country, and it is doubtful that he willfully placed Israel's interests ahead of ours in such a vile and despicable manner. Therefore, we are left with only one alternative, and this is that President Johnson was in a position such that he had no other choice other than to obey the Zionists who were running the show.

How can an American believe that our president was subservient to the Zionists to the extent that he would facilitate the murder of American servicemen and drop nuclear bombs on an unknowing and defenseless city? Unfortunately, we can believe it because the facts and circumstances of the situation leave us with no other choice. Furthermore, if this conclusion is not true, why did our government go to such great lengths to cover up this incident?

As a matter of course, the following are the investigations that were convened by our government to address the USS Liberty Incident:[2]

- US Naval Court of Inquiry (1967)
- Joint Chiefs of Staff's Report (1967)
- CIA Intelligence Memorandums (1967)
- Clark Clifford Report (1967)
- Senate Foreign Relations Committee Testimony (1967)
- House Armed Services Committee Investigation (1971)
- The NSA History Report (1981)

All these investigations exonerated Israel of wrongdoing. Every member of the *Liberty*'s crew disagreed with these results. From their perspective, these investigative efforts were a whitewash and part of the cover-up, the purpose of which was to let Israel off the hook and hide our government's role in this sordid affair. According to the *Liberty*'s crew, important and crucial information was omitted while false and erroneous data was allowed to be heard. Furthermore, all the damning testimony that conflicted with Israel's version of events was deliberately excluded from these proceedings and not heard. According to the USS *Liberty* Veterans Association, the orders to falsify (the naval inquiry) came directly from President Johnson.

Since 1967, the USS *Liberty* Veterans Association has persistently tried to get Congress to launch an investigation into the matter, all for naught. Article 1, section 8 of our Constitution gives the House of Representatives the power "to define and punish piracies and felonies committed on the high seas and offenses against the Law of

Nations." Certainly, the USS *Liberty* Incident is a situation that meets these criteria and thereby demands the attention of Congress. Despite this, Congress has steadfastly refused to conduct an investigation and the cover-up continues to this day.

This brings us to Operation Cyanide! According to the USS *Liberty* Veterans Association, they possess documentation that proves that the Liberty was an integral part of this Israeli plan.

Thus, Operation Cyanide had to be a joint undertaking by the United States and Israel. This means that during the Six-Day War, America was not an uninvolved spectator of this war but instead a secret ally of Israel with an agreed-upon role to play. Unfortunately, the available documentation has been censored such that it does not reveal the extent and nature of the United States' involvement. Despite this, there is much we can discern from what we already know to be true.

For example, the name of this sinister joint Israeli-American operation speaks volumes about its nature. Cyanide is a poison used to kill unsuspecting victims. From this name, it should be clear that Operation Cyanide was a joint effort between our government and Israel to make unsuspecting victims of one or more groups of people. Who are the people associated with the USS *Liberty* Incident who fall within this criterion? Two groups come to mind; the crew of the USS *Liberty* and all those in Cairo when the Sixth Fleet A-4s were heading their way with nuclear cargo. The crew members of the USS *Liberty* certainly became victims and had no idea they would be a party to such an atrocity. As far as the people in Cairo are concerned, being vaporized in a nuclear blast assuredly was going to be a surprise to them.

Thus, we can be confident that we have nailed down Operation Cyanide. Cyanide was a joint effort between Israel and our government to sink an American ship with all hands-on board and blame this attack on Egypt. With the American public enraged over this development, our government would have the excuse it needed to enter the war on Israel's side. As horrible as it is, America's entry into the war was going to be made with a bang—a bang that would vaporize Cairo and all those unfortunate enough to be in the city when our nuclear weapons were unleashed. Understanding all this, we can reasonably be certain that Operation Cyanide was the Israeli code name for the USS *Liberty* Incident itself. Everything that transpired was a part of this diabolical plan, and we can thank providence that the *Liberty* was saved from total destruction by a torpedo that was slightly off its mark.

To believe any American, especially the president of the United States, would be party to a plan to kill American servicemen is lunacy. But as insane as this is, it does not change the fact that this is what happened. Surely, President Johnson must have made his regrettable decisions under tremendous pressure. This raises the question of who could possibly hold such power over a sitting president. The answer to this question is the same group of people who overthrew our government in 1913 and played a key role in establishing the State of Israel, the Zionist Banksters of the New World Order. Furthermore, President Johnson became president after the assassination of President Kennedy. This being the case, it is possible that President Johnson feared he was dealing with the people who brought about the death of one of our most loved and admired presidents. Surely this possibility must have tempered his actions.

This is a difficult scenario for Americans to accept because it is so fantastic. Granted, the Zionist Banksters hold tremendous sway and influence over those who lead us, but to maintain that they have the power to order a sitting president to commit irrational war crimes is difficult to swallow. However, swallow it we must if we are going to understand our true history and how the world we live in functions. As we delve into subsequent chapters, the absurd will become more and more reasonable, such that we will reach a point where believing the absurd is the only option we have if we wish to live by the truth.

CHAPTER 8:
Fingerprints of the New World Order

When something monumental occurs, the situation may be such that it is not readily apparent what caused the event to happen. However, as events pile up over time, it becomes easier to discern what is really going on. This is only true when a person has an open mind. It certainly isn't the case if one assumes everything our government tells us is true. Keeping this in mind, let's recap what we know to be true:

- The Federal Reserve Bank is the central bank of the United States.
- The Federal Reserve Bank is nothing its name implies and is a privately owned money pump for the New World Order.
- The Federal Reserve Bank does nothing beneficial for the United States or its citizens.
- The New World Order is made up of the rich and powerful banking families who own and control the Federal Reserve Bank.
- The banking families of the New World Order overthrew our government in 1913.
- The vehicle used to accomplish the overthrow of our government was the Federal Reserve Act.
- The Federal Reserve Act, in conjunction with Amendments XVI and XVII (all of which came into being in 1913), changed our government from being a federation of state governments into an all-powerful national government.
- Our new national government owns a piece of the time and labor of every working American.
- Our government was overthrown to give the Banksters enhanced control over our government and citizens.

- The New World Order is not new but instead is the *old-world order* with an upscale name.
- The house of Rothschild, the richest and most influential banking family of them all, championed the creation of the State of Israel.
- In order to secure the future of Israel, the United States and Israel executed and aborted a false flag attack to murder the entire crew of the USS Liberty, so as to give the United States an excuse to enter the Six-Day War on the side of Israel.

Incredibly, many Americans have no problem with the Zionist/New World Order agenda. They believe that despite its flaws, the world is pretty much as it should be. Some of us even believe it is a Christian obligation to support the State of Israel. People think this way because this is what they have been led to believe by the church they attend. The rationale used to substantiate this belief is in the Old Testament of the Bible—the Jews are God's chosen people and the promised land (Palestine) was given to them by God. There are a multitude of flaws associated with this kind of thinking, not the least of which is that Jesus came into the world to establish a New Covenant, not with just the Jews, but with all of mankind. Under the New Covenant, all men are brothers and equals in the eyes of God. There are no more chosen people, and there is no more "promised land." A Christian establishes his relationship with God through love and a commitment to righteousness. Spiritually, a piece of dirt or land has no significance whatsoever to a Christian.

Oddly enough, as far as Palestine is concerned, this last truth is also true for our Jewish brothers. According to the Torah, the Jews had sinned, and because of their sins, God took away the promised land and dispersed the Jews throughout the nations of the world. There, the Jews were to stay until they had atoned for their sins and God once again called them together as one people. It is for God and God alone to deem when this will occur. It is definitely not the place of any Jew or group of Jews to make this decision for God. According to the New Covenant, Christians are under no obligation to help establish the State of Israel. According to the Torah, the Jewish Bible, it is wrong for a Jew to do this as well. However, this situation is far more serious for a Jew than a Christian. If a Jew works to establish the State of Israel, they do so contrary to God's will.

Jesus Christ taught that all men are brothers and equal in the eyes of God. Zionists Jews subscribe to the notion that all Jews have a right to return home to Palestine. These two schools of thought are opposed to each other. A Jew returning home to a land he has never seen or lived on has to displace someone from the land he covets, the problem being that those being displaced have occupied the land in question for centuries. This raises the question, who has the right to own and live on the land formerly occupied by the Palestinians? Civil law is clear on this: the Palestinians own the land, have clear title to it, and no one has the right to take it from them. Case closed! Unfortunately, it is not closed if you are a Zionist. Zionists believe they are God's chosen and being "chosen" means their rights to Palestine overshadow and supersede those of the Palestinians.

No Christian or American, under any circumstance, can agree with this point of view. It is contrary to the concept of equal justice under the law and the fact that all men are equal in the eyes of God. The truth of the matter is that what the Zionists believe is racial discrimination because it makes second-class citizens out of a group of people whose only crime in life is not being Jewish. The situation is no different from apartheid in South Africa, which was condemned by the nations of the world. However, the situation is more complex than this. If an individual is one of God's chosen, then it follows that there is something about this person that makes them better than other people. If a person is better than other people, then they are superior to these people. There is grave danger in this kind of thinking. The Nazis believed they were superior to everyone else, and we know full well where such thinking led them.

When the Jews sinned against God, as punishment, God took away the land he had given them and dispersed the Jews throughout the other nations of the world. This severed their claim to the promised land. However, after thousands of years, this long-dead claim was resurrected by the Zionists who decided the time had come for the Jews to once again have a nation of their own. Unfortunately for the Palestinians, the location selected for this new nation was the Jews' former biblical home in Palestine. This is unfortunate because once again, the Palestinians were going to be evicted from the land of their forefathers.

This situation is also unfortunate for America because the Zionists have convinced many Americans that it is fitting and proper for us to help Israel achieve its goals. Americans believe this despite the fact this goes against everything America is supposed to stand for. Regrettably, we have also done this at the expense and detriment of the Palestinian people. We have no right or justification for taking the Israeli side of this issue. If choose sides we must, then justice demands that we stand with the Palestinians. Presently, we are wrongfully fighting on the side of the aggressors against people who are fighting to recover what was wrongfully taken from them. Furthermore, if we sided with the Palestinians against the Israelis, Israel would be more disposed to accept a negotiated settlement instead of using every minor provocation as an excuse to rain death and destruction upon those living close to their borders.

The United States holds the key to a peaceful settlement of the Middle East crisis. However, in order to achieve lasting peace, it is incumbent upon us to take up the Palestinian cause. Only then will Israel negotiate in good faith. The problem is that the NWO Zionists who control our government will never allow this to happen. Zionist thinking has been dominant within the Western world for the past one hundred years. During this time, the world has been preparing for war, fighting wars, or recovering from war. WWI, WWII, the War on Terror, and the USS *Liberty* Incident are Zionist-instigated abominations. Therefore, it is safe to assume that the other major events that have occurred over the past one hundred years will also bear evidence of Zionist meddling and interference. Following are several events that demonstrate this to be true.

The Great Depression

One of the main reasons Congress passed the Federal Reserve Act was because its backers assured us that the Federal Reserve Bank (Fed) would dampen business cycles and eliminate depressions. Recently, former Fed chairman Ben Bernanke admitted that instead of doing this, the Fed intentionally created the Great Depression of 1929.[1] Let's add this up! One of the reasons the Federal Reserve Act was passed was because proponents promised that the Fed would eliminate depressions. Instead of doing this, they intentionally created a depression. Doesn't this mean that the Federal Reserve Bank is guilty of fraud?

It is shocking that former Fed chairman Ben Bernanke owned up to the fact that the Fed is guilty of fraud. The Great Depression was a curse upon the people of this nation and everyone else in the world. Fortunes were lost, lives were ruined, suicides ensued, and the entire world was engulfed in misery and depredation. Despite all these things, Ben Bernanke makes this terrible admission with as much concern and empathy as if he were telling us what he had for breakfast. Why can he be so casual about something so horrendous? The Fed is so powerful and well entrenched that those who own and control it, care less about what Americans know or think. This speaks volumes about the Fed and the nature of the government we live under. The Fed publicly admitted to a crime that destroyed lives and brought abject misery to the entire world, and there is nothing that our government will do about it.

The Assassination of President Kennedy

President John F. Kennedy was beyond doubt one of America's great presidents. He was in league with George Washington, Thomas Jefferson, Abraham Lincoln, and Theodor Roosevelt. One may not agree with this assessment, but it can be shown to be true in consideration of what John Kennedy attempted to accomplish as our president. The following is an excerpt from a speech he made before the American Publishers Association on April 27, 1961. The speech is often referred to as the speech that got John F. Kennedy killed. It is described this way because the speech takes to task what would eventually come to be known as the New World Order:

> For we are opposed around the world by a monolithic
> and ruthless conspiracy that relies on covert means
> for expanding its sphere of influence—on infiltration

> instead of invasion, on subversion instead of elections, on intimidation instead of free choice, on guerrillas by night instead of armies by day. It is a system which has conscripted vast human and material resources into the building of a tightly knit, highly efficient machine that combines military, diplomatic, intelligence, economic, scientific, and political operations.

Although he does not name the organization to which he is referring, there is no doubt that in his speech, President Kennedy is talking about the incipient New World Order. Of course, during Kennedy's term of office, this name was not yet used. However, what other group of people can be described as being a "monolithic and ruthless conspiracy that relies on covert means for expanding its sphere of influence" and "is a system which has conscripted vast human and material resources into the building of a tightly knit, highly efficient machine"? The New World Order is the only organization that fits this description, and President Kennedy's speech is a declaration of war against them.

Who killed President Kennedy? According to the Warren Commission, it was Lee Harvey Oswald and he did this acting alone. However, in order for this to be true, we need a magic bullet, and there is no such thing as a magic bullet. Therefore, Oswald did not act alone, and if this was the case, it follows that the president was murdered by a group of conspirators. While both the Mafia and the Cubans harbored grudges against our president, to conclude that they were the masterminds behind his assassination does not make sense. Such a horrific event could only have been pulled off by the people who held sway over the law enforcement and investigative agencies of our federal government. This points directly to the New World Order! Clearly, they had the most compelling motive for killing our president. In his speech, President Kennedy had taken a stand against them. This left the NWO with little choice! President Kennedy was going to upset their apple cart, and he had to be stopped. If he wasn't, their plans for a New World Order would be foiled.

In June of 1963, President Kennedy issued Executive Order 11110. This executive order instructed the Treasury Department to print United States Treasury notes instead of Federal Reserve notes. These Treasury notes were backed by silver in contrast to Federal Reserve notes, which were *backed by nothing*. These actions are why we can be assured that President Kennedy is one of our greatest presidents. His executive order sidestepped the Federal Reserve Act of 1913 and shut off the Fed's money pump. President Kennedy, to his credit, was attempting to restore our republic by undoing the Fed-engineered overthrow of our government in 1913. Unfortunately, he failed to accomplish this because he was murdered.

Upon President Kennedy's death, Vice President Lyndon Johnson assumed the office of president. Among the first things Johnson did as President was to *dutifully* recall the United States Treasury notes that were in circulation. No president after Johnson has ever reissued these notes even though Executive Order 11110 still stands. By recalling these Treasury notes, President Johnson demonstrated his willingness to accommodate the wishes of what would eventually be called the New World Order. Why else would he reverse an executive order that was so tremendously beneficial to the people of this nation? Whether the New World Order murdered JFK or not, his assassination gave them tremendous sway over President Johnson, and this was also true for the presidents who followed. What American President would defy an organization that may have murdered the most popular president in modern times, and gotten away with it? Perhaps this is the reason why President Johnson recalled the USS *Liberty* rescue efforts and why he ordered our military to nuke Cairo.

The 9/11 Attack on World Trade Center

On September 11, 2001, the World Trade Center (WTC) was destroyed by a terrorist attack. A reasonable question to ask is, why the attack wasn't foiled before it came to fruition? Evidence exists that numerous people and organizations within our government were aware of the impending disaster. For example, an FBI field agent had reported to his superiors in Washington that a group of Arab nationals was learning how to fly commercial aircraft. The previous truck bomb attack on the twin towers on February 26, 1993, brought into sharp focus the fact that the WTC was a prime terrorist target. In response, the subject of a second attack by terrorists using hijacked commercial airliners was a common topic of discussion among military strategists and think tanks throughout the nation. A report by a field agent that something was amiss should have sparked an immediate response from this agent's superiors in Washington. For them to have ignored such a report is too incredible to believe. They are professional people who are paid to be on top of such matters. Obviously, they did not do the job they were paid to do, and to think this failure was an honest mistake does not make sense.

The time from when the first airliner was known to be in trouble until the last plane crashed, was about two hours.[2] This being the case, why weren't any of the hijacked airplanes intercepted by American fighters? If an aircraft inadvertently flies through the Air Defense Identification Zone (ADIZ) without clearance, the offending aircraft will have a fighter escort on its tail in minutes.

The North American Aerospace Defense Command (NORAD) is tasked with this responsibility. As a matter of routine, NORAD scrambles armed and ready jets specifically for this purpose. If an aircraft experiences difficulties in the skies such as being off course or losing communication, NORAD reacts immediately. In the ten-month period preceding 9/11, NORAD completed sixty-seven interceptions with an average intercept time of twenty minutes from the time the FAA knew an aircraft had a problem to the time the intercept was accomplished. In no instance was an intercept unsuccessful.

It is incredible to think that none of the four hijacked airplanes on 9/11 were intercepted. Therefore, it is reasonable to conclude that officials at the highest levels of our government allowed the attack to proceed. This should not be hard to believe. If President Johnson called back airplanes launched to save American lives during the USS Liberty Incident, it is not unreasonable to believe that President George W. Bush would not have any reservations about preventing American fighters from intercepting the hijacked airliners. While it is true that a group of amateur Saudi nationals pulled off the attack, it is also true that the attacks would never have succeeded if our government officials had done their jobs properly. The attack on the USS Liberty was a false-flag attack to get the United States into a war with the Arab nations. This plot failed only because the Liberty did not sink. However, on 9/11, a second attempt to bring the United States into war with the Arab world succeeded. The nation is still embroiled in this war and will be for many years to come.

Our Wars in the Middle East

Saddam Hussein invaded Kuwait when George H. W. Bush was president. A coalition of forces led by the United States, in an operation called Desert Storm, forced the Iraqi military to abandon their conquest and flee back to Iraq. This should have been the end of the story. However, 9/11 happened under the administration of George W. Bush, the son of George H.W. Bush. The younger Bush responded by orchestrating a campaign of lies against Saddam Hussein, Iraq's president, who had nothing to do with 9/11. This didn't matter to the younger Bush. He was intent upon upstaging his father and also was deferring to the New World Order Zionists who wanted the United States embroiled in fighting Israel's wars in the Middle East.

Toward this end, on March 20, 2003, we invaded Iraq in an operation called Shock and Awe. We were led to believe the goal of this offensive was to depose Saddam Hussain and those loyal to him. However, belying this limited goal was Bush's decision to disarm and dismiss the Iraqi police, military, and intelligence forces. This was a fateful decision, and to say the least, it was a blunder of biblical proportions. The Iraqi government had huge quantities of weapons stashed everywhere throughout the nation, and the Iraqi military and police had access to these weapons. By telling them to go home with no job and no way to feed their families, we ensured that these people would use these weapons to start an insurgency against us. Instead of firing these people, we should have realized they were our greatest asset for building a new Iraq. Had we used them for this purpose, there would have been no insurgency, and the United States would not be caught in the quagmire we are in today. This decision was so foolish and so detrimental to the interests of this nation, there had to be a sinister hand behind it.

The USS *Liberty* Incident was engineered by the Zionists to draw us into fighting Israel's wars in the Middle East. The attack on 9/11 was allowed to happen for this same reason. Therefore, to think that our intention was to depose Saddam Hussein and leave Iraq after cutting off the head of the snake does not add up. This is especially true in light of the fact that we alienated and made enemies of the very people we needed to make our invasion a success. The real purpose of our invasion of Iraq, in deference to the Zionists, was to establish a foothold in the Middle East so we could become embroiled in fighting wars on Israel's behalf. This is why we are fighting today, and this is why we will be fighting for many years to come.

Dual Citizenship

The following United States Oath of Citizenship, also known as the Oath of Allegiance, must be recited by every prospective citizen before he or she receives a naturalization certificate:[3]

> I hereby declare, on oath, that I absolutely and entirely renounce and abjure all allegiance and fidelity to any foreign prince, potentate, state, or sovereignty, of whom or which I have heretofore been a subject or citizen; that I will support and defend the Constitution and laws of the United States of America against all enemies, foreign and domestic; that I will bear true faith and allegiance to the same; that I will bear arms on behalf of the United States when required by the law; that I will perform noncombatant service in the armed forces of the United States when required by the law; that I will perform work of national importance under civilian direction when required by the law; and that I take this obligation freely without any mental reservation or purpose of evasion; so help me God.

The wording in this oath is quite clear: in order to be a citizen of the United States, one must renounce their citizenship in their country of origin. Until 1967, there were a number of laws on the books ensuring this was the case. These laws date back to the early days of our republic. Indeed, in 1958 in *Perez v. Brown*, the Supreme Court ruled in favor of one of these laws when it was legally challenged. However, in 1967, nine years after the *Perez v. Brown* decision, in *Afroyim v. Rusk,* the US Supreme Court reversed itself and ruled that naturalized citizens cannot be deprived of their citizenship by the government under any circumstances.

The crux of this case was that Beys Afroyim, a Polish-born immigrant who had become a naturalized citizen, voted in an Israeli election in violation of the oath he swore to be a United States citizen. This ruling by the US Supreme Court demonstrates that the court believes that willingly violating an oath taken to become a citizen of this nation means nothing, and defrauding the people of this nation by violating said oath is something our government is powerless to address. Only a Zionist thinks this way, and we can thank them for being behind this Supreme Court decision. This decision is just one more example of a never-ending series of actions taken by the Zionists to dismantle our Republic.

Notes

1. The Fed deliberately caused the Great Depression. (http://www.wnd.com/2008/03/59405/)
2. 9/11 Time Line: (http://www.wanttoknow.info/9-11cover-up10pg)
3. Dual citizenship (http://en.wikipedia.org/wiki/Afroyim v. Rusk)

CHAPTER 9:
The Economics of Disaster

The economy of this nation has been in and out of recessions for the past decade. However, despite what the pundits in this field think or say, the recessions we have been experiencing are far different from the ones we have experienced in the past. The reason for this is we have a monetary system that is being managed primarily to benefit its owners instead of the people of this nation. Furthermore, our present economic downturn is not the result of uncontrollable market forces but, instead, the result of actions taken by the New World Order moguls to consolidate their power and control over the world's economies. The best example we have of this is the passage of the General Agreement on Tariffs and Trade (GATT) in 1994. Despite the fact that various world markets have rebounded over the past few years, the average American has been left behind. The situation is such that we will never again experience the level of prosperity we enjoyed over most of this nation's history.

Upon passage of GATT, the United States lost its sovereignty to the World Trade Organization (WTO), an organization whose bylaws make it a ruling authority superior to Congress, our president, and Supreme Court. The justifications offered by our elected representatives for their vote for GATT were that this trade agreement would help our economy by reducing tariffs, eliminating barriers to American goods and services, minimizing protectionism, and enhancing America's leadership position in the global economy. Belying these claims is the fact that the standard of living of the American worker is among the highest in the world. In contrast, the vast majority of the world's workers are slaves to their employers, earning barely enough to provide their families with the essentials of life. If all tariffs and barriers to trade are lifted, American workers will be in level competition with the low-paid workers of the third world who greatly outnumber us. This being true, logic and basic economics tell us that the tendency will be for the American worker to be pulled down to the salary level of the third-world worker, not the other way around.

As predicted, in keeping with the actions of Congress, reduced tariffs, the absence of barriers to trade, and minimized protectionism have allowed American corporations to move overseas where labor is cheaper and environmental regulations are almost nonexistent. It has also encouraged corporations remaining here to outsource American jobs so they can take advantage of the underpaid and unprotected labor forces of the third world. The end result is that employee benefits for American workers are disappearing, their earning power is being reduced, and they are being forced into menial jobs of what is now euphemistically called a consumer economy. A consumer economy is a service economy, and what this means is that instead of the basis of our economy being the production of goods, it is now providing services to others.

However, our situation is worse than just described because of our monetary system. If you ask the average American where money comes from, their response probably will be "from the government." This is true to the extent that our government prints our money, but this is where its involvement ends. Money at the national level comes from debt, or more specifically, the national debt. When our government needs money, it borrows this money from the Federal Reserve Bank, which despite its name is privately owned. In other words, instead of creating money as provided for in our Constitution, Congress, through the Federal Reserve Act, has outsourced this responsibility to a private corporation. As a result, our government must pay the principal and associated interest on money that it is supposed to create for itself at no cost. The money created by this process is called *fiat money* because it is not backed by gold and silver as in the past.

Fiat money is not the only money that fuels our economy, and it is only about 5 percent of the total amount in circulation. This being true, where does the remaining 95 percent come from? This elusive money does not have a name because Americans are not supposed to know it exists.

For lack of something better, let's call it *debt money* because, like fiat money, it is created out of debt. Fiat money is created when the

Federal government borrows money from the Fed, but debt money is created when you or I borrow money from our bank. When we go to a bank to apply for a loan to buy a car or a house, upon approval of our loan, the bank credits our account with the amount borrowed. This credit is newly created money available for our purchase. Naturally, most Americans think that the money placed in our accounts come from the bank, but this is not true. To be sure, the bank is required to maintain reserves to cover part of our loan, but it doesn't put this money into our account. Instead, all the bank does is make a bookkeeping entry that creates the money we borrowed. Thus, the bank has loaned us money that did not exist before we took out our loan. At this point, the only real value involved in the transaction is the collateral pledged by our promissory note, which is an asset to the bank.

While this seems crazy, the system is even crazier than this. Once we buy our car or some other item through a bank loan, the person receiving the money from this sale will eventually deposit these funds in their bank. This new deposit is an asset to the bank in question, and this being the case, they are allowed to make additional loans to their customers for up to 90 percent of the amount deposited. This deposit-loan-deposit process keeps repeating with ever-smaller amounts so that eventually, the debt money created by the banks is nine times the original amount we borrowed. For example, if we borrowed $10,000 to buy a car, our bank conjures up this amount by crediting it to our account, thus making it available for our purchase. As a consequence of our purchase, eventually, our original loan turns into $90,000 in other loans made by other banks. The money used for all these loans exists only as notations on paper, but these notations allow those involved to obtain possessions equivalent to the sum of all the individual loans. Now here's the rub; while the money the banker loaned us was created by the bank out of thin air, the principal and interest, which eventually will have to be paid, are not. This money must be earned by the borrowers through work or some other means. Yes, the borrower ends up with something of value that was purchased with the borrowed money, but incredibly, the bank ends up getting real money earned by the borrower plus interest even though the bank contributed nothing of real value to the transaction and only acted as a facilitator.

The reality of our situation is that our monetary system has made us akin to rats running on a treadmill. We keep running faster to get to the end, to be out of debt, but the faster we run, the faster the treadmill turns. The truth is that we will never reach the end. Instead, we continually fall behind, and our total debt keeps increasing. This is the financial state of affairs of our nation today. Our national and personal debt is reaching astronomical figures, and there is no way to ever pay it off because we can never earn enough money to keep pace with the growing debt. Indeed, if all the money in circulation today were used to pay our existing debt, there would not be enough to cover all the outstanding loans.

To summarize,

- Our monetary system is owned and managed by private individuals answerable to only themselves. This is an unacceptable situation. No private group of people should exercise this level of authority over our lives and economy.
- Our monetary system is based upon debt instead of value, and as a result, interest-bearing debt is the driving force behind the creation of money
- Borrowing by our government, corporations, and individuals creates money, but the money created is really debt owed to the banks. In truth, the banks own all our money.
- The interest paid for a loan, in many cases, is as much as the principal, and many borrowers pay back twice the amount borrowed in real money even though the bank created the principal out of thin air through a bookkeeping entry.
- Because of the above, as a nation, we are locked into a perpetually increasing debt, most of which would not exist if our government provided this service as required by our Constitution.

Let's go back in time to when the Western world embarked upon its age of exploration. Indeed, early on, we didn't know if the world was round, and it appeared to be infinite. People looked at the horizon, and it seemed to go on forever. What better way was there to get rich than to go out into the unknown and grab a piece of the action? However, this takes money, and if one doesn't have any, it has to be borrowed. The issue is that no one wants to loan money unless there is something in it for them. Perhaps usury isn't such a bad idea after all. In the real world, if I am going to get mine and this takes borrowing, what's wrong with sharing a portion of my newfound wealth with those who provided me with the means of finding it? This makes sense.

Fueled by money-lending at interest, the Old World expanded, and eventually, we discovered the New World. When we did, our flat infinite world changed into a round finite one. Despite this, the world was still relatively empty, and its resources seemed to be unlimited. In time, our ingenuity and resourcefulness produced the Industrial Revolution. As a species, we could no longer expand territorially, but our bountiful earth was there to be exploited, and the moneylenders were more than willing to help us do this. In this nation, we exploited our environment with a vengeance, and in time, we became an industrial giant. Our success and prosperity made us the envy of the world, and it was credit and the moneylenders who helped us achieve this.

The above being true, what is so terrible about a privately owned, debt-based monetary system? The answer to this question, simply put, is

- A debt-based monetary system in private hands is immoral because it allows the lender to reap windfall profits for doing essentially nothing.
- Extreme wealth gives those who have it an unfair advantage over everyone else in society.
- Extreme wealth enables those who have it to corrupt everything they touch, including key institutions of society and governments.
- A debt-based monetary system in private hands is driven by the profit motive. Other important considerations that come into play are ignored.

The Federal Reserve System is a criminal enterprise and is a system of usury in every sense of the word. We fought a revolutionary war against Great Britain, but what most Americans do not realize is that one of the reasons for the Revolutionary War was to free ourselves from the bankers who held England and the rest of Europe in their grip. We won the Revolutionary War and thought this was the end of the story. We had established ourselves as an independent nation and were free to march west to pursue our manifest destiny. What we didn't realize was that the forces of evil were relentless, and in time, we would grow complacent. In 1913, our naivety paid off for the Banksters. While no one paid attention, they cajoled and hoodwinked Congress into passing the unconstitutional Federal Reserve Act. From this day forward, Americans were no longer free and independent people. Our future and well-being would be in the hands of a gaggle of greedy men who would make us pay dearly for their presence. The bitter irony of our situation is that these Banksters enslaved us with our own money and are now using our resources, wealth, and military to enslave the rest of the world.

But if this were all there was to be concerned about, it wouldn't be so bad in comparison to what is eventually in store for us. Usury is a crime, and our hijacked Congress made this crime the basis of our monetary system. But the real tragedy of our situation is that the health and viability of our economic system are wholly dependent upon the continued expansion of our economy. We are told by the moneylenders that our economy should expand around 3 percent yearly to remain healthy. This seems reasonable, but appearances are deceiving. The truth behind this seemingly innocent number is that an annual growth rate of 3 percent is not a straight line on a graph as one would think. Instead, the 3 percent each year is applied to the previous year's total. Therefore, a yearly growth rate of 3 percent means that economic output and activity must increase not linearly over time but along an increasingly steeper quadratic curve.

For example, assume at any point in time that our economic output is one hundred widgets, and our target growth rate is 3 percent yearly. This being the case, our economic output will double approximately every twenty-three years. If one hundred widgets were necessary for year one, two hundred widgets will be needed in twenty-three years, and sixteen hundred widgets in ninety-two years. After ten cycles, the total amount of widgets produced would have to be 102,400 or a 1,000 percent increase over our base year. If a nation embraces a debt-based monetary system where private banks control the money supply by issuing debt, the inescapable consequence of such a course of action is that the nation so cursed must expand its economy at an ever-increasing rate just to maintain its supply of money. If it fails to do this, recession or depression will be the result, the problem being that a continually accelerating rate of growth is physically impossible in a finite world with a finite amount of resources.

However, there are more sinister downsides to the monetary system we have. Not only have we lost control of our government, we will also eventually lose everything the system allowed us to create. Collectively, we will always owe more than we own. Furthermore, because the viability of our monetary system is dependent upon ever-expanding growth, not only are we rapidly depleting the resources of our planet, but we are also destroying our planet's ability to support life. We do this at the behest and for the benefit of a small group of greedy and morally bankrupt men. One of the reasons for all the wars we fight today is to keep our monetary system going. We are locked into fighting these wars in perpetuity because if we stop, the world will experience another Great Depression.

Nothing important in life happens unless there is a reason, and this is especially true for politics. Our economy is driven by a debt-based monetary system, which among other things, necessitates that we use and exploit our resources at an ever-increasing rate to maintain its health and viability. Therefore, everything our government does today is done with an eye toward increasing economic activity, and this means accelerating exploitation of the limited resources of our planet. The mantra of our government today is buy, spend, borrow, use, consume, construct, build, expand, grow, and do this faster and faster. Such things as conservation, responsible use, limited growth, balanced budgets, sustainable development, sustainable population levels, and sanity are incompatible with our monetary system. This being the case, they are also repugnant to our government and the power brokers who control it. We are cursed to live under a government that only pays lip service to the things that are not only worthwhile but necessary to our survival on this tiny overstressed planet.

Our former government was conceived in tyranny and born in freedom. Beyond all doubt, it was the greatest government devised by man. As Americans, it was our profound and sacred responsibility to bequeath this precious jewel to our children. What else is there to say? In this, we have failed miserably. Unfortunately, there *is* more to say. We have also failed our children by not passing to them a planet where their survivability is assured. We are a species that has fouled its own nest to such a degree that our children will not be able to live here in peace and contentment.

We did this because making money for the Banksters was more important than the world we live in. They are to blame for this, but we also share this blame because we allowed them to do this to us. The truth we will take with us to our graves is that our children will suffer grievously because we were sound asleep when greed became the dominant force in the lives of men.

CHAPTER 10:
What's Happening?

What is happening to us? This is a good question because very few people know what is really going on. Those who do either are complicit in the con or remain silent because of the consequences of speaking out. The reality of our situation is that religion is being used as a means of controlling our thinking and behavior. Most people will think this contention is preposterous, but so is everything else in this book. Being preposterous does not mean it isn't true. In any case, in order to proceed with this discussion, we must pretend that God does not exist. This is not easy for most people because thinking *no God* is repugnant to them. However, this must be done if we are going to see and understand the basic natures of the religions we will be discussing.

There are two things that drive religion: fear of the unknown and wishful thinking. We fear death because we are not able to fathom what it is. All we really know about death is that it is the end of life. This lack of knowledge makes us fearful, and out of fear, we create God to provide us with an answer to what we don't know. Aside from our fears, we also want to live a worthwhile and happy life. Because we are frail and unsure of ourselves, we turn to God and ask him to help us find the path to happiness. These are the two prime motivating factors behind religion. Knowing this, it should also be apparent that these attributes are weaknesses that can be exploited by others. It would be foolish not to realize this is true and that there are people who would use this state of affairs for their own self-serving purposes. For example, human nature being what it is, any person who aspires to a position of leadership in society, is a suspect for this kind of underhanded manipulation. Even the most trusted community leader could have unscrupulous motives and a hidden agenda. In times long gone, we had names for people like this. We called them witch doctor, shaman, or medicine man. In modern societies, the names have changed, and we call them priest, rabbi, caliph, minister, imam, etc.

The first primitive religion assumed everything around us had a spirit or soul that interacted with our world. This being the case, to live a good and proper life, people believed it was necessary to befriend or at least placate the spirits around us. To fail to do this was to invite misfortune, sickness, or even death. The question is how does one go about befriending or placating a spirit that cannot be seen or felt? Praying and paying homage to these spirits is one obvious answer to this question, but the situation is such that we really do not know the proper way of doing this. No problem! There is always a willing and able shaman available to help us through the darkness. Herein is the fundamental nature of many early religions. In the final analysis, it is the basis of most religions. Someone who claims to know more than we do about what is impossible to know steps up and helps us find the one true way.

The next step up from this primitive form of religion was to raise the spirits around us to being entities. In other words, inanimate objects, plants, or animals did not possess a spirit like us, but instead, there were a plethora of gods that were similar to us. These gods were extraordinary beings and were responsible for various areas of human activity. This more advanced form of religion moves us ahead to ancient Greece and Rome, where religious belief entailed a world of men and a parallel world of the gods. Naturally, it was believed that the gods could affect and shape events in our world. This being the case, once again, we were in need of someone to intercede and ensure that we did not offend the gods and, more importantly, induce them to behave in some manner that was to our benefit. This arrangement was a more sophisticated form of religion. However, the underlying factors had not changed. People were frightened and mystified by the world around them and, through knowledgeable intermediaries, sought to influence and control what is not possible to influence or control.

The next advancement for religion in the world of man was someone at some point in time decided there wasn't a gaggle of gods to deal with. Instead, there was only one God. The reason this thinking came about is obscure, but it is likely that some shamans came to the conclusion that a plethora of gods was too complicated and diverse to control. If there was only one God, things would be simplified and more manageable. For whatever reason, monotheism was born. This was an astounding development! There wasn't a spirit in everything; there wasn't a plethora of gods with different personalities and predilections. Instead, there was only one God who made everything and ran the entire show.

The first monotheistic religion was Judaism. Of course, along with this new conception of God, we needed a rabbi to tell us what God wanted and required of us. Without a rabbi, people would not know how to behave to remain in God's favor. The development of monotheism by early Jews was a giant leap forward for mankind. To be sure, this new concept eventually took over the Western world. However, despite this giant leap forward, early Judaism was a primitive religion.

Many will be offended by this last statement, but it has to be said. We are trying to find the truth, even if it offends people. In any case, Judaism is a primitive religion for three reasons: it does not offer the promise of an afterlife, it assumes non-Jews are enemies, and it is a behavior-based, carrot-and-stick kind of religion. If you obey God and unfailingly follow his rules, you will be rewarded. This is the carrot! On the other side of the coin, the stick is that if a believer does not obey God, they will suffer consequences. These doctrines are fundamental to the Old Covenant. A *covenant* is an agreement or contract between two entities, and as far as Judaism is concerned, the contract that the Jews had with God was simple and straightforward. However, Judaism is more complicated than this because, like all religions, it is also a way of life. These other aspects of Judaism were molded by the realities faced by the early Jews who had to survive in a hostile world populated and ruled by pagans.

With the advent of monotheism, the situation was such that there was a relatively small group of people who thought differently from everybody else. Unfortunately, in days gone by, there was danger in this. Being different often meant being singled out for persecution. Thus, early Jews had to develop clever ways to survive in a hostile pagan world. As a people, they needed a cohesive bond that would unite them against the rest of the world. An obvious candidate for this bond is the fact that the Jews had chosen one God to be the master of their lives. This being true, it does not take much of a leap of faith to turn this around and posture that their one God chose them. Thus, the Jews became God's chosen people, and this was the bond that would help them survive.

Because the Jews were "chosen," it follows that they were special, and being special meant they were better than everybody else. This became their creed, and this is what bound them together. However, there is danger in such thinking. If the pagans knew that Jews viewed them as being lesser human beings, they would have real problems with this. Here again, in days of yore, having problems with something usually meant you did it mortal bodily harm. Therefore, to survive, the early Jews developed two faces: one that they showed to each other and another to show everyone else. The face the pagans saw disarmed them, and this helped the Jews survive.

In our distant past, fighting each other was a great sport and a common practice. In order to survive, under such circumstances, the early Jews needed to find a way to avoid these situations as much as possible. What good or purpose would be served by siding with one side or the other in these never-ending conflicts? Thus, early Jews, being more intelligent than the pagans around them, used cunning and deception to avoid becoming involved in the pagan's petty squabbles. The Jews knew and understood that all pagans were potentially dangerous enemies, and they were far outnumbered by them. In such a situation, a good strategy for survival would be to pit your enemies against each other while pretending to be friendly with both sides.

Playing both sides against the middle is a dangerous and difficult game, but the Jews were up to this challenge, and over time, they became masters at it. They understood that if one group of pagans was preoccupied with fighting the other, neither group would have the time to worry or care about what the Jews were up to. Admittedly, this is the essence of duplicity, but it makes a lot of sense. Why would anyone want to choose sides in a conflict where the outcome was irrelevant? Furthermore, if you are special in the eyes of God and the world is full of potential enemies who happen to be godless heathens, whatever action you take to survive, no matter how wrongful or unethical, will have God's blessing.

In keeping with this situation, the Jews developed two books for their religion, one being the Torah, which includes the first five books of the Christian Bible. These Old Testament books are the face of Judaism that the world is meant to see. The other book is the Talmud, and it is intended for Jewish eyes only. This is because the Talmud contains many rabbinical writings which non-Jews would find offensive. These writings are a hangover from pagan times, and they assume that all non-Jews are enemies or, at the very least, potential enemies. This being the case, according to some passages of the Talmud, it is permissible for a Jew to lie or commit crimes against non-Jews. What this boils down to is that early Judaism was a clannish religion made up of an elitist group of insiders who distrusted everyone who was not a Jew. While these beliefs are not shared by most Jews today, unfortunately, they are views well entrenched within modern-day Zionism.

In the days before Christianity, the concept of monotheism was exclusive to Judaism, and a majority of the known world was pagan. As a result, the early Jews were an embattled people who were set upon by others. Because of this, their prophets talked of a messiah who would come into the world to save the Jews from the oppression they lived with. In time, Jesus Christ was born, and many Jews believed their prayers had been answered. Jesus Christ was born to free and save the Jews, but not in a way most of them expected. Christ was born in fulfillment of Old Testament prophecy, but to the consternation of many Jews, he also was born to establish a *New Covenant* not just for the Jews but for all of mankind.

This New Covenant did away with the concept of a "chosen people" and proclaimed that all men are brothers and the children of God. Furthermore, people would no longer find favor with God by following the law or a set of rules. Instead, people would be judged by their love for God, their love for their fellow men, and by what they believed in their hearts. These developments were revolutionary. They also were a giant leap forward for mankind because this new dogma freed us from the tyranny of religion. As Christians, people were able to establish their own personal relationship with God, and no one was empowered to judge others in this respect. Jesus Christ freed mankind from tyranny, but this is only part of the story. He also proclaimed that man was a spirit similar to God, and that by accepting him as Lord and Savior, we would earn a place in God's heaven.

Through his New Covenant, Jesus Christ did not expand upon or add to Judaism. Instead, he created an entirely new and different religion. By doing so, he freed mankind from the tyranny of *the law* and returned us to an intellectual Garden of Eden where the witch doctors and shamans no longer decided how people should behave. These revelations did not sit very well with the Pharisees, who were a ruling sect of Judaism at the time Christ was born. Clearly, Jesus was a threat to their authority, and this they could not tolerate. To rid themselves of this upstart rabbi, the Pharisees brought charges against him before the ruling Roman authorities, and while the Romans could find no fault with Jesus according to their laws, in deference to the Pharisees, they tortured and crucified him. But Jesus did not die. His body perished, but his mind and thoughts created a new religion that eventually would give rise to the greatest nation in all of history—the United States of America.

However, America, at this juncture, was still a long way from being founded. After Jesus Christ was crucified, his followers were perceived as being enemies of the Roman Empire because they refused to swear allegiance to its emperor. For this reason, Christians were imprisoned, tortured, and fed to the lions for the amusement of the Roman gentry and citizens. However, a good idea is hard to keep down, and over time, Christianity became more and more popular until it was no longer possible to suppress it. Therefore, in AD 313, Roman emperor Constantine decriminalized Christian worship. Unbeknownst at the time, this was the beginning of Christianity's demise. This is not to say that decriminalization wasn't a good thing; it's just that after Constantine, the influence of the church grew by leaps and bounds such that Christianity became impossible for government leaders to ignore.

Eventually, Christianity was embraced by the ruling authorities of Europe and morphed into Catholicism. Once Christianity became Catholicism, it became a religion not of ideas and principles but instead of rules that had to be religiously obeyed. Thus, Catholicism moved away from the New Covenant and back toward the Old. In time, Catholicism had little to do with Christianity; instead, it philosophically resembled Judaism. Granted, the rules were different, but the emphasis was on obeying the rules, not doing the right thing. Thus, several hundred years after the death of Christ, Christianity died. The capstone of this transformation came during the Spanish Inquisition of 1478 when people were tortured to death in the name of Jesus Christ. They deserved this fate because they didn't adhere to the rules established by the Spanish authorities.

With the advent of Christianity as a state religion, Christianity died. This is how things stood until the prophet Muhammad came along at the close of the fifth century. Mohammad loved his people and recognized that Catholicism was not the faith of the early biblical prophets. As a result, he created a new religion called Islam. Muhammad believed Islam returned religion to its fundamental roots. To the Muslims, Muhammad was a prophet next in line following Jesus. However, despite what Muslims believe, Jesus Christ was not the same ilk as Adam, Abraham, or Moses. As previously discussed, Jesus did not teach his followers to find favor with God by following a set of rules as these earlier prophets did.

This important point, apparently, was lost upon Islam. As a result, Islam is a religion that has more in common with Judaism than Christianity. True, like Christianity, Islam offers an afterlife with God in heaven, but this is as far as the similarity goes. Islam is more like Judaism because it is a religion of rules that must be religiously followed. Furthermore, like Judaism, Islam considers nonbelievers to be enemies who are less in the eyes of God than true believers. To be sure, Islam's rules are different from Judaism, but they are rules nonetheless, and like Judaism, following them is important and necessary.

Christianity was dead! Behavior-based religions reigned supreme, and waging war had become a religious responsibility. Such thinking, in the guise of Islam and Catholicism, dominated the European and Middle Eastern worlds. As a result, mankind entered the Dark Ages, which persisted for seven hundred years, from the sixth to the thirteenth centuries. During this time, the Crusades were fought over a piece of dirt called the Holy Land. Think of the pain and suffering humanity experienced during those terrible years all because people thought it was so important to follow their particular set of rules, that it was incumbent upon them to kill anyone who followed a set of rules different from theirs.

Fortunately, in 1483, a man was born who was destined to bring an end to this madness. His name was Martin Luther, and he rekindled a light in the world by resurrecting Christianity. Martin Luther was the father of the Protestant Reformation. Note the basis of *protestant* is the word *protest*. The thing being protested was the world that had been created by the Catholic Church. The basis of *reformation* is the word *reform*. The things being reformed were the unchristian teachings of this same church. Martin Luther returned true Christianity to Europe, and this eventually ushered in the age of enlightenment.

The Protestant Reformation gave rise to a number of Protestant sects, which allowed people to return to God in a manner of their choosing. This is what Christianity is about, worshiping God in your own personal way. What a tremendous blessing for man; what a tremendous honor to God. But this wasn't good enough for the ruling powers of Europe. Such thinking was a threat to their authority and control. You cannot have people thinking for themselves and worshiping God in any way they wish. Such behavior must be stamped out. This is exactly what these despots tried to do. But it was all for naught because Columbus had discovered a New World. Who cares about the kings and queens of Europe? If we can't worship God the way we wish, there is a land across the ocean where we can go to be free.

Here we are in 2015, and of late, we are seeing a blending of Christianity and Judaism in the minds of many Americans. The thinking is that because Jesus Christ was Jewish and was born in accordance with the Old Testament prophecy, the roots of Christianity lie within Judaism. Furthermore, there is only one God, and this same God ruled in both the Old and New Testaments. All the foregoing being true, it follows that Christians and Jews are brothers who should love and help each other. This is all well and good, but there is a fly in this ointment, which is a grave and serious problem for Christians; the fly being that just because Christians believe in the Old Testament and just because the God of the Old Testament gave the Holy Land to the Jews, it does not follow that Christians have a responsibility to help the Jews return to and take ownership of Palestine.

Unfortunately, far too many Christians in America believe the opposite, and they believe this way because this lie is being taught in many Christian churches. These beliefs are not Christian. Christians care nothing about ownership and nationhood. Instead of being Christian, these beliefs reek of Zionism, and it is Zionist thinking that is being passed off as Christian doctrine. The roots of Christianity are not in Judaism. Jesus Christ was a Jew, but he came into the world to establish an entirely new religion and a New Covenant that replaced the Old in its entirety, not just for the Jews but for all of mankind. A fundamental tenet of this New Covenant is that no one is special and all men are equal in the eyes of God. This includes the Jews.

People came to the New World to be free so they could worship God in any manner of their choosing. To ensure freedom, these people joined together and created the United States of America. Unfortunately, Christianity, once again, has become an establishment religion. As a result, Christianity has died a second time, and America, its stepchild, is dying along with it. All this has come to pass as a result of the passage of the Federal Reserve Act in 1913. The Pharisees, or in today's parlance, the Zionists, are now in control. Freedom is anathema to these people. As a result, Americans are no longer free. They want us under control and have us fighting wars that have nothing to do with us. God reached out to us once, but we let his love slip away. He reached out to us again, but because we were lazy and stupid, we let his love slip away a second time. As a result, the world has entered a new dark age where hell on earth once again is the order of the day. The question is who is going to save us this time?

CHAPTER 11:
Judaism versus Zionism

This book has made many shocking revelations that came as a great surprise to many readers. This speaks volumes about what is going on in America today. We are supposed to be a free people, and the only way we are truly free is if we are informed. To be informed, we need an independent and freely operating news media. Without this, we are victims and at the mercy of those who lead us. When this is the case, instead of providing factual information about events and issues, the press follows a hidden agenda dictated by those who control our government. This makes a mockery of democracy because it is not possible for citizens to vote intelligently if they are fed inaccurate information. Furthermore, when the press withholds information, people have no idea about what is really going on. This is the status quo in the United States today. We think we are a free people, but our freedom is only an illusion, and we are hopelessly brainwashed.

At first glance, it does not appear reasonable to criticize the media for not alerting Americans to the overthrow of our government in 1913. After all, very few people knew what was really happening, and it is possible to assume this included the publishers and editors of the nation's newspapers. However, belying this assumption is that just four years later in 1917, the Zionists struck a deal with England such that they agreed to bring America into the war on the side of the Allies if the British agreed to help establish the State of Israel. The Zionists knew they needed the cooperation of the nation's newspapers to make good on their end of this agreement. Therefore, they had to be confident of the media's cooperation before they struck this deal. This implies that the press was in their pockets many years before the passage of the Federal Reserve Act in 1913. It is also reasonable to conclude that the media played a role in facilitating the passage of this ignoble and unconstitutional legislation.

One of the best examples of the American press being all too willing to accommodate the Zionist agenda is the USS *Liberty* Incident and its aftermath. The deliberate attack on the *Liberty* should have been headline news across the nation. Instead, many newspapers and television stations did not carry the story. The *New York Times* published one short article about the incident on page 29 of its daily paper. The USS *Liberty* Veterans Association meets yearly to keep alive the memory of the *Liberty* in the hope that someday Congress will hold hearings and investigate the incident. Despite these efforts and the importance of what they are trying to accomplish, the nation's media never mentions these people or their organization. As a result, Americans are clueless about this grave and serious American tragedy.

Some little-known facts about the USS *Liberty*, which are not newsworthy enough to appear in the nation's newspapers, are as follows:[1]

- The USS *Liberty* is a converted WWII victory ship retrofitted to listen to the communications of other nations. Incredibly, as a result of the Israeli attack, this noncombatant's vessel is the most decorated ship in US Naval history, for a single action. Not even the aircraft carriers that fought the Battle of Midway in WWII can make this claim.
- The survivors of the Israeli attack on the USS *Liberty* were ordered not to talk about this occurrence. If they did, they were told they would be fined and/or imprisoned.
- President Johnson ordered the official records concerning the USS *Liberty* to be falsified such that they show the Israeli attack on the USS *Liberty* was an honest mistake.
- Military orders were issued prohibiting any monument or document from stating that Israel was the nation that attacked the USS *Liberty*.
- Captain McGonagle was awarded the Congressional Medal of Honor for his actions during the attack on the USS *Liberty*. Instead of this honor being presented in the White House by our president, as is customary, it was presented to Captain

McGonagle by the Secretary of the Navy in one of Washington's navy yards.

- The survivors of the USS *Liberty* Incident, in his honor, have placed a star for Captain McGonagle on the Walk of Fame in Palm Springs, California, near Sonny Bono's statue.

The USS *Liberty* Incident, while near the top of the list of stories our media never writes about, is not the best example we have. The premier story that almost no one has heard of is the battle being waged between Zionism and Judaism. The reason for this is because the Zionists want people to believe that Zionism and Judaism are inseparable and that every single Jew in the world is solidly behind the State of Israel. Nothing could be further from the truth. Incredibly, our media works to ensure that Americans remain ignorant and uninformed about this subject. This speaks volumes about the control the Zionists wield over our nation's press.

Zionism is not a religion. Instead, it is a political movement that established the State of Israel and now works to ensure its existence. Judaism, on the other hand, is a religion. Yes, Israel is a religious state, and Judaism is its religion, but Judaism, the religion, had nothing to do with the establishment of the State of Israel. Such doings were a Zionist initiative alone, and the fact that people believe otherwise is an example of how well the Zionists have sold this lie to the world. All Jews are not Zionists, and those who aren't are opposed to Zionism. Furthermore, there are many Jewish citizens living in Israel who oppose its existence. This seems too incredible to believe, but it is true. Unfortunately, most people fail to understand that Zionism hijacked Judaism and uses it as a shield to protect the nation of Israel from legitimate criticism of its rogue and criminal behavior. The world is convinced that anti-Zionism is anti-Semitism. This is a lie! Anti-Zionism is not anti-Semitism, but woe be unto anyone foolish enough to criticize Zionism or Israel. Such a person, according to the Zionists, is a rabid anti-Semite and neo-Nazi.

To understand what is happening between Zionism and Orthodox Judaism, you have to read the Torah, the holy book of Judaism. According to the Torah, the glory of God shined upon the Jews, and he blessed them in two ways: they would be his people and, accordingly, would live in the land he promised. However, the Jews sinned against God. As punishment for their sins, God dispersed them throughout the nations of the world where they are fated to serve mankind through good deeds and by setting an example. This is the fate of the Jews as ordained by God until such time as they redeem themselves in his eyes. There is nothing the Jews of today can do to change this, and their redemption and reunion are dependent upon God and God alone.

For anyone or any group of people to take it upon themselves to call the Jews home in God's name is contrary to his will. According to many Jews, to do this through the force of arms as the Zionists have done is a sacrilege. Therefore, for many Orthodox Jews, the establishment of a Jewish State by the Zionists is diametrically opposed and contradictory to Judaism, the Jewish people, and the people of Israel—not Israel the political entity but Israel the chosen people of God. There is no equivocation or wiggle room here. According to many Orthodox Jews, either you are with Zionism or you are with Judaism. You cannot have it both ways. The Zionists do everything within their power to censor and suppress this information for reasons that should be obvious.

Following is a list of Jewish organizations opposed to Zionism and the State of Israel:

- *True Torah Jews against Zionism*—This organization believes that Zionism is contrary to Jewish law as embodied within the Torah. According to them, Zionism wrongfully advocates a political and military end to Jewish exile, fosters pseudo-Judaism based on secular nationalism, seeks *armed materialism* as opposed to divine understanding, and has created a Zionist state instead of one that is Jewish.

- *Not in My Name*—This is a predominantly Jewish organization that works toward a peaceful and just resolution of the Israeli/Palestinian conflict. They oppose the illegal West Bank and Gaza occupations, the West Bank and East Jerusalem settlements, Israel's wall of separation, the unjust punishment of Palestinians and Israeli Arabs, and Israel's blatant abuse of human rights.

- *Jewish Voice for Peace (JVP)*—JVP is a group of American Jewish community activists who came together to work for peace, social justice, and human rights. They call upon the United States and other nations to end the violence and support Palestinian self-determination free from occupation and Zionist oppression.

- *Brit Tzedek v'Shalom*—This organization is a Jewish alliance for justice and peace. It bills itself as being America's largest grassroots Jewish organization with around fifty thousand supporters, one-thousand of whom are Rabbis. The organization subscribes to a two-state negotiated resolution of the Israeli/Palestinian conflict.

- *Neturei Karta International (NKI)*—NKI is a group of Orthodox Jews who used to live in Jerusalem. They are opposed to the existence of the State of Israel and once held demonstrations and protests to make their views known. Because of this, they were harassed, arrested, and physically tortured by the Israeli police.

Most of these organizations' members now live outside of Israel where they have established synagogues, educational institutions, publishing houses, and other organizations that espouse their beliefs. NKI opposes the State of Israel because members believe that the concept of a sovereign Jewish State is in violation of Jewish law.

Clearly, there is a serious schism between Zionism and certain elements of Orthodox Judaism. It is also true that the views of these Orthodox Jews are shared by a minority of Jews in the world today. However, this was not the case one hundred years ago at the beginning of this past century. At that time, the situation was reversed. Most Jews in the world agreed with the Orthodox position, and it was the Zionists who were a small minority within the Jewish community. This is truly an astounding reversal and came about because the Zionists were successful in achieving their goal of establishing the State of Israel. Everybody loves a winner, and the Zionists won. However, winning is one thing, and being right is another.

The Zionist movement came about primarily through the power and influence of the house of Rothschild, the richest and most powerful banking family in the world. Why the Rothschilds picked up this torch is not known, but pick it up they did. If it wasn't for the Rothschilds, Israel would not exist today. Two things are certain: no Rothschild is the long-awaited Jewish messiah, and none of them is a prophet of God. Therefore, even though they created the State of Israel and most Jews believe the state they created was blessed by God, Israel did not come into being in accordance with Torah scripture. According to the Torah, the Jews had sinned, and as a result, God took his *promised land* back and dispersed the Jews throughout the nations of the world. This is their fate until such time as God brings them back together as one people. Thus, the creation of the State of Israel by the Rothschild Zionists is counter to Torah scripture and contrary to God's will. Furthermore, to establish the State of Israel through the force of arms, on top of the bodies of millions of Jews murdered in the Holocaust, is a sacrilege to many Jews.

Americans wrongfully believe there is a biblical justification for the creation of the State of Israel. This erroneous belief has become entrenched throughout the world because of Zionist power and influence. The truth is that, as espoused by many Jews, the State of Israel exists contrary to God's will. This is confirmed by the Torah and also by the events that have transpired because of the State of Israel. Two world wars were fought so Israel could exist. Furthermore, the Palestinian people are being evicted from their homes, which in turn are given to foreign Jews who have no right to them. This particular injustice has given rise to the war on terror and destabilized the world. However, as bad as all this is, it is not the worst thing that has happened because of the State of Israel.

The United States was the greatest nation in the history of the world because of its system of government. In 1913, this changed because New World Order Zionist bankers took control. Americans were sound asleep when this happened, and they continue to be asleep today. Presently, we are fighting a war on terror, and it is this war that has given those who rule us an excuse to dismantle every remaining visage of law protecting our God-given rights. Today, because of the Zionists and their stepchild, Israel, nothing in the world is as it should be, and the recent history of mankind is a chronology of lies and atrocities. The truth hidden by these lies is that the citizens of this once great nation have lost their government, the greatest government in the history of mankind, so the Zionists can have their religious state.

Notes

1. The USS Liberty Story – Pamphlet distributed by the USS Liberty Veterans Association and available from them.

CHAPTER 12:
The Only Solution

The first step necessary to solve a problem is to admit you have one. The second step is to identify what the problem is. The first eleven chapters of this book made a good-faith effort to demonstrate what's wrong with this nation and the world we live in. Human nature being what it is, upon completing this book, many people will dismiss what they read for a multitude of reasons—the foremost one being that they refuse to accept anything that upsets the cushy and comfortable world within which they prefer to live. These people are in denial for denial's sake, and they are the biggest impediment we face if we are to ever reach a point where solving our problems is possible.

This book so far has approached our situation *microscopically* and examined a plethora of details and information in the hopes of demonstrating that the official explanations for things do not make sense. It went on to offer alternative explanations that were a common thread in all the events discussed. However, there also is a way to approach this matter *macroscopically*.

We know the New World Order exists. Therefore, the government we think we have no longer exists because the two entities are incompatible with each other. A government of the people, by the people, and for the people cannot be subservient and beholden to an oligarchy of rich and powerful dictators. The NWO is a world government that makes decisions and is capable of implementing these decisions such that they become viable and operative. It follows that such decisions must be supported by our government. There are two reasons for this: the NWO needs the authority and military might of the United States to provide the backbone for their decisions, and it also needs the cooperation of our government to ensure that the people of this nation are on board with and accept their agenda.

Our government, the one we are supposed to have, is constituted to be independent and sovereign. It is also supposed to be free of hidden agendas and work solely for the benefit of the citizens of this nation. These facts present us with a problem. The government we presently have is not free, not independent, not sovereign, and works from a hidden agenda beneficial to the NWO and to the detriment of the citizens of this nation. Therefore, it should be obvious that the government we have is very different from the one we are supposed to have. The only way such a change could come about is if our government had been overthrown. If the word *overthrown* is too strong, perhaps *taken over* would be more appropriate? In any case, the final result is the same. We no longer have a government that serves us. Putting this into one sentence, it is sufficient to say that instead of having a government ruled from the bottom up, we have one ruled from the top down.

Many Americans have no problem with this deplorable state of affairs. After all, what is so bad about a world government? Technology has turned our once immense world into one where miles no longer matter. Isn't world government an idea whose time has come? These points are well-taken. A technology-shrunken world cries out for some kind of international organization to oversee and ensure equity across our dissolving borders. The question that screams out to be answered is whether those who brought us the NWO are the best people to be running the show. According to David Rockefeller, they are. In a speech before the Trilateral Commission made in 1991, he said, "The supranational sovereignty of an intellectual elite and world bankers is surely preferable to the national auto-determination practiced in past centuries."

It should be clear that David Rockefeller believes that a group of super rich, egotistical, and amoral bankers who hoodwinked the working people of the world out of their wealth and earnings should run things. Obviously, Mr. Rockefeller has a very short memory because the people he is talking about have been in charge for the past one hundred years. When we add up what their leadership has wrought, it is not a pretty picture. To relieve Mr. Rockefeller of his illusions and delusions, the following is offered:

World War—If the NWO Zionists did not embark on their quest to establish the State of Israel, they would have had no reason to engineer America's entry into WWI. If America had stayed out of WWI, it is highly likely that the war would have ended two years earlier than it did. Furthermore, with a just and equitable end to WWI, the seeds of WWII would not have been planted and the chances are that WWII would not have taken place.

Anti-Semitism—As part of their plan to create the State of Israel, the NWO Zionists fostered hatred for the Jews in Europe. They did this, among other ways, by supporting and financing Hitler's rise to power. This ultimately led to six million innocent Jews being murdered by the Nazis. In regard to this terrible state of affairs, Neturei Karta International, a worldwide Jewish organization, in an article entitled "Why Orthodox Jews Are Opposed to a Zionist State," wrote;

> If one contemplates the two thousand years of our (Jewish) exile, take any hundred years even the hardest, one will not find as much suffering, bloodshed, and catastrophes for the People of Israel as in the period of the Zionists.

The War on Terror—The State of Israel would not exist if not for the Zionists. If the State of Israel did not exist, there would be no Muslim terrorism. If there were no Muslim terrorism, there would be no war on terror. Without a war on terror, it is possible that the world would be at peace.

The Police State—If there were no war on terror, there would be no need for the Patriot Act, no need for the Department of Homeland Security, and no need to militarize the nation's law enforcement agencies. Without a war on terror, there would be no reason for America to be turned into a police state.

International Law—International law, or the rule of law among nations, is a casualty of the establishment of the State of Israel and the resulting war on terror. Iraq invaded Kuwait to steal its oil, and the NWO Zionists invaded Palestine to steal its land. Both actions should be condemned because they are both instances of a stronger group of people imposing their will upon a weaker people. The United States and its allies, on one hand, helped the victimized Kuwaitis. On the other hand, we helped victimize the Palestinians by siding with the Zionists. The Israeli invasion of Palestine was a violation of international law. Therefore, international law has been reduced to the philosophy of might makes right. Furthermore, on Israel's behalf, the United States kills, tortures, and jails people whose only crime is their willingness to fight to help people whose homes have been stolen from them. We have even resorted to murdering our own citizens for Israel's benefit.

The Treadmill—The good life entails being able to enjoy the fruits of one's labor without reservations or fear of losing what has already been earned. Under our present monetary system, we are on a treadmill where the harder we run, the faster we fall behind. Contributing to this untenable state of affairs is the fact that inflation insidiously robs us of our savings and the value of our work. At the turn of the previous century, only one member of a household had to work to support a family. Today, in far too many instances, both mother and father work to make ends meet. Sometimes, it is necessary for members of a family to hold two jobs. In 1913, when the Fed took over our monetary system, the dollar was worth a dollar and was backed by precious metals. Today, it is worth about four cents and backed by nothing.

The Income Tax—The income tax we pay has no legitimacy under constitutional law. A tax on the wages of working Americans is illegal and was imposed upon American workers to provide the Banksters with a way to siphon our money into their pockets while doing nothing for us in return.

The Truth—The truth is sacred and is one of the things a citizen should expect and demand from public officials. On the other side of the coin, it is the duty and responsibility of public officials to tell the truth because when they don't, it means they are following a hidden agenda. In America today, because our government is a puppet to the New World Order, lying and deceiving the public is endemic to the system and not only considered to be a prerogative of public officials but a duty and responsibility.

Principles—The founders subscribed to a number of governing principles, which were inviolate. The government they created was limited in power, and these powers were shared and allocated between the three branches of our government. If the governing principles enshrined within our Constitution are dysfunctional, then so are the checks and balances upon which the system depends. When this happens, the powers of the government become unlimited. So, it is with our government. Principles no longer exist, and our government is free to do anything it wishes without reservation or justification.

Freedom—Americans hold freedom sacred. Despite the fact that most Americans think we are free, the opposite is the case. This is true because our government enjoys unlimited power over us. In America today, it is the government that is free and we are its subjects. Granted, we are free to take a walk or watch television when the mood strikes us, but we are not free politically because we have no say in most everything our government does. If we are not free politically, then we are not free.

Human Rights—Three fundamental and inalienable rights enumerated within our Declaration of Independence are life, liberty, and the pursuit of happiness. Today, these rights are no longer inalienable, and we enjoy them solely at the discretion of our government.

Economic Sustainability—A monetary system based upon privately issued debt operates under the assumption that we live in an infinite world, with infinite resources and an infinite capacity to absorb the end products of human activity. The world we live in is not infinite. This being true, to continue as we have in the past ensures that the fate we face is a world cataclysm of biblical proportions.

Population Growth—More people translate into more workers and consumers, the very thing a debt-based monetary system requires. Our world has a finite capacity to support human activity, and this means that there is a limit to how many people can live on this planet and maintain healthy and viable ecological systems. Presently, global temperatures are increasing, the oceans are being polluted, ocean dead zones are expanding, fish stocks are being depleted, and the extinction of species is proceeding at an alarming rate. Despite these regrettable things, the governments of the world ignore these problems and pretend that we have nothing to worry about. This is the biggest failing of the NWO Banksters. Because of them, humankind has fouled its own nest and is presently faced with a future of want, destitution, and anarchy.

Many people go through life assuming that what we find before us in the world is as things should be. Nothing is further from the truth. Things are the way they are because those who wield authority and power made decisions that brought us here. It doesn't take a genius to see that the present state of humankind is worse than horrible. Our NWO masters have brought upon us needless wars, depressions, suffering, a rapid depletion of the world's resources, and a deterioration of the world's ability to support life. Presently, the world is forced to endure a perpetual war on terror as a result of the establishment of the State of Israel. In consideration of these things, Mr. Rockefeller is wrong. The rule of the NWO bankers is not preferable. Instead, it is a curse and pox on all of humanity. If we are going to save ourselves from the fate they have bestowed upon us, we must be rid of them.

Being rid of the NWO Banksters is easy to say but difficult to achieve because they have been entrenched in power for so long. This has afforded them the opportunity of placing their minions in positions of authority and power throughout most institutions of society. To rid ourselves of the curse we live under, we face the almost impossible task of convincing all these people that the best interests of everyone, including themselves, is to remove the NWO Banksters from power. This will be a difficult undertaking because we are talking about greedy people who got to where they are because of their willingness to compromise themselves. Their prime imperative is *loyalty to the boss*. This loyalty transcends loyalty to the nation, loyalty to the citizens who pay their salaries, loyalty to the governing principles upon which this nation was established, and loyalty to their religion and the moral principles upon which it rests.

With a clear understanding of what we are up against, as far as the mechanisms of accomplishing what we want is concerned, it is a simple matter of taking four steps:

1. Our president should invoke President Kennedy's long-dormant Executive Order 11110 and order the Treasury Department to issue United States Treasury notes in lieu of Federal Reserve notes. By so doing, our president will nullify the Federal Reserve Act and stop the flow of money into NWO coffers. This is a step in the right direction, but it will not deprive these criminals of the wealth they have already stolen from us. More has to be done.

2. The next step in disenfranchising the NWO Banksters is to have Congress repeal and repudiate the Federal Reserve Act. Repealing this act will get it off the books, but repudiation is also necessary to declare null and void all debts and monies this nation owes these criminal bankers. Repudiation will wipe the slate clean and provide us with a new beginning as far as the national debt is concerned. However, this is not where we should stop because these Banksters would still have the wealth they stole from us.

3. To recover this money, the Department of Justice, under our RICO statutes, should file charges of felony fraud and conspiracy to commit fraud against the owners and principles of the Federal Reserve Bank. If convicted of these charges, those involved should be sentenced according to the provisions of our laws and also be ordered to forfeit to the United States government all funds and assets in their possession that were obtained through fraudulent activities.

4. Finally, in order for justice to be done and for the sake of those who lost their lives, the United States should draw up formal charges against the NWO Banksters and file them with the appropriate international tribunals. These charges should include inciting and abetting theft, torture, murder, war, and genocide. To be sure, at Nuremberg, the world brought the Nazi war criminals to justice. However, left out as defendants in these trials were the Zionists whose meddling brought on WWII and the Holocaust. If it weren't for these criminals, the Nazi party would have never risen to power and would never have committed the crimes it did.

Admittedly, achieving all the above is a tall order. However, taking such actions is not only justified and warranted, but necessary if humanity is going to recover from and climb out of the cesspool within which we presently live. If we fail to meet this challenge, then we truly are a pathetic species and deserve the fate that is presently barreling down upon us.

APPENDICES
The Selected Writings of Alan R. Adaschik

This appendix contains thirty-nine selected articles and essays written by Alan R. Adaschik, which comprise the majority of this book. The first twelve chapters of this book are the end result of twenty-one years of study and research by Alan Adaschik. At various points during this period of time, he felt compelled to take a pen in hand and write about the issues he was studying. Most of these articles serve to clarify the prime message of this book, which is that our government is not our government because it has been overthrown. By reading these articles, you will learn how our government has failed us. The breadth and scope of these failures are further validation that an overthrow of our government has occurred.

The articles about religion and our environment are included because they address important issues relevant to our times. Religion is supposed to be a liberating and uplifting aspect of life.

Unfortunately, in America today, religion is being used as a means of controlling the masses. This purpose can only be served by ignoring the essential message of Jesus Christ and reducing Christ's teachings to a list of dos and don'ts, enforced by a God diminished to being the alter ego of an over-controlling government.

Next to life itself, our environment is the most important thing we have. It is a precious but fragile jewel that can only be protected by the authority of the government. Unfortunately for us all, the prime motivation of those who lead us is greed. Therefore, environmental issues are of no concern to them. The consequences of this state of affairs are that we live on a deteriorating and dying planet, which will become a living hell for our children.

APPENDIX A1
Imposter or President?

November 2011

Most Americans are aware of the controversy surrounding Barack Obama's birthright to be president of the United States but, as usual, have no clue as to what is really going on or the importance of this issue to us as a nation. From a practical point of view, the resolution of this problem is simple: either he is or isn't qualified, and it is incumbent upon Barack Obama to settle this question. However, nothing in politics is reasonable or simple anymore, and the fact that this controversy continues to rage exemplifies everything that is wrong with America and demonstrates why we are a failed nation.

The alleged facts are that Barack Obama was born in Hawaii to an American mother and a foreign-born father. To substantiate this, Mr. Obama has given us a Certificate of Live Birth (COLB). To him and his supporters, this settles the matter. However, a COLB is easily forged, and to many Americans, the document settles nothing, especially when Mr. Obama's own words have confirmed he is in possession of his original birth certificate issued at the time of his birth. This being the case, numerous Americans have filed suit in federal court to force Mr. Obama to make public his original birth certificate. To date, he has spent almost one million dollars fighting these lawsuits. So far, the courts have sided with our alleged president by refusing to hear these cases or by dismissing them on issues of standing. Therefore, it should be clear that our judicial system does not consider the particulars of these cases to be worthy of consideration.

To the founders, such circumstances would have been absurd. Article II, section 1, paragraph 5 of our Constitution provides that our president must be a natural-born citizen of this nation. This being the case, it follows that a candidate for the office of president is obligated to prove he is qualified because being able to refuse to do so means that an individual has the power to unilaterally void this provision of our Constitution. It also follows that by refusing to fulfill this constitutional requirement, a person has forfeited his or her right to be president. Never in their wildest dreams did the founders imagine a president or a candidate for president would be allowed to decline providing definitive proof of his or her citizenship. And never in their worst nightmares did they imagine that the legal system of this nation would help a sitting president break the law, especially a high sacred law enshrined within our Constitution. But these absurd dreams are now the reality that Americans are forced to live with.

Barack Obama is our president-elect and as such took an oath of office to preserve and protect our Constitution. To be sure, in order to preserve and protect our Constitution, the president must make every possible effort to ensure that its provisions are followed, and this includes providing definitive proof of his eligibility to hold the office he has been elected to. Not only has Barack Obama failed to do this in clear and flagrant violation of his oath of office, but he has also spent almost one million dollars to stonewall the issue. Surely a remedy to this sad and deplorable situation must exist within the scope of our Constitution. If none does, then what does this say about the founders and the document they bestowed upon us?

The founders were not stupid, and the constitution they created to govern our government is a wondrous document with a plethora of checks and balances to ensure that our government functions properly. However, these checks and balances will only function if there are people in government willing to honor their oath of office and fulfill their constitutional duties and responsibilities to the people of this nation. Unfortunately, our government stopped being our government many years ago and is now a criminal enterprise. I know that many Americans will cringe at this last statement, but "criminal enterprise" is the only appropriate description for a government peopled by those who deliberately violate their oath of office by conspiring to violate our Constitution for the sole purpose of ensuring their position and status in life. Unfortunately, this includes every government official presently holding office, elected or otherwise, save a precious few. And those precious few have been rendered impotent by the corruption that totally engulfs them. The situation within our government, as it really exists today, is so pathetic that "criminal enterprise" is not an overly harsh description but instead the nicest way possible to describe it.

If President Obama was truly our president, he would, without hesitation or reservation, produce valid documents that prove his eligibility to occupy this position. If our attorney general was truly our attorney general, he would appoint an independent special prosecutor to look into this matter. If Congress was truly our Congress, they would demand that President Obama provide them with definitive proof of his eligibility to be president and hold him in contempt if he refused. If the House of Representatives was truly our House of Representatives, they would impeach President Obama for being in violation of article II, section 1, paragraph 5 of our Constitution. If our judicial system were truly our judicial system, judges would honor the oath they have taken and ensure that the provisions of our Constitution are obeyed by ruling that President Obama must surrender documents that will settle this issue. And finally, if our government was truly our government, the issue on hand would not be an issue at all, and we would not be forced to endure the farce, which has unfolded before us within the courts of this nation.

The present situation is such that no one in our government is willing to take responsibility for ensuring that the provisions of our Constitution are obeyed, and yet every single government official has a sworn duty and responsibility to do so. Can it really be true that Congress and members of the judicial branch of our government would have us believe that article II, section 1, paragraph 5 of our Constitution is a meaningless and useless provision such that under it, Barack Obama is not accountable to the people of this nation? Apparently, he isn't because the alleged president has been successful in holding off our fellow citizens who have called him to task in this regard. How can anyone explain the obvious contradictions and absurdities associated with this state of affairs? Can anyone truly say that our elected officials and government authorities are trying to do the right thing and what is best for the people of this nation? If you think this is the case, then send me your address because I have a bridge in Brooklyn I would like to sell you.

Looking at this dilemma from a different angle, we should ask ourselves what course of action is best for this nation. If Barack Obama is constitutionally qualified to be our president and he is required to prove it by providing a copy of his original birth certificate, then no harm has been done and an important precedent has been set for future presidential candidates. Furthermore, the many citizens who are concerned about this issue will have had their concerns satisfied. On the other hand, if this is not done, this controversy will remain unresolved and forever be a stain on the history of this nation. On the other side of the coin, if Barack Obama is not qualified to be our president and is required to provide us with a copy of his original birth certificate, a liar and a fraud will have been exposed and removed from office to the benefit of all Americans. Conversely, if no action is taken, Americans will be forced to suffer an imposter as their president, and this terrible truth will far outweigh any good this usurper may accomplish while in office. To argue otherwise is sheer sophistry. Let's allow a fraud and con artist to be our president because he is the most qualified to lead and will do a good job. The absurdity of this contention should be self-evident.

All of the above being true, what about the sixty-four million Americans who voted for Barack Obama as president and the majority of Americans who feel his qualifications to hold office are not an issue? First and foremost, we are supposed to be a constitutional republic where the rule of law is paramount. Therefore, the votes and opinions of citizens, even majority opinions, should play no role in the settlement of this issue. The question is one of fact and legality, not one of perceptions and personal preferences. Either Barack Obama is qualified to be our president under the Constitution or he is not. The onus is upon Mr. Obama to establish his credentials in this regard. If he refuses or fails to do so, he should be impeached and removed from office because no individual is more important than our republic. To hold otherwise is the epitome of demagoguery, and a nation ruled by demagoguery is a wellspring of tyranny.

Unfortunately, today, America is ruled by demagoguery, and as a result, those of us who truly care about what is happening will be forced to live through the next several years wondering if our president is a liar, fraud, and usurper. No citizen should have to live under such a deplorable state of affairs, but this is exactly the position our leaders will place us in because they dance to the tune of a different master, and they are indifferent to the pain we suffer. They have "arrived," and this is far more important to them than truth, honor, and their oath of office.

Postscript

I am a citizen of the United States of America. As such, I have a constitutionally provided right to know if my president is qualified to hold the office he was elected to. Presently, the situation is such that members of our judicial system, in violation of our Constitution and their oath of office, are working to deny me and every other citizen of this nation this constitutional right. If you disagree, then either you are constitutionally challenged or, for some ignoble self-serving reason, have wrongfully chosen to side with those who oppress me. In either case, you are an enabler of tyranny and an American in name only, and I challenge you or anyone else to demonstrate why I am wrong to reach these conclusions.

What most Americans fail to realize is that in a constitutional republic, it is the citizens who are ultimately responsible for ensuring that the law is obeyed. If the situation is such that government officials have joined together in a conspiracy to break the law, then a time has come for each and every one of us to stand up and be counted. In the United States of America, clearly and without any shred of doubt, this time has come. If you, as an individual citizen of this once great nation, decline to join the ranks of those of us who stand against such tyranny, then you are part of the problem and a traitor to the rest of us. This is what our constitutional contract is all about, and this is the most fundamental aspect of being an American. Those who fail this test forfeit the right to call themselves an American. What in God's name do they think separates us from everyone else in the world?

A truly lamentable and tragic aspect of our situation is that a strong majority of Americans, through ignorance, fail to comprehend what is being done to us. Therefore, against their own best interests, they foolishly stand with the oppressors and detractors who lead us.

This is exactly why these charlatans ignore the fact that we are, first and foremost, a republic, and why they trumpet the word *democracy* like a sacred and holy mantra. In a republic, the rule of law is paramount. In a democracy, the ignorant and misinformed trump common sense, reason, the law, and yes, even the fundamental principles that are the bedrock foundation of a republic. Thus, our leaders hide behind the illusion of democracy so the majority will perceive those of us who go against the grain as a threat to society. We are not a threat to society or to anyone. However, we are a threat to the established order of things because the order we now live under is no longer the ideal established by the founders but, instead, a criminal enterprise wrongfully established to benefit those who lead us in violation of our Constitution's provisions.

APPENDIX A2
Impeachment and the Constitution

May 1999

There are many momentous events in the 210 years of our nation's history, and the impeachment of President William Jefferson Clinton ranks among them. Unfortunately, most Americans do not comprehend the significance of the president's impeachment trial. President Clinton was impeached by the House of Representatives and found not guilty by the Senate. This article will not argue the president's guilt or innocence but instead will attempt to shed light upon misconceptions and mistakes evident during his impeachment trial. These misconceptions and mistakes strike at the heart of our constitutional form of government and have transformed this nation from one that is ruled by law to one ruled by demagoguery.

The Constitution

The Constitution of the United States of America is a document written by citizens in layman's terms. Its purpose is to establish our government and the laws that guide and control it. If the wording of the Constitution sounds awkward, it is because our style of writing has changed over the past 210 years. Most words and phrases in the Constitution can be taken at face value. However, in certain cases, to understand the intent of our founding fathers, an understanding of the common usage of words at the time is necessary.

Following is the verbatim text from our Constitution, which addresses impeachment:

- Article I, Section 2—The House of Representatives shall have the sole Power of Impeachment.

- Article I, Section 3—The Senate shall have the sole Power to try all Impeachments. When sitting for that Purpose, they shall be on Oath or Affirmation. When the President of the United States is tried the Chief Justice shall preside: and no Person shall be convicted without the Concurrence of two-thirds of the Members present. Judgment in cases of Impeachment shall not extend further than to removal from Office, and disqualification to hold and enjoy any Office of Honor, Trust, or profit under the United States: but the Party convicted shall nevertheless be liable and subject to Indictment, Trial, Judgment and Punishment, according to Law.

- Article II, Section 2—The President shall have Power to grant Reprieves and Pardons for Offenses against the United States, except in Cases of Impeachment.

- Article II, Section 4—The President, Vice President, and all civil Officers of the United States, shall be removed from Office on impeachment for, and Conviction of, Treason, Bribery, or other high Crimes and Misdemeanors.

- Article III, Section 2—The Trial of all Crimes, except in Cases of Impeachment, shall be by Jury.

At first glance, these words appear straightforward and easy to understand. A procedure has been established for removing high officials from office for committing "Treason, Bribery, or other high Crimes and Misdemeanors." But what other crimes are impeachable under these guidelines? President Clinton's supporters maintain that only crimes that are an obvious threat to the nation are impeachable and that perjury and obstruction of justice do not meet this constitutional standard. We know of two crimes that are definitely impeachable: treason and bribery. Treason is an obvious threat to the nation. However, bribery may or may not be a threat dependent upon the circumstance, and clearly, there are many bribes that are not a threat. Therefore, some types of bribes may be impeachable while others are not. How do we determine the difference?

Perhaps an answer to this question lies in the phrase "high Crimes and Misdemeanors." This is a curious arrangement of words. Why is the word *misdemeanor* used in conjunction with *high crimes*? Is there such a thing as a high misdemeanor? Can a misdemeanor crime be detrimental to our nation? If not, we are left with the disturbing conclusion that this part of our Constitution does not make sense, and the founders erred when writing it. But wait, this contradiction is resolved if the word *high* does not refer to a hierarchy of crimes but instead to the status of the official committing the crime. In other words, a *high crime* is not a crime worse than others but a crime committed by a "high" government official. Under this interpretation, both high crimes and high misdemeanors are possible, and the Constitution makes sense as written. The fact that the words *crimes* and *misdemeanors* are capitalized while *high* is not, supports this conclusion.

Our new understanding of *high crimes* is the only one that makes sense because it is not possible to reconcile *misdemeanor* with the word *high*. A *misdemeanor* can never be a high crime, and there is no such thing as misdemeanor treason or misdemeanor bribery. Therefore, the contention that only high crimes detrimental to our nation are impeachable is false. Our Constitution holds government officials accountable for all crimes committed while in office, irrespective of how serious those crimes are.

How could the founders give Congress the power to overturn a national election because of a misdemeanor crime? To understand why, it is necessary to understand their frame of mind at the time the Constitution was written. We had just fought a terrible war to throw off the yoke of British tyranny, and at best, the government was considered a necessary evil. This was clearly established by Thomas Paine in his pamphlet "Common Sense," which was very popular and widely read just prior to the Revolutionary War. Furthermore, the thirteen colonies were populated by people who had fled the Old World to escape the oppression and tyranny of their former governments. Therefore, our founding fathers, to a man, were distrustful of government. Knowing this, it is not hard to understand why they subscribed to the notion that criminals of any kind should not be allowed to hold public office—more so our highest office, the presidency. The saying, "A public office is a public trust," held real significance to the founders.

Are we really left with the disturbing prospect that the president can be removed from office for jaywalking or parking at an expired meter? The founders were not that dogmatic. To be sure, a president will be removed from office if impeached by the House and convicted by the Senate, but this will only happen if the House exercises its constitutional authority to impeach. There is nothing in the Constitution that compels the House to act. Impeachment, therefore, is an option for the House to exercise at its discretion. If the House impeaches, it is incumbent upon the Senate to hold a trial; the *sole* purpose of which is to determine if the offending official is guilty as charged and thereby removed from office. No other course of action is permitted, and under no circumstances does the Senate enjoy the option of questioning whether a crime is impeachable or not. The House has already ruled, and the Constitution reserves this right for the House alone.

Under what circumstances can we expect the House to exercise its power of impeachment? For jaywalking? Obviously no! For treason? Obviously yes! Where is the middle ground between these two crimes? For an answer, we must look to bribery, a crime that was given special mention by the founders. Irrespective of bribes affecting national security, what is it about a bribe that makes it repugnant? When a public official takes a bribe, he is acting in his own interest to the detriment of the public. Bribe-taking entails a lie because concurrent with accepting a salary to work for the public's best interest, an official secretly accepts a bribe to work for someone else's interest. Clearly, a public official who accepts a bribe, any bribe for any reason, has violated the public trust, and by doing so, he has forfeited the privilege of holding office.

We have now identified our middle ground. The Constitution holds that the president, vice president, or other high officials should be impeached and removed from office for treason, bribery, or any crime that constitutes a breach of the public trust similar to bribery. This interpretation stands the test of reason and is in keeping with sound governing principles and also with the mindset of our founding fathers at the time the Constitution was written.

Truth is an undeniable pillar of good government, and this is especially valid in our judicial system where the truth is held sacred. The public's best interest is always served by the truth, and any lie told in an official capacity is a breach of public trust because it supports the furtherance of a hidden agenda. This being so, obstruction of justice, the end result of which is to establish a lie, is also a breach of public trust. The common essence of bribery, perjury, and obstruction are lies and deception to pursue a hidden agenda contrary to the public's best interest. Therefore, these crimes are clear violations of public trust and are impeachable. According to article I, section 3 of the Constitution, judgment in cases of impeachment is limited to removal from office and permanent disqualification to hold office. Once removed or if found not guilty and not removed from office, the offending official is subject to being charged and tried in a court of law. From this wording, it should be clear that an impeachment trial, while being called a trial, is really an administrative procedure for removing offending officials from office to protect the public's best interests and also for the purpose of allowing officials to be tried in a court of law as a private citizen. Judgment in cases of impeachment is limited to removal from office and disqualification to hold office specifically to ensure that the impeachment process does not infringe upon the prerogatives and mandates of our criminal justice system. This being so, an impeachment trial has a lower threshold of guilt than a criminal trial and does not replace or supersede one. It is also possible for an official to be impeached and removed from office and then subsequently found not guilty in a court of law.

To understand why the founders had no problem with this last possibility, which seems so terribly unfair to us, we must revisit the mindset they had when writing the Constitution. The founders did not view removing the president and replacing him with the vice president as overturning an election but instead as a sacred duty performed for the good of the nation on behalf of its citizens. The founders believed public officials should not only avoid improprieties, but also the appearance of impropriety. Isn't this the essence of good leadership and a standard that should be expected from government officials? A guiding principle in law is that it is better to have a guilty man go free than to convict an innocent one. The converse is true for impeachment. It is better to remove an innocent president from office than have a guilty one remain there.

The impeachment process was placed within our Constitution to ensure that government officials serve the public's best interest and to remove them from office when they do not. Its purpose, most assuredly, was not to establish a privileged class of government officials for whom the rule of law can be suspended or denied. Unfortunately, in the trial of President William Jefferson Clinton, this perversion prevailed.

The President's Trial

Should the president have been removed from office for being unfaithful to his wife? While this moral transgression is lamentable, obviously no. No one should be removed from office for a moral lapse that is private in nature. However, in addition to being unfaithful, the thrust of the Paula Jones's lawsuit was that the president used the authority of his office to prey upon female subordinates. Irrespective of whether this is true or not, it was the Paula Jones's lawsuit that resulted in the exposure of the president's relationship with Monica Lewinsky. His actions during the investigation of this relationship led to his impeachment.

President Clinton was impeached for lying under oath and attempting to impede an investigation of his sexual activities. However, because these transgressions resulted from actions that are private and personal, many people conclude that they are forgivable and not impeachable. Despite popular opinion, there are no mitigating circumstances for not telling the truth under oath or for obstructing a duly constituted legal investigation. This is especially true for the president of the United States, the highest law enforcement official within our nation, and this holds true irrespective of how much we like the president and how well he does his job. Popularity and competence should never overshadow the principles upon which good government is based and the principles that support our criminal justice system.

The Senate voted "not guilty" to the articles of impeachment, and the president's supporters declared a victory for democracy and constitutional government. Unfortunately, the opposite is true. The system worked properly through the swearing-in of senators as jurors, but immediately following this ceremony, the Senate trial degenerated into a political circus.

Upon receipt of the articles of impeachment, the Constitution mandates that the Senate hold a trial. Before this trial begins, each Senator swears an oath that he will judge the president by the evidence. This never happened. Immediately following the swearing-in ceremony, the Senate tendered a motion to dismiss the charges against the president. This vote was taken because it was understood that not enough votes were there to convict. Apparently, this was determined by asking each senator how they would vote, and having prejudged the president, they wrongfully revealed their intentions. This would constitute a mistrial in a court of law. Furthermore, because the House retains the *sole* power to impeach, it follows that it is not constitutional for the Senate to tender a motion to dismiss the charges against the president. A vote to dismiss is the same as a vote to not impeach because both votes determine if a Senate trial will be held. This being so, the vote to dismiss by the Senate was an affront to the House of Representatives and constituted a usurpation of their impeachment authority.

After the motion to dismiss failed, the Senate had to decide how to proceed. These procedural deliberations focused on the number of witnesses that would be called and the method of presentation of their testimony. In a criminal trial, no such limitations are allowed. To be sure, evidence can be ruled inadmissible due to legal technicalities or because it is irrelevant, but justice demands that all material evidence be heard. The Senate swore an oath to judge the President by the evidence. It is not possible to reconcile this oath with a vote taken to place limitations on the evidence presented. Therefore, the vote in question was unconstitutional.

During the Senate trial, many senators voted to acquit because they believed that perjury and obstruction do not rise to an impeachable level. It has been established that this is not the case. Irrespective of whether this is true or not, to allow this belief to determine how they would vote was also an affront to the House of Representatives and unconstitutional. The Constitution provides that the House retains the sole power to impeach. Therefore, a vote to impeach by the House establishes that the crimes in question are impeachable. Furthermore, when the Constitution establishes that the Senate retains the sole power to try impeachments, it follows that the Senate is duty-bound to determine if the impeached individual is guilty as charged and nothing more. The Senate prides itself on being a deliberative body superior to the House of Representatives. Unfortunately, this point of view clouded their judgment, and during the president's impeachment trial, their deliberative instincts led them to ignore their oath as jurors and their duty under the Constitution.

It is disturbing and incomprehensible that so many Americans seem to agree that the crimes of perjury and obstruction are not impeachable. How is it possible for anyone to think the framers would create a constitution that allows government officials to remain in office if they perjure themselves or obstruct justice? Put yourself in the place of the framers: a new nation is being formed, and you are a delegate to its constitutional convention and a member of a subcommittee that will draft articles addressing impeachment. In the course of doing so, you return to the convention floor with a draft document establishing that it is permissible within the proposed constitution for the president and other government officials to lie to the public, lie under oath, and obstruct the investigation of crimes. Clearly, if you did this, the other delegates to the convention would conclude that you were insane and laugh you off the convention floor. Yet incomprehensibly, this obvious absurdity has been accepted by many Americans as being the intention of our founding fathers, and as a result, this travesty has been established as a constitutional standard for the future of this nation.

A stated justification for attempting to dismiss the charges against the president and limit the evidence presented was that the polls indicated that a majority of Americans did not want the president removed from office. At first glance, this seems very democratic, but in the final analysis, it signifies that we have been transformed from being a nation of law to a nation where the majority rules even when the majority is misinformed. The sad reality of this state of affairs is that the president was not properly judged as prescribed by the Constitution but instead was judged by polling the opinions of people who had not been sworn to judge the president by the evidence, had very limited knowledge of the evidence available, had never read our Constitution, and even if they had, would be mystified about its legal precepts and nuances. Is this how a representative form of government is supposed to function? The definition of *demagoguery* is to maintain a position of leadership and authority by appealing to the prejudices and misconceptions of common citizens. These doings are the very essence of demagoguery.

Analysis

Consider the following concerning the state of mind of Americans as polled and our Congress during the president's impeachment proceedings:

1. Approximately one-third of us believe the president is not guilty.
2. Approximately one-third of us believe that the president is guilty of perjury and obstruction but also wrongfully believe these offenses are such that he should not be removed from office.
3. Approximately one-third of us believe the president should be removed from office because of his crimes.
4. Over one-half of the House of Representatives believe that the president should be removed from office because of his crimes.
5. One-half of the United States Senate believes the president is guilty of obstruction.
6. Forty-five percent of the United States Senate believes the president is guilty of perjury.

The president's supporters base their case for vindication upon the fact that if you combine items 1 and 2 above, it is correct to state that two-thirds of the people do not want to see the president removed from office. However, what is wrongfully being ignored is the fact that two-thirds of us believe the president is guilty of perjury and obstruction, and one-half of Congress agrees. Furthermore, one-half of the two-thirds majority against removal are laboring under the misconception that the president's crimes do not warrant impeachment. If these people were enlightened, it is possible that many of them would change their minds. It follows, therefore, that if the president's impeachment trial were replayed before a fully informed electorate, the outcome may have been different.

Conclusion

The impeachment of a president is one of the most important and sacred tasks our Constitution asks of Congress. Unfortunately, many people believe that the impeachment trial of President William Jefferson Clinton has been a waste of time. Regrettably, they are correct in their belief only because the president's impeachment trial was not conducted in keeping with the provisions of our Constitution and therefore was unconstitutional. Our forefathers, 210 years ago, gathered together to create a document, the purpose of which was to establish our government and the laws that it must obey. This document, called the Constitution, is the most magnificent document ever created in the history of mankind. However, it will only serve us if those we entrust to preserve, protect, and defend it are honest and trustworthy. The impeachment trial of President William Jefferson Clinton has established that these attributes are no longer required for high government office. As a result, our Constitution will no longer fulfill the purpose for which it was created.

APPENDIX A3
Change

May 2010

A buzzword used by many presidential candidates is *change*. Indeed, for the past several years, *change* has been a prominent word in presidential campaigns. However, just as conspicuous in most of these campaigns is the fact that the candidates do not tell us specifically what changes they are talking about. Sure, we get generalizations about ending the war and changing the way Washington does business, but the actual changes being promised by both the Republicans and Democrats are a mystery to us. The problem is that change can be bad or good, and without specific information about what changes a candidate is proposing, we really have no idea what we are voting for.

President George W. Bush brought about many significant changes to this nation. He established that a president may take our nation to war on a lie and use war as a pretext to take away the rights given to us by God and protected by our Constitution. President Bush has also established that human beings, especially foreigners, have no inalienable rights and can be tortured when deemed necessary by government authorities. Finally, he has created a mega-governmental agency called the Department of Homeland Security that has put new meaning into the phrase "Big Brother is watching." Barack Obama, in his presidential campaign, promised to change some of these things. The problem is he made these promises with fingers crossed behind his back, and as his second term of office passed, he has changed nothing promised.

Americans are hungry for change. We want the jobs and corporations that have fled overseas to come home and rehire those they fired. We would like gas to be two dollars a gallon and not have to pay one hundred dollars for a few bags of groceries. We want the tornados in the Midwest to go away and the glaciers to stop melting and falling into the sea. We pray that the perpetual wars in the Middle East will end and for our troops to come home. We want an end to foreign aid, secure borders, a balanced budget, and for America to stop policing the world. We want our government to stop lying to us and want a president who is accountable for his actions. Finally, we wish to leave this world a better place for our children as our parents and grandparents have done before us. In other words, we want what we had before. Therefore, Americans do not really want change. We have had a bellyful of change and what we really want is *reform*.

Reform! What an easy word to say, but what a difficult thing to bring about. Politically speaking, reform means going back to where we are supposed to be. But where is that? Ask Americans and you get different answers from everyone. We all know something is very wrong, but we are unable to agree on what needs to be done to turn things around despite the fact that the answer to our problems is self-evident. We need to return to the fundamental constitutional roots that made this nation what it was for most of the past century. In other words, we need a constitutional government with all the checks and balances designed to ensure that the wrong changes do not take place and our government behaves the way we want it to. While this is what Americans should want, we do not have a snowball's chance in hell of ever seeing this happen because this is not what our leaders want. Our leaders want to be free, and for them to be truly free, they need to be free of our Constitution and free of accountability to us. And the two best ways of achieving this freedom are through perpetual war and an economic system that turns us into the downtrodden economic slaves of the Banksters.

America changed in 1913. This was the year that Congress wrongfully, and in violation of our Constitution, created the Federal Reserve—a private foreign banking cartel given authority to control our money supply and economy. It should be clear that if a group of people can control our money supply and economy, then they can control everything including our government. There is no equivocation here; either we control our government through our Constitution or they control it through the power of the dollar. Unfortunately, human nature being what it is, the dollar always trumps an oath of office, and this being the case, we are left with a government that pays lip service to our Constitution and lies to us about everything.

All of the foregoing being true, the first thing that any president should do upon entering office is work to repeal the Federal Reserve Act. Has Barack Obama ever mentioned this kind of change? Other than Ron Paul, has any Republican or Democrat ever mentioned this kind of change? No, of course not! The simple truth of the matter is that almost all Republican and Democrat leaders work for them (the Banksters) and not for us. Can you imagine a high-level corporate executive informing his board of directors that they are fired? Well, this is exactly what is necessary for our president and Congress to do for us to be a free people again. In order to serve and save us, they must tell the Banksters that they are no longer needed because they were never needed in the first place.

Concurrent with the above actions, our government should repeal GATT and get us out of the World Trade Organization (WTO). When we joined the United Nations, to ensure that this organization would not control the course of our nation, a security council was created, which gave the United States veto power over all actions taken by the UN. No such veto power exists for actions taken by the WTO. Instead, we have agreed to make all of our laws, policies, and procedures conform to the decisions of the WTO—without reservation. In other words, the WTO is a governing body that controls our government. By quitting the WTO, we would regain our lost sovereignty and return to the day when we can trade freely with other nations without a group of foreigners telling us what to do.

The reality this nation faces today is that we are in a permanent recession called poverty, and this is exactly where our government has placed us to the benefit of our New World Order masters. Americans want this to change, and as a result, presidential candidates paint themselves as agents of change while, in truth, they intend to change nothing of substance. On the other hand, to his credit, Barack Obama has actually changed something. Instead of having a white oppressor for a president, we have one who is black.

APPENDIX A4
Immigration Reform

April 2003

During his campaign, President George W. Bush promised Hispanic voters that if reelected, he would "reform" immigration. By reform, he intends to provide three-year work visas for an undetermined number of the millions of illegal immigrants that presently reside in the United States. These so-called guest workers could then apply for permanent legal status, provided their employers assure government officials that the jobs the guest workers held could not be filled by Americans.

Labor unions and conservatives opposed the proposed reform because they believe it would encourage illegal immigration, take jobs away from American workers, give employers too much say in deciding the fate of the illegal immigrants, and because it essentially is an amnesty program for undocumented workers. President Bush declared that he was not swayed or deterred by these arguments because the only jobs affected would be those that Americans are unwilling to fill and because his proposal is a "worker" program, not an amnesty program. President Bush also maintains that legalizing the flow of worker immigrants into this country would free up the Border Patrol and allow them to concentrate on drug smuggling and other security concerns.

First of all, it is acknowledged that there are millions of illegal immigrants presently in this country. If the Border Patrol is presently preoccupied with stemming their flow at the expense of addressing drug smuggling or other security concerns, then they aren't doing any aspect of their job very well. The Border Patrol's primary job is to prevent illegal entry into our country. You do not enhance one aspect of this job by ignoring another. The opposite is true; if you improve your performance at interdicting one kind of illegal interloper, you necessarily improve your performance at interdicting all kinds of interlopers, whatever their reason for crossing the border. To put this another way, if I were a terrorist intent upon entering the United States to do mayhem and I knew that illegal immigrant workers were not being intercepted by the Border Patrol, then I would enter the country posing as an illegal immigrant worker.

President Bush is also wrong when he argues that the only jobs affected will be those that Americans are unwilling to fill. To be sure, there are many undesirable jobs in this nation, but they are undesirable for two reasons: the nature of the work and the level of associated pay. Therefore, the problem of unfillable jobs is one more of compensation than the nature of the work performed. From this, it should be clear that if the level of pay of any job is raised high enough, it will be possible to find workers to fill it. This is especially true when so many people are presently unemployed because of the outsourcing of manufacturing jobs. The converse is also true. If you have a job where the nature of the work is acceptable or desirable, the job will become unfillable if the pay offered is lowered enough. This truth is being ignored by President Bush.

The real problem with letting illegal workers legally fill jobs is that employers will be able to offer far less money for existing jobs across the employment spectrum, and this will dissuade Americans from applying for these jobs, thus qualifying them for illegal immigrants. Therefore, pay scales for unskilled and semiskilled work will decline in all sectors of our economy as more and more jobs are filled by peasant labor willing to work for lower pay. The end result of this is that to stay employed, American workers will be forced to accept less and less pay for the work they do until, pay-wise, they are on par with the illegal immigrants. Thus, American workers will inevitably become low-paid peasant workers. Basic economics and the law of supply and demand deem this to be true.

President Bush maintains that his proposal is a worker program and not an amnesty program. Here again, the president uses half-truths and inappropriate language to make his proposal seem more palatable. First of all, the fundamental aspect of his proposal is to ignore the illegal status of illegal immigrant workers. Beyond doubt, this constitutes amnesty for employed illegal immigrants and future illegal immigrants who find jobs when they get here. As a result, the number of immigrants who would legally enter this country would depend strictly upon the wiles of those who are able to illegally come here and the resourcefulness of businessmen seeking to reduce the cost of their labor force. Congress, national policy, and the Border Patrol will no longer be a part of this all-important equation.

President Bush is essentially correct when he describes his proposal as being a "worker program," but he ignores the fact that he is not talking about American workers but instead foreign workers who broke our laws to get here. He also fails to clarify that what he really means by his "foreign worker program" is an "employer program" that delivers cheap foreign labor to American businesses at the expense of American workers. Of course, President Bush could counter these points by pointing out that cheaper labor will mean cheaper goods and services for American consumers. But by doing so, he conveniently ignores the fact that American consumers without jobs cannot afford to buy most goods and services no matter how cheap they are.

In conclusion, the critics of President Bush's immigration reform proposal are woefully correct in their concerns. The president's proposal is first and foremost an amnesty program for those who broke the law to get here. Furthermore, his proposal will greatly encourage illegal immigration and take away a substantial number of jobs from American workers. However, left unsaid by the proposal's critics is that it will also result in lower pay scales and reduced benefit packages for workers in all sectors of our struggling economy. This being the case, Bush's proposal is anything but immigration reform. Instead, it is an immigration free-for-all and another example of a president who cares nothing for the people who pay his salary and one who thinks nothing of helping outsiders plunder this nation's wealth and heritage.

APPENDIX A5
The Telecom Immunity Fiasco

August 2008

Upon Senate passage of the updated Foreign Intelligence Surveillance Act (FISA), Representative Russ Feingold (D-Wisconsin) commented that passage of this bill was an assault upon our Constitution and its darkest hour. Representative Feingold was directing these comments to the bill's provision of immunity from lawsuits for telecom companies that cooperated with President George W. Bush's illegal spying on overseas communications of American citizens. While at first glance Congressman Feingold's comments are a refreshing breath of fresh air that we rarely get from our national leaders, upon analysis, he was remiss in not describing the depth and true nature of the assault he was talking about. Furthermore, although this current assault was horrific, it was not as damaging as other assaults on our Constitution that have occurred in the past. Unfortunately, these transgressions are never talked about by politicians of today. From this perspective, it is reasonable to wonder if Representative Feingold is not really concerned about the violation of our Constitution but instead made his comments solely to create the illusion that he is concerned.

The original FISA was passed in 1978 following Watergate, the spying scandal that occurred during that decade. Its purpose was to ensure that the president would never again unilaterally spy upon the communications of Americans. Following 9/11, President Bush saw this act as an inconvenience to his war on terrorism, so he ignored the act and enlisted several telecom companies to assist him in spying upon American overseas communications. President Bush deliberately broke the law, and to induce telecom executives to cooperate with his illegal program, he gave them written assurances that the spying was legal. With these bogus assurances in hand, these executives also willingly broke the law to gain favor with the White

House because they feared possible future reprisals. Lending credence to this, is the fact that Qwest CEO Joseph P. Nacchio declined to participate in President Bush's illegal spying program, and subsequently, his company lost several lucrative government contracts. He is presently facing charges of insider trading.

All of the foregoing being a true and an accurate description of the situation, sixty-nine out of the ninety-six voting Senators thought that, under the circumstances, offending telecom executives deserved to be granted immunity from the forty-six lawsuits filed by citizens seeking redress in the matter. The White House argued that immunity should be granted because the executives in question were given assurances that the illegal spying was legal and because punishing the executives would dissuade their cooperation with the White House in the future. Some senators also postured that although the telecom executives knowingly broke the law, they did so out of patriotic duty, and this justified their actions.

While some people will see an element of cogency in these arguments, in the final analysis, they pale in comparison to the horrific fact that the rights of Americans were deliberately and grievously violated by President Bush in consort with the offending telecom industry executives, and now Congress has denied these citizens redress in the matter. There are many things that can be said about this development, but the most telling is that, apparently, members of Congress care more about their relationship with the offending telecom executives than they do with the citizens who pay their salaries. Adding insult to injury, although the granting of immunity does not extend to criminal prosecution of the participating telecom executives, the chance of this ever happening is now nil to none. The agency responsible for filing such charges is the Department of Justice, and unfortunately for justice, the Department of Justice reports and answers directly to George Bush, the person who orchestrated these felonious criminal acts in the first place.

Congress took it upon itself to grant immunity to the offending telecom executives in an official piece of legislation that President Bush will sign. This is a tragedy for this nation because, in a legal sense, the immunity being granted is unprecedented, unjustifiable, and contrary to the principles that underpin our criminal justice system. In the past, immunity was granted to induce a minor participant in a crime to testify against principles instrumental in perpetuating the crime. Therefore, granting immunity is a form of bartering, the purpose of which is to use the little fish to capture the big fish. The immunity granted by Congress to the telecom executives in question by way of legislation is nothing like this. Instead, it is a blanket immunity granted for the sole purpose of letting the guilty parties off the hook when we do not know specifically who they are, the extent of their crimes, or their level of guilt. Granting immunity under these circumstances is an absurd miscarriage of justice that makes Congress a party to the cover-up of these crimes.

Beyond a cover-up, granting blanket immunity for any reason by Congress is unconstitutional. Our Constitution clearly defines the duties and responsibilities of Congress. Amendment X of the Constitution provides that the powers not delegated to our federal government by the Constitution are reserved for the states or the people. In other words, no branch of our federal government can assume a power not granted specifically to it by the Constitution. The power or authority to grant blanket immunity for criminal acts appears nowhere in our Constitution. Therefore, for Congress to unilaterally assume this power and let the telecom executives off the hook is unconstitutional. Furthermore, article I, section 9 of our Constitution provides that Congress will pass "no ex post facto" laws. *Ex post facto* means laws that are retroactive and apply to past situations. The FISA law just passed by Congress provides retroactive immunity to telecom executives and is unconstitutional for this reason as well.

In conclusion, the recently passed FISA legislation passed by Congress is unconstitutional for two reasons: its immunity provision is a power assumed by Congress that is not provided for anywhere in our Constitution, and it provides after-the-fact retroactive immunity, which is specifically prohibited by our Constitution. The unfortunate and dismal reality of this situation is that President Bush knows this, our Justice Department knows this, and so does all of Congress. Under these circumstances, it is time for Americans to ask why sixty-nine United States senators willfully and deliberately violated their oath of office to pass this ignoble legislation. The obvious answers to this question are to protect the offending rich and powerful telecom executives involved and to also protect President Bush, who was the perpetrator of these crimes. In other words, damn the Constitution, damn the truth, damn justice, and damn the people of this nation. The most important thing to members of Congress is feathering their own nests by protecting the ruling establishment at all costs.

APPENDIX B1
Good Government?

August 2006

The New World Order (NWO) is presently dissolving our borders, working toward a common economic union between Mexico, Canada, and the United States, and fighting a war of subjugation in Iraq with our troops and resources. As Bob Dylan said, "The times they are a changin", and unfortunately, what's changing is how we are governed. Most Americans are unaware of what is happening, and even more incredibly, of those in the know, many condone and support what is being done. I do not, and this is why I sit at this keyboard trying to wake people up.

Americans take pride in our government. This is because the government we think we have was something to be proud of. However, the simple truth of the matter is that this government is long gone, and in its place, we have a puppet government that is beholden and subservient to the NWO. This being the case, the questions we should ask ourselves is should we be proud of our new government, and should we pledge allegiance to it? My answer to both of these questions is no, and in case you fail to get my drift, let me state for the record that I am an American who is ashamed of the kind of government we have and also ashamed of my fellow Americans who, by pledging allegiance to what essentially is a scam, are living in denial and are unwitting participants in our subjugation and enslavement.

The problem is that the NWO, up until recently, has planned and plotted in secret. Fortunately, this has changed, and we now know a lot more about who they are and what they are trying to accomplish. Recently, David Rockefeller, an NWO principal and a founder of the Trilateral Commission, in an address to the Trilateral Commission given in June of 1991, said the following:

> We are grateful to the Washington Post, the New York Times, Time Magazine, and other great publications whose directors have attended our meetings and respected their promises of discretion for almost forty years. It would have been impossible for us to develop our plan for the world if we had been subjected to the light of publicity during those years. But now the world is more sophisticated and prepared to march towards a world government. The supranational sovereignty of an intellectual elite and world bankers is surely preferable to the national auto-determination practiced in past centuries.

The *we* David Rockefeller refers to is the NWO. Let's not mince words here. If you wish to choose another name for what Mr. Rockefeller is talking about, then you are free to do so, but whatever you call this fledgling world government, it should be clear that David Rockefeller has assured us that one exists. This much is certain, and now that one of the NWO's founders has let the cat out of the bag, according to Mr. Rockefeller, we can also be sure of the following:

- The leadership of the New World Order met in secret for almost forty years to develop their plan to rule the world.

- The directors of major news publications of our mainstream media have attended these meetings and failed to report what was going on to the American people.

- The leadership of the New World Order has met in secret for almost forty years to develop their plan to rule the world.

- If the American people had been aware of what was going on, they would have been opposed to the decisions being made and stopped these changes from happening.

- A world dictatorship of the moneyed elite is superior to democracy.

Mr. Rockefeller's words tell us a lot about the New World Order, and it should be evident that the government we are talking about is peopled by unelected individuals who rule for life. This being the case, two issues are of concern: what is the nature and character of the government under question, and what is the nature and character of the people we are talking about? If we are stuck with this government and these individuals for the foreseeable future, knowing their nature and character is very important.

The first thing evident is that our NWO masters have an ego problem. They think having unconscionable amounts of money makes them better than everyone else, and even more incomprehensibly, they think that it bestows upon them a special right to rule the world. However, the situation is far worse than this. Their ego problem has rendered them out of touch with reality. If they are better than everyone else, then it follows that they believe they are superior human beings. This being the case, it logically follows that the rest of us are inferior human beings. Therefore, not only do they believe they have a special right to rule the world, they also think they have a duty and obligation to do so, because us lesser human beings are not capable of governing ourselves.

This kind of warped and perverted thinking is similar to the philosophies that gripped Nazi Germany under Adolf Hitler's rule. The Nazis also believed they were superior to everyone else in the world. In fact, if we substitute Aryan for "intellectual elite," we find that David Rockefeller and Adolf Hitler are cut from the same block of wood. Furthermore, if Adolf Hitler suddenly arose from his grave, he undoubtedly would shake Mr. Rockefeller's hand and congratulate him for a job well done. History teaches us that we are in real danger when individuals in positions of authority think they are better than other people, and unfortunately, history is now repeating itself. Once again, a group of megalomaniacs is trying to take over the world.

However, this is not the entire story. David Rockefeller admits that if Americans had been aware of what he and his fellow conspirators were up to, they would have been opposed to their plans. This is shocking! What kind of despicable human being brags about being able to fool an entire nation and sees nothing wrong with forcing his will upon a free and independent people? At least Adolf Hitler was honest enough to announce his intentions to the world before he assumed power.

No such claim to candor can be made by David Rockefeller and his coconspirators. Their actions are not the mark of honest men or honorable human beings. Furthermore, they also fall short of the bar when it comes to integrity. From my perspective, Mr. Rockefeller and his cronies, including the depraved corporate moguls from the fourth estate who watched in silence while these people plotted against us, are not only not as good as the rest of us, but in truth are despicable human beings who deserve our contempt and ridicule.

This now brings us to a far more sinister topic. For the most part, our NWO masters are Americans who were born in this country. Therefore, they are citizens of this nation who, like the rest of us through the years, have pledged allegiance to our flag and the republic for which it stands.

Apparently, this pledge meant nothing to them because, for the past forty years, they recited our pledge of allegiance before God and the people of this nation while meeting in secret to plot against us. It is highly ironic that a group of people labeling themselves "intellectually elite" and who think this gives them the mandate to rule the entire world, upon analysis, are nothing more than a cabal of lying traitors who have corrupted the nation of their birth and had the unmitigated gall to reduce their fellow citizens to subjugation and bondage.

A bedrock principle of good government and the American experiment in democracy is that a government's legitimacy depends upon the consent of the governed. If the New World Order had to fool us in order to assume power, how legitimate is the government they created? I certainly didn't give them my consent, and I certainly do not approve of the way I am being governed. And what *way* are we talking about?

The overriding characteristic of the abomination they created is that they decide and we abide—the hallmark of a dictatorship! You can call it communism, fascism, totalitarianism, imperialism, or whatever *ism* you like! All these terms fit our situation quite well, but irrespective of what you wish to call it, the bottom line is that the government of the people, by the people, and for the people of which Abraham Lincoln spoke has perished from the earth, and President Lincoln, our founding fathers, and all the other great Americans we have held in reverence throughout our lives are turning over in their graves.

APPENDIX B2
The Fed Is a Ponzi Scheme!

June 2007

Most Americans are proud of their country and consider the United States to be the greatest nation in all history. This is because there are many things we can point to which substantiate this belief. However, everything in life is transitory, and when the final judgment for this nation comes to pass, history will record that, instead of being something special to be admired, Americans were suckers who fell hook, line, and sinker for the worst Ponzi scheme the world has ever seen: the Federal Reserve Bank.

A Ponzi scheme is a swindle that was conceived and run by an Italian immigrant named Charles Ponzi. Mr. Ponzi defrauded his investors out of millions of dollars during the 1920s. The con, like most cons, was deceptively simple. Its perpetrator convinced his clients that he was a skillful investor who would make them more money than they could make investing elsewhere. Once people are hooked and give their money to the perpetrator, they are paid what they think are legitimate earnings with money conned from newer investors. The scheme functions smoothly for a while, but an increasing number of new investors are required to pay off the older investors and keep them at bay. Of course, over time, this becomes an impossible situation, and eventually, the scheme collapses with those still in the game losing everything they invested.

Understanding this, it should be clear that the Federal Reserve Bank has many of the same characteristics as a Ponzi scheme. Like a Ponzi scheme, it began with a lie concocted solely to suck in its intended victims. The lie used to get this nation into bed with the Fed is that they promised to regulate our economy such that booms and busts would be eliminated. In truth, the opposite has been the case, and the Fed has admitted that it played a role in bringing about the Depression of 1929 as well as the deep recession that presently grips the nation. Similar to a Ponzi scheme, the Fed takes our money and gives us nothing in return. The money we give to the Fed is not earned for any service it provides nor is there any reasonable justification for us to give it to them. Finally, similar to a Ponzi scheme, the eventual collapse of our economy is inevitable.

While the similarities between a Ponzi scheme and the Fed are such that it falls into the same category of crime, the truth of the matter is that the Fed is far more diabolical than a simple Ponzi scheme. The victims of a Ponzi scheme are motivated by greed and make a deliberate choice to join the scam. In contrast, the Fed has made victims of all the citizens of this nation who were never given a choice because Congress decided the matter for us. In a Ponzi scheme, victims lose their investments but are left with the money they did not invest. The Fed also keeps the money we give it, but because fiat money is a key element of the scam, it is continually being printed. As a result, the money we keep and save for ourselves loses value over time and will eventually be worth nothing. Thus, under the Fed, not only do we lose the money we give it, we eventually lose all the money we have. For example, the Federal Reserve notes we have in our pocket today are worth only 4 percent of what they were in 1913, when the Fed first came to power. If you had one million dollars then, it is only worth forty-thousand dollars now. This would not be the case if our government managed our money supply. Not only would we be able to avoid the curse of inflation but the income taxes we pay would be unnecessary.

The Federal Reserve Bank truly is a den of con artists who have stolen the wealth and prosperity of an entire nation. Our problem today is that their diabolical scheme was legitimized in 1913 by the passage of the Federal Reserve Act. This abominable act was a product of subterfuge and deception. Every congressman who voted for it did so in violation of their oath of office. The time has come for Congress to make amends for what it did to the people of this nation. This can only be accomplished by repealing the Federal Reserve Act and returning the power to create money to Congress, where it rightfully belongs. Those perpetuating this con should be brought to justice, the debts we owe them declared void and the assets they obtained with our money confiscated. Only these actions will make things right and free America from the financial bondage that the Fed and their stooges in Congress have bestowed upon us.

Don't hold your breath waiting for this to happen. The huge amount of money the Fed has stolen has made these criminals rich beyond anyone's ability to comprehend, and they use this money to corrupt everything they touch. Their ill-gotten gains have enabled them to keep those we elect to office under their thumbs. An exception to this was President John F. Kennedy, who worked to reign in the Fed while he was in office. In June of 1963, President Kennedy signed Executive Order 11110, which authorized the United States Treasury to print Treasury notes in lieu of Federal Reserve notes. This returned the power to create money to our Treasury Department. Unfortunately, President Kennedy was murdered in 1963. Subsequent to his assassination, the money issued in accordance with his executive order was removed from circulation, never to be seen again.

There is another aspect to our present situation that also costs Americans dearly. The Fed has created an atmosphere of corruption throughout the nation that pervades all our institutions. The result of this is that men of integrity, who will not compromise themselves, never advance in the hierarchy of our governing institutions. The primary attribute looked for in those being considered for advancement is loyalty to the boss beyond all other considerations including legalities and the public's best interest. The higher one goes up the ladder in public service, the truer this becomes. Our government is led by a criminal enterprise, and because of this, it has become a criminal enterprise.

Far too many government officials obtain wealth and position through illegal and dishonorable means. Those who are honest and aware of what is going on look the other way because they know that doing otherwise will be the kiss of death to their careers. The inevitable result of this dismal environment is that our government does nothing right anymore no matter what resources are available. We only have to look to our war on terror, our war on drugs, how we protect our borders, military procurement, and how government contracts are issued and managed to understand why this is true. The Fed has turned our government into an ineffectual nightmare, and the cost we pay for this is enormous.

APPENDIX B3
My Opinion of Barack Obama

March 2009

A short time ago, a friend of mine sent me a request from his daughter in college. She was writing a paper on what people thought about Barack Obama, our newly elected president, and asked me for my impressions in two hundred words or less. Following is my offering:

Barack Obama is intelligent, articulate, handsome, and dedicated to his beautiful family. He also wants to be a president for all Americans and not just those with six-figure incomes. On the other side of the coin, the president-elect is a Democrat, and his party shares responsibility with the Republicans for the mess this country is in. Therefore, being a loyal Democrat, Barack Obama is handicapped in regard to the options available to him to help this nation. Also, as an accepted member of this nation's ruling establishment, he is committed to keeping Americans in the dark about how we are really governed. Therefore, his most grievous character flaw is his willingness to participate in deception. Proof of this is his use of the word *democracy* to describe America, his wrongfully calling Bill Clinton a great president, and the fact that he has taken his oath of office with his fingers crossed behind his back. In conclusion, appearances are that Barack Obama is the answer to this nation's prayers, but the truth is that instead of being our salvation, we are in for politics as usual, and politics, as usual, means the American experiment in Republican democracy is over.

Apparently, upon reading my offering, my friend's daughter received more than she bargained for because she never wrote back to thank me for fulfilling her request. To be sure, my response is a highly critical assessment of a popular and newly elected president. However, despite the severity of my assessment, the real truth is that I was far too easy on him.

There are three key organizations that are part of the New World Order: the Bilderbergers, the Council on Foreign Relations, and the Trilateral Commission. The leadership of these groups meets in secret to decide things, but we are never told what they decide, even though their decisions have shaped the world we live in today. David Rockefeller is a prime mover in these organizations, and in order to understand what they are about, all we have to do is read a statement he made in 1991:

> The world is more sophisticated and prepared to march toward a world government. The supranational sovereignty of an intellectual elite and world bankers is surely preferable to the national auto-determination practiced in past centuries.

No matter how you slice it, Mr. Rockefeller and his associates have declared themselves to be rulers of the world. And in case you have been living in la-la land for the past several years, it should be clear that these are the people who have shaped the world within which we live. However, something is very wrong with this because there is no way possible to reconcile a world governing body with our Constitution. Our Constitution mandates that Congress will decide the issues that affect this nation, not a group of self-appointed dictators who hold themselves superior to Congress, our president, and the Supreme Court. The bottom line is that any government official who is a member of any one of the organizations stands in violation of his or her oath of office, and this being the case, that government official is a traitor. This having been established the question that cries out to be answered is, how well do the members of Barack Obama's administration stand up to scrutiny in this regard?

Barack Obama is a member of the Council on Foreign Relations. As far as the top fourteen officials in his administration are concerned, three are not members of any of these organizations, three belong to at least one of them, four belong to two of them, and five belong to all three organizations at the same time. This being true, what does this tell us about the kind of government we have in Washington? Can it be said that their interests lie with the people of this nation or with those who have appointed themselves dictators of the world?

The New World Order exists, and its goal is to dominate and govern the world. Unfortunately, in many instances, the goals and aspirations of the New World Order run counter to those of this nation and its people. When this is the case, government officials are bound by sacred oaths to do what is best for us, not what is best for a world government or some other group of people. Unfortunately, the situation is such that a strong majority of the people Barack Obama has chosen to serve in his administration are committed to serving the agenda of the above three organizations at our expense. This being the case, it follows that these people take their oath of office with their fingers crossed behind their backs, take the salary we pay them under false pretenses, and when necessary, will stab the nation they pledge allegiance to in the back at the drop of a hat. Thus, the administration of Barack Obama is not an instrument of change. Instead, it is an instrument that will ensure that our government remains subservient to the New World Order, and one that will also ensure that the American people remain ignorant, compliant, and subjugated.

APPENDIX B4
Deception and the WTO

December 2002

In the editorials published recently, entitled "Bush Had No Choice on Repeal", in the Erie Times-News, and "WTO Steel Maneuver Heartens Free Traders", by William Buckley, both authors conclude that political realities forced President George Bush to back off on steel tariffs.

First of all, the Europeans and Japanese did not just get together and decide to impose sanctions upon us. Instead, they were acting at the behest of the WTO, which authorized the sanctions in keeping with its administrative procedures. Article XVI, paragraph 4 of the GATT accord states, "Each member [of the WTO] shall ensure the conformity of its laws, regulations and administrative procedures with its obligations as provided in the annexed agreements." In other words, as a member of the WTO, we have pre-agreed to abide by a dispute-settlement mechanism that is binding upon member nations, including us.

The real story of what happened to the United States when it imposed tariffs on imported steel is that upon taking this step, the other steel-producing members of the WTO challenged our tariffs before a WTO ruling panel that ruled in their favor. This having been accomplished, we were now legally obligated to remove the tariffs as agreed when we joined the WTO. If we refused, we would be in violation of prior agreements in the GATT Accord and, as a result, would face WTO-imposed sanctions in the form of retaliatory tariffs from member nations.

In conclusion, our situation is now such that the government of the United States no longer retains the power to regulate commerce with foreign nations as required by article I, section 8 of our Constitution. Instead, we have entered into a treaty that permanently assigns this power to the WTO. The fact that Americans are not being told about the true nature of our relationship with the WTO, speaks volumes about our government and the mainstream media of this nation.

APPENDIX B5
When Corporations Rule?

March 2004

Modern corporations span the globe and possess resources that exceed those of many governments. The only protection people have against the excesses of these rich and powerful organizations is the government, and the only thing that ensures that a government will fulfill its responsibilities to its citizens is its constitution. However, these protections will be there only if the constitution in question is a viable and functional document.

A *constitution* is a document that is supposed to define and control government. Once it has failed in any way, even once, it has been rendered useless for the prime purpose for which it was written. A government with a failed constitution is free to pick and choose which provisions it will obey and which it will not. Like dominos, one by one, key provisions will be violated until the government in question is out of control, and those elected to serve are free to sell themselves and their nation to the highest bidder.

So, it is in the United States of America. Corporate thinking totally dominates every aspect of our government, and indeed the situation has progressed to the point where our government works primarily for the corporations instead of us. Unfortunately, far too many Americans have no problem with this state of affairs because they are blind to the difference between capitalism, our prevailing economic system, and our government, which we created to govern our affairs and provide essential services necessary for the common good. Two of the most important services provided by a government are defense and leveling the playing field between competing elements in society.

There are grave consequences for society when corporations dominate a government. Corporations exist to earn profits. To do so, they seek advantage in the marketplace. This goal is at odds with government's prime function of leveling the playing field. When corporations call the shots, this important responsibility is grievously compromised. However, in order for this to happen, accountability must also be compromised. With accountability gone, corruption will thrive and eventually engulf every aspect and area of government. This is our situation in America today. Our government not only keeps secrets on matters of national security but also hides how it works and makes decisions so we will not have a clue as to what it is doing. Our government is now so corrupt that we are no longer just customers of corporations but their victims.

A corporation is run by a president or chief executive officer. This individual is responsible only to his board of directors and is in total charge of every aspect of the corporation he heads. In other words, a CEO is a dictator. He *decides* and everyone else obeys. In a republic, a president is responsible to a congress of elected representatives who serve as the nation's board of directors. When corporations take over government, this key check and balance break down because both Congress and the president are controlled by the same people. The end result is that a nation's president will be transformed from being an administrator with well-defined and limited responsibilities to a dictator in total control of everything that a government does. In the United States today, President George W. Bush, "the Decider," has dismantled almost every check and balance that controlled and limited the prerogatives of his office. He truly has become a dictator above the law and answerable only to the special interests that were instrumental in getting him elected.

This state of affairs is truly regrettable not only because Americans no longer have a say in how we are governed but also because our government only addresses issues that are important to corporations and ignores important issues critical to the common good. When push comes to shove, our government always sides with the corporations when the interests of citizens and corporations clash. Of late, the best examples of this are our border with Mexico, environmental concerns, global warming, and overpopulation.

In the past, most corporations operated within the confines of national boundaries, and their markets were defined by those boundaries. As a result, corporate executives had no problem with the concept of nationhood as it once existed. However, now that globalization is upon us, national boundaries are an inconvenience and annoyance to corporations. Therefore, they want them ignored and dissolved, which is exactly what our recent presidents have been doing to our border with Mexico. They are doing this against the will of the American people. What Americans want is not what global corporations want, but because they are in charge, we do not stand a chance of ever having our will prevail over theirs. This truth speaks volumes about the democracy we think we have and in which we take so much pride.

Congress pays lip service to stopping the flood of illegal immigrants while our president does nothing to stop it. But our situation is far worse than this. In defiance of the wishes of the American people and in disregard of the provisions of our Constitution, recent presidents are forging an economic union with Canada and Mexico that will dissolve our borders even more and reduce being an American to something akin to being a fan of a sports team. The team is there, and people take pride in being associated with its name, but the relationship is meaningless and of no real consequence to anyone. Most Americans would not vote for or approve of this economic union, but it is happening anyway because this is what our corporate masters want.

Presently, President George W. Bush has the worst record on environmental and quality of life issues than any other president in history. He has ensured that the revolving door between private industry and governmental regulatory agencies is well-oiled and swinging freely. From the exploitation and sell-off of public lands to the wholesale corruption of governmental agencies created to protect the public's interest, there is no limit to the abominations and atrocities that President Bush and his corporate cronies are ramming down our throats. While this happens, Congress sits back and does nothing. Every time President Bush refuses to obey a law passed by Congress or issues a signing statement that nullifies the law being passed, he is in contempt of Congress and should be impeached. Does any of this concern Congress? Of course, not because both our president and Congress bow to the same corporate masters. It is not likely that Congress will reign in a president who is doing the bidding of the same people who control Congress.

The threat of global warming and its inevitable consequences have been known to modern science since the 1950s. We are now over fifty years down the road from the first scientific evidence that global warming was happening and only recently has our federal government acknowledged the phenomenon. Even now, their candor has not come about because the threat is real but because the problem has become so clearly evident that it cannot be denied any longer. However, despite acknowledging its existence and despite the clear and present danger to us all, the federal government is still doing nothing of substance to address the problem. We spend billions to fight a war of subjugation in a foreign nation but do nothing to fight a threat that is far more dangerous than world terrorism.

This bitter irony exists because corporations believe that taking steps to counter global warming will reduce profits and affect their ability to plunder and exploit the world's resources. Therefore, they are against the science of global warming and are spending huge sums of money to discredit not only the science but the scientists who work in this field. Former vice president Al Gore championed the case for global warming for most of his life. However, when he was vice president, we heard nothing from him about this issue because our corporate masters kept him from bringing this threat to the attention of the American people. Only after leaving public office was Mr. Gore finally able to freely serve the public by doing what he wasn't allowed to do as our vice president.

Fifty years of opportunity have passed. During those fifty years, we could have addressed the problem of global warming when the solutions were relatively cheap and easy. Now the situation has progressed to the point where the solutions are no longer cheap and easy, and even if we begin to make the sacrifices necessary to address the problem, we still will suffer its effects for years to come. Indeed, the possibility exists that it may be too late to do anything at all. Our corporate masters are directly responsible for the missed opportunity to address global warming sooner and for putting us in the terrible situation we now face. Profits are more important to them than anything, including the quality of life on this planet and the well-being of all humankind.

Nowhere is the depravity of corporate thinking and priorities more evident than when it comes to the issue of overpopulation. Overpopulation transcends global warming as an issue because it is the root cause of global warming. Furthermore, it is the underlying driving force behind every other serious problem that mankind presently faces. Flying in the face of these truths is the fact that corporations believe population growth is good for business. More people mean cheap labor and more customers. Who cares that more people also result in more global warming, more pollution, more crowded roads, more crowded cities, more crime, more urban sprawl, more extinct wildlife, less green space, and a lower quality of life for all concerned, with the exception, of course, of our corporate masters? Why should they care if you or I breathe noxious fumes while we sit trapped in traffic on the way to the store to buy a loaf of bread? Such mundane things are of no concern to them as they fly around in their corporate jets and are shuttled to their spacious mansions and mega-yachts by helicopter. Presently, the world population hovers at about six billion people.

At this level, everything we have that makes life possible and worthwhile is being stretched to its limit, and almost nothing we do is being done on a sustainable basis. Our climate, our food supply, our sources of clean drinkable water, the planet's wildlife, and our quality of life are at risk. Our federal government is doing nothing to address any of these problems because "it is bad for business." Their position is that we have no reason to be concerned about the future because such concerns will reduce corporate profitability. The truth be damned when there is money to be made by ignoring it.

World population is exploding. It took us four thousand years to reach a population level of six billion people. At this level, life on this planet as we know it is at risk. What will happen to us over the next fifty years as the world's population climbs to nine billion people, as presently projected? Is there any way for a reasonable person to deny that we are in for a disaster of biblical proportions? Incredibly, this is exactly what our corporate masters do because thinking otherwise puts profits at risk and because they believe their wealth and power will make them immune to the realities the rest of us are facing. Yes, this kind of thinking is absurd, but what do you expect from a group of people concerned only with making money and feathering their nests?

Corporate thinking now reigns supreme over our government and has corrupted it to the point where it is a criminal enterprise. But our situation is far worse than this. Our government is really not our government but the brainchild of the New World Order and is only the shell of what it once was. The problem is that a corporate-run world is nothing more than a dictatorship of people whose only motivation in life is and increasing their wealth and power. They, more than any other group of people, are the least qualified to rule, and in consideration of the great challenges we face in an overcrowded and shrinking world, their shortsighted and self-serving leadership will spell disaster for all of mankind.

In 1991, David Rockefeller said, "The supranational sovereignty of an intellectual elite and world bankers is surely preferable to the national auto-determination practiced in past centuries." By his statement, Mr. Rockefeller clearly demonstrates that he and his cronies are out of touch with reality. People like this in charge, at this critical time in history, is a recipe for disaster not only for Americans but also for every other living thing on the planet. We have a difficult road ahead, and the last thing we need is a cabal of amoral, self-serving egotists not only making the road more difficult but actively working to destroy every possible chance we have of succeeding.

APPENDIX C1
Freedom and Democracy

July 2004

Language defines the world within which we live because, through language, we define and shape ideas and concepts that are the basis of what we think. In turn, what people think determines how they behave. Therefore, controlling the behavior of people is simply a matter of shaping their world by defining the concepts that form the basis of their thoughts. There are three ways to accomplish this:

- redefine concepts and ideas slowly over time to accommodate desired changes
- allow unwanted concepts and ideas to fade into obscurity
- prevent undesirable concepts and ideas from developing

In America today, the process of controlling people through language has been developed into a fine art by those in government with the cooperation of the media, our educational institutions, and the entertainment industry. The use of the socially acceptable phrase "politically correct" exemplifies this. In the final analysis, politically correct thoughts are nothing more than those acceptable to the ruling establishment. The unfortunate aspect of this situation is that they are correct only because they are acceptable. Merit, reality, principle, reason, logic, and/or constitutional concerns have nothing to do with determining their degree of acceptability. During the cold war, communists subscribed to the notion of politically correct thought, the only difference was that we called their politically correct thoughts *propaganda* or *brainwashing*.

The end result of a successful thought-control process is the general acceptance of change because those affected are not aware that a change took place. The situation changed, but the description of the situation changed along with it, and to someone not paying attention, nothing changed. While this is all well and good for harmony and tranquility's sake, there is an inherent grave danger when those in government can wield this kind of power. It enables them to make changes at our expense and not in our best interest. This is why our founding fathers added an amendment procedure to our Constitution. They strongly believed that it is morally repugnant for government officials to use stealth to make fundamental changes to how we are governed, and that the only acceptable way for such changes to be made is by informed consent of the citizenry after careful consideration of the implications associated with the change being considered.

Unfortunately, in the United States of America today, governmental change by stealth is the order of the day, and things have progressed to the point where not only is consent of the governed a dysfunctional concept, it has been almost entirely replaced by deception and illusion. We are truly a nation of the con and conned, and we euphemize this lamentable state of affairs by calling it "politics." Unfortunately, the end result of the politics we are talking about is that not only have we been robbed of our heritage and birthright, we are now being ravaged and looted economically with the complicity and cooperation of those entrusted to protect us.

The above statements and conclusions are anathema to most Americans, which does not in any way reflect upon their validity or truth but instead, indicates how successful the change makers have been in achieving their ends. This can be clearly established to anyone's satisfaction by a careful examination of two of our most revered and sacred concepts: freedom and democracy. These words exemplify the very essence of Americanism and roll off our lips as sacred and inviolate truths. Millions of Americans have died for the sake of these words, and it is taken for granted that those who made this supreme sacrifice have not died in vain, but have they?

The *real* truth out there for anyone to see, if they just open their eyes, is that what we call freedom today is not the same freedom we enjoyed in the past, and this nation is democratic in name only. If our founding fathers suddenly arose from their graves and surveyed our present situation, to a man, they would hold that not only are we not free and not a democracy but instead a subjugated and downtrodden people.

Freedom is an easy concept to understand. One is free when able to do as one wishes. However, there are obvious limitations to our freedom, the first one being physical reality. We are free to jump off a building if we wish, but if we do, there are severe consequences for exercising this kind of freedom. Similarly, other people are a limitation to our freedom. An individual's freedom ends where another person's begins. From this, it necessarily follows that the more people there are around, the less freedom everyone has. This is why people in a young and relatively unpopulated United States enjoyed far more freedom than Americans do today. But this is not why our founding fathers would conclude we are not free.

To understand their point of view, it is necessary to realize that there are two distinct aspects to freedom: personal freedom and political freedom. Personal freedom is the freedom to make personal choices, such as which channel to watch on television, what to eat for dinner, who to marry, whether to take a walk or not, etc. However, political freedom was far more important to the founders than personal freedom because they clearly understood that the only way to have and ensure personal freedom was to protect and preserve political freedom. They believed that without political freedom, personal freedom was at risk because it could be compromised at any time. Therefore, when drafting our Constitution, foremost in the founders' minds was to create a document that ensured and protected political freedom. As an afterthought, they later added the Bill of Rights to ensure that some highly important personal freedoms were specifically protected.

What is *political freedom*? Political freedom is the inalienable right of self-government, and it was identified by Abraham Lincoln when he described our government as being "of the people, by the people, and for the people." Unfortunately, in America today, most people do not realize the significance of these words and only think of them as a historical curiosity, but in truth, they are the very touchstones of political freedom.

Of the people means that private citizens hold office, not professional politicians. *By the people* means the people as a group determine how they will be governed, and this function is most emphatically not the providence of elected officials alone. *For the people* means that our government is our servant and not our master. This is what the Constitution of the United States of America is all about, this is the primary goal the founders had in mind when drafting it, and these are the principles they enshrined therein. Underscoring these principles is necessary to ensure their perpetuation is our inalienable right to free speech, to petition the government for the redress of grievances, and to hold those in government accountable for their actions under the Constitution. In addition to the foregoing, the final elements necessary to ensure political freedom are the two underlying principles of enlightened democracy: majority rule tempered by the protection of minority rights.

The issue on hand that would be of major concern to our founding fathers, and should be to us, is, how well does the government we presently live under measure up to the above-described principles? Unfortunately, upon examination, the answer to this question is painfully obvious: it does not.

First and foremost, we do not have a government that is *of the people.* Instead, our elected representatives are lifelong professional politicians whose first order of business is feathering their own nest and protecting the status quo. However, this is not the worst of it because in the United States of America today, it takes a tremendous amount of money to run for national office. Therefore, in keeping with a desire to look out for their own interests, the very first order of business of a professional politician is to ensure that those providing him with money and support continue to do so. The only way to do this is to do their bidding. No one with power and influence contributes to and supports politicians so they can independently vote their conscience in the best interests of this nation and its people. Therefore, the real first order of business for a professional politician is to vote to please those who contribute money and do favors for them. Doing what is best for the people of this nation is secondary.

By the people: Instead of living under the government created and bestowed upon us by the founders, how our government functions and operates has been changed through the years, not by amendment as required by our Constitution, but, wrongfully, by simple legislative acts. In other words, the government we presently live under is not the brainchild of our founding fathers as we delude ourselves into believing but instead the handiwork of professional politicians whose loyalties and motives have just been discussed.

For the people: A healthy economy is in everyone's best interest, and many politicians, especially Republicans, subscribe to the trickle-down theory of economics as follows: when corporations earn profits, for the most part, they are reinvested in our economy thus creating jobs and adding to the prosperity of all concerned. This kind of thinking is used by politicians to justify catering to special interests. True, it is self-serving to a degree, but in the past, such thinking had validity and did no real harm to the nation. However, this is no longer true. Special interests and the corporations they represent have become globalized. In other words, our situation is now such that those who call the tune that politicians dance to are concerned with global issues and have no concern for the well-being of Americans and the American worker. This being the case, the trickledown theory, as far as Americans are concerned, is bankrupt. When politicians cater to special interests and help corporations earn money from Americans, this money is invested overseas where it is cheaper to do business. The end result of this is a steady flow of wealth out of the country that is robbing us of our prosperity. Our elected representatives pretend to be for us but in deference to those who back them, knowingly act to allow this to happen, belying what they pretend to be.

Freedom of speech: It takes great courage for someone to speak out against what is wrong with the government in America today, and this doesn't just mean running the risk of being ridiculed or labeled politically incorrect. Speaking freely about how we are governed in the United States of America today will affect your job, opportunities for employment, opportunities for advancement through promotion, and your ability to earn a living for you and your family. If the consequences for speaking freely are this severe, then free speech is not free and has a terrible cost associated with it.

Petition Government: In America, today, writing to elected officials is a waste of time for matters of substance because professional politicians cater to special interests when it comes to deciding such matters. This being the case, our final redress should be the courts. However, the courts have wrongfully and unconstitutionally ruled that citizens have no legal recourse over the actions of Congress that affect all citizens equally as a group. It is more than ironic that the judicial branch of our government, which is constitutionally tasked with ensuring that the other branches of government abide by constitutional precepts, has acted in an official capacity to ensure that the other branches of government do not have to and no one, not even all of us acting together, can do anything about it. Not only is this a gross and flagrant violation of our Constitution, it abrogates one of our most important inalienable rights.

Accountability: Americans can no longer achieve redress of their grievances by petitioning government officials or by suing them in a court of law. Thus, we have no means of holding them accountable other than voting them out of office. However, voting them out of office will only produce results if there are alternative candidates who hold different views from the incumbent official that coincide with ours. While some third-party candidates offer such options, the simple truth of the matter is that the two major parties have such a lock on the electorate and elective process that addressing issues about how we are governed through the ballot box is impossible. The result of all this is that elected government officials are accountable to no one other than the special interests that help get them elected and keep them in office.

Majority Rule: The only thing that the majority really decides in America today is to decide whether Twiddle Dum or Twiddle Dee will hold office. However, average citizens have absolutely no say in who becomes Twiddle Dum or Twiddle Dee, and once either one is elected, as far as our system of government is concerned, they are one and the same person. Furthermore, there are many important actions taken by our government today that, if the truth were known, the majority would be dead set against, yet our government is able to take these actions anyway.

Minority Rights: Minority rights in America have come to mean rights solely associated with one's color, creed, gender, sexual preference, or national origin and no longer include protecting the rights of an individual against majority preferences and excesses. Not only are the minority rights of an individual no longer afforded any special kind of protection by government, we have also been stripped of our God-given inalienable rights. Our perception of rights and minority rights has changed, and because of this, we docilely accept a government that instead of protecting our rights extends or takes them away at will.

In conclusion, Americans are free to go to the bathroom when the need arises, but when it comes to enjoying the elements that comprise political freedom, all of them have been compromised and are essentially dysfunctional. Yet we go about our business thinking this is not the case. We think we are free because we confuse personal freedom with political freedom, and no one in government, the media, or our educational institutions will risk their jobs or future well- being by clearing up our misconceptions. We have lost the only thing that ensures our personal freedom, our political freedom, and the inevitable result is that we are now losing our personal freedom as well.

If we have been robbed of our political freedom by those elected to serve us, what then does this say about the kind of democracy we have? No American would intentionally vote away our political freedom, yet it is gone and has been taken from us without our consent. This makes a mockery of democracy and establishes that the democracy we have is only an illusion.

For several generations, this nation was locked in a cold war with communism. Indeed, we called ourselves the free world and looked upon those living in the Soviet Bloc as enslaved and downtrodden.

The question is how free are we today in comparison to those who used to live under Communism? The truth is that we are now not much better off than the citizens of the Soviet Union during the Cold War. We have a two-party system that in matters of substance is one party, we no longer have inalienable rights, we no longer own the fruits of our own labor, our property is not safe and secure from confiscation and seizure, we are being systematically robbed of our wealth and heritage, and we can be arrested and held without being charged or tried at the discretion of government bureaucrats. Where then is the freedom that we take such pride in having?

Americans are no longer free, and democracy is just an illusion kept alive by the ruling establishment so they can have their way with us. This would be the verdict of our founding fathers if they were alive today, and this is the verdict that would be reached by any intelligent individual who impartially examines our present situation.

APPENDIX C2
A Letter to Cousin Jerry

March 2002

Dear Jerry,

It was a pleasure visiting you this past weekend. However, our discussion following breakfast left me concerned, and as a result, I am compelled to put my thoughts in writing. Please understand that I do not feel this way because you disagreed with me. As a student of philosophy, I know many people will disagree on any given topic, and to take issue with this is foolishness. However, your position from my perspective amounted to a denial of the truth. I believe our government denies the truth in a similar manner, and it is the implications associated with this state of affairs that has me concerned.

There are no direct consequences associated with citizens denying the truth. However, this is not the case when government officials do so, because it means they are concealing the reasons behind their actions and operating from hidden agendas. With the exception of matters concerning national security, no public servant or elected official has the right to hide the reasons why they have chosen an official course of action. Furthermore, when government officials deny the truth, lying and deceiving become acceptable and an imperative of government. This state of affairs gives government officials a vested interest in keeping citizens as ignorant as possible about matters that concern them. This is why, in America today, most citizens know very little of our heritage and nation's history.

Our discussion focused upon a single topic: does our government routinely violate our Constitution? Before proceeding, several issues that arose during our discussion need to be addressed.

You asked by whose authority and by what right do I have to make judgments about matters of constitutionality. From my perspective, it is shocking that an American would ask a question like this. In concert with other citizens, I own our Constitution, and being its owner, I have a right to read it, study it, and pass judgment upon the actions of government according to its precepts. Our government has no claim of ownership to our Constitution. As citizens, it belongs to us alone. We wrote it, imposed its provisions on our government, and passed it on to posterity. Unfortunately, while all of the foregoing is self-evident, you do have a point because the government we presently live under has wrongfully assumed the authority to change how we are governed without our permission. And worse, taken steps to separate *we the people* from our Constitution. By so doing, they have denied us our right to self-determination and the right to petition government for the redress of grievances.

Our discussion ended with you stating that you disagreed with me and that we should agree to disagree. Under any other circumstances, I would accept this as being the gentlemanly thing to do. However, considering the importance of the matter under discussion, it is not possible for me to be this understanding. If you are right and I am wrong, there are no consequences associated with agreeing to your proposal. However, if I am right and you are wrong, there are serious consequences, which shouldn't be ignored. Therefore, from my perspective, agreeing to disagree about the issue under discussion means that we ignore our present state of affairs and, by doing so, agree to live under corruption, deception, and tyranny. Therefore, I do not agree to disagree and challenge you or anyone else, especially those in government, to sit down with pen in hand and properly respond to the points and arguments I am making in this letter. While you enjoy the luxury of ignoring my challenge, in a Republic, government officials have a duty and obligation to intelligently respond to issues raised about how they behave and how we are governed. This is the essence of accountability, and without it, our republic is dead and we are subjugated.

In our discussion, you said I was being nitpicky with words and seemed to think that this was a valid response to my arguments. It should be self-evident that this is not the case. The Constitution is nothing more than a collection of words. However, it is the meaning and intent of those words that make it such an important document.

Therefore, to be "nitpicking" with the verbiage of our Constitution is necessary and a virtue. To accuse someone of nitpicking when discussing constitutional issues is tantamount to saying, "I have no intelligent response to what you are saying, and I am going to think I am right no matter what you say; end of discussion." The proper thing to do when impasses like this occur is to stop and reach an agreement as to the meaning of the words in question and then proceed on common ground.

The truth is not something that should be trifled with, and this is especially true for government officials. Unfortunately, those who lead us talk of "spin doctors" like being one is a legitimate calling or profession. As a result, putting a "spin" on known facts or situations is considered to be normal and acceptable in politics. This kind of convoluted thinking has turned knowing the truth into an exercise in futility, and it is the key that opened Pandora's box for our nation. Spin doctors acknowledge that a fact is something that is true. However, they refuse to accept that there are two kinds of facts: observed facts and inferred facts. Observed facts, also called known facts, are those discerned by one or more of the five senses. Inferred facts cannot be seen directly but are arrived at by logically extrapolating from a set of known or given facts. An inferred fact is just as true as a known fact, provided all of the supporting facts are true and the reasoning and logic used to discern them are valid.

A "spin doctor," while acknowledging the validity of observed facts, uses them to arrive at a preconceived conclusion through the use of faulty reasoning and logic. The average voter, being uneducated and willing to accept any feel-good explanation, is easily fooled by this kind of intellectual chicanery. Those who lead us are masters at this game and have given it a special name. They call it *democracy*. However, the use of this word is inappropriate to describe what is really going on. Forgive me for nitpicking, but the word that best describes how we are led is *demagoguery*. However, for reasons that should be obvious, this word is shunned because it doesn't have the right "spin" to it.

Within the above framework and understandings, I believe our government routinely, and as a matter of policy, violates our Constitution, and this can easily be proven to any reasonable person willing to examine the facts with an unbiased eye. Furthermore, despite your opinion on these matters, unless you or someone else can demonstrate where I am wrong through fact, reason, or logic, then the truths established are universal and independent of whether or not other people agree with them. Of course, everyone has the right to disagree if they choose, but I strongly object to those who do so arbitrarily and then insult my intelligence by expecting me to accept their unsubstantiated disagreement as being valid or on par with my logically derived position. Only a spin doctor, politician, or someone with an axe to grind would so posture. This having been said, I offer the following for consideration:

Fact: Amendment II of our Constitution states that, "the right of the people to keep and bear arms shall not be infringed."

Fact: *Infringed* in the context within which it is used means that the right to bear arms will not be inhibited, reduced, or violated in any way.

Fact: Hand grenades, bazookas, machine guns, nuclear warheads, chemical and biological weapons, etc., are arms prohibited to citizens by our government.

Conclusion: The government's prohibitions of the above armaments are incompatible with and repugnant to Amendment II of our Constitution.

If the above facts are true, then logic dictates that the conclusion reached is also true. Furthermore, if the conclusion reached is true, it is a fact. This having been established, it can also be stated with certainty that our government routinely operates in violation of Amendment II of our Constitution because of two other known facts: it has prohibited the arms listed for many years and has no intention of amending our Constitution to make these prohibitions legal. This last conclusion, based on the two new facts and the previous conclusion, is inescapable and cannot be dismissed by saying I have an axe to grind, I am nitpicking words, I don't know what I am talking about, I have no right to discuss such things, or the prohibition of such armaments makes sense so this invalidates my arguments. The prohibition of such weapons does make sense, but this does not in any way modify, mitigate, or invalidate the conclusions reached. While it is true that people hold the right to deny them if they choose, but if they do so without proper justification, they are being unreasonable and in denial for reasons that have nothing to do with the topic under discussion.

I fully recognize that the prohibition of the arms in question is reasonable, desirable, and necessary. As citizens, we truly have much to fear from other citizens owning such weapons. However, this being the case, ample justification exists to amend our Constitution to accommodate this reality. The real issue here is, why hasn't this been done? Our founding fathers held that we should be fearful of any government that would legislate something contrary to constitutional provisions without first amending the Constitution. Why? Because the Constitution is the highest law of the land, and if government can violate one provision, then it holds the power to violate all provisions, rendering the Constitution dysfunctional for the primary purpose for which it was written. This truth is not lost upon those who lead us, and this is why they have ignored the amendment process in certain instances. They desire absolute and total control over us, and our Constitution stands in the way of achieving these ends.

Article I, section 8 of our Constitution states that "Congress shall have the Power to regulate commerce with foreign nations", and to "make all laws which shall be necessary and proper for the Execution of this power." The GATT accords state that "The WTO creates laws that govern international trade between its members." Paragraph 4 of the GATT accord also states that "Each member (of the WTO) shall ensure the conformity of its laws, regulations, and administrative procedures with its obligations as provided (for) in the annexed Agreements." Based upon these facts, the proof that GATT is unconstitutional follows:

Fact: Congress is empowered by our Constitution to enact laws that regulate trade with foreign nations.

Fact: The WTO is empowered by the GATT Accord to establish laws that regulate trade between member nations.

Fact: By joining the WTO, Congress agreed to change our laws so they are in agreement with those established by the WTO, both now and in the future.

These are the givens, and from them, it should be clear that while Congress still retains authority to pass laws regulating trade with foreign nations, it can only do so when they are in agreement with the laws established by the WTO. From this it follows that:

All laws passed by Congress regulating trade with foreign nations are subject to review and approval by the WTO, at the WTO's discretion.

The final authority in regard to laws passed by Congress to regulate trade with foreign nations is the WTO and not our Supreme Court.

Therefore, the enactment of GATT and our resulting participation in the WTO as members is unconstitutional for three reasons:

1. It is repugnant to article 1, section 8 of our Constitution, which gives Congress the power to regulate trade with foreign nations. If, as is the case, Congress has subordinated and/or assigned part of this power to someone else, then it no longer retains this power for itself, and this is unconstitutional. The Constitution does not give Congress the power to subordinate and/or assign any of its power to anyone else, even if we can reverse this decision or quit the WTO at some time in the future.

2. It is repugnant to Amendment X, which reads, "The powers not delegated to the United States (government) by the Constitution, nor prohibited by it to the States, are reserved

to the States respectively, or to the people." Therefore, the Constitution prohibits Congress from assuming or exercising any power not specifically provided to it within the Constitution (more on Amendment X later). When Congress subordinated and/or assigned some of its powers to the WTO, it assumed the authority to do this in violation of Amendment X.

3. It is repugnant to article III, section 2, which reads, "The judicial Power (of the Supreme Court) shall extend to all Cases in Law and Equity, arising under this Constitution, the Laws of the United States, and Treaties made, or which shall be made, under their Authority." By pre-agreeing to ensure that all our laws will conform to those of the WTO, Congress has precluded Supreme Court authority over the laws in question and thereby abrogated the constitutionally provided powers of the Supreme Court. Our present situation is such that if the Supreme Court ruled that a conforming law to GATT was unconstitutional, this ruling would violate the GATT accord, subjecting the United States to WTO approved sanctions by its member nations. How supreme is our Supreme Court if a higher authority can penalize the United States for not following its rulings, irrespective of how our Supreme Court rules?

Finally, the clearest example of a constitutional provision that is routinely violated by Congress involves Amendment X, introduced above. The founding fathers, to a man, wished to limit the scope and power of our federal government. Toward this end, they included Amendment X in our Constitution, which simply means that if the federal government passes any law or takes any action not specifically provided for elsewhere in the Constitution, then that law or action violates Amendment X and is unconstitutional. Therefore, all that is necessary to conclusively prove that our government, as a matter of routine practice, violates provisions of our Constitution, is to demonstrate that it routinely does things not authorized anywhere in it. Toward this end, I offer Social Security, the Interstate Highway

System, the National Park System, OSHA, FEMA, the FCC, HUD, the EPA, the FDA, the EEOC, foreign aid, welfare, aid to education, the minimum wage, income tax, etc.

None of the above federal agencies, programs, or activities, no matter how well intended and/or necessary for us as a people, are provided for anywhere in the Constitution and therefore, are instituted by usurpation in violation of Amendment X. Furthermore, most members of Congress and the Supreme Court, being lawyers, know this is the case but have no problem posturing otherwise. They lie to us or "spin" the truth to maintain appearances of propriety and legitimacy. This is shocking, but it is not hard to understand in consideration of the fact that their first act as a congressman or Supreme Court justice is to violate their oath of office by swearing to preserve a constitution, which they intend to routinely violate. I apologize for nitpicking words here, but *preservation*, to them, means that they jam the Constitution in a mason jar, seal it with wax, and put it on the shelf only to be considered again if it suits their purposes.

In this letter, I believe I have offered proof that our government operates in routine violation of our Constitution. Furthermore, if what I have established is true, then it is also true that we live under and swear allegiance to an illegitimate and corrupt government. This having been established, it is incumbent upon those who lead to demonstrate that this is not the case by demonstrating where I have erred in fact, reason, or logic. They should not enjoy the luxury of ignoring such serious allegations, but ignore them they will for two reasons: they have no valid rebuttal to my arguments, and they know there are no consequences associated with ignoring me because most citizens, out of ignorance and apathy, accept this kind of behavior from our elected representatives. Furthermore, to ensure that a concerned citizen will not be able to force attention to these issues through our nation's judicial system, rulings therein have made it impossible for anyone to obtain a court ruling on these matters.

I do not want to live in a nation where the government routinely violates its constitution. I do not want to live in a nation where government officials and members of its judicial system violate their oath of office the moment it is taken. I do not want to live in a nation where everyone pledges allegiance to a nonexistent form of government. I do not want to live in a nation where the government decides how it will govern without the consent of those who are governed. I do not want to live in a nation where elected officials can arbitrarily ignore the legitimate concerns of citizens. Finally, I do not want to live in a nation where government officials have embraced lying to citizens as their prime imperative.

I do not believe our success as a nation and the present state of our economic well-being came about because those who lead us do all these things. I also do not believe those who lead us have to continue doing these things in order to ensure our future security and economic well-being. In fact, I believe the opposite to be the case, and we are presently being led down the path of reduced security and eventual economic collapse. I sincerely hope I am wrong. As an ex-naval officer, fighter pilot, and former public servant, I loathe to believe the things I do about our government, but my loathing is not a reason to deny the truth. I cannot bury my head in the sand and hide from it like many of us choose to do. I also cannot stand at the side of the road and declare the emperor regally clothed when he is as naked as a jaybird. I understand why many of my fellow Americans do these things. But what I cannot understand is how any American, knowing the truth, can ignore these issues—or worse, actually conspire against their fellow Americans by willfully acting to preserve the status quo. Finally, I cannot understand how anyone cannot see the dreadful consequences that inevitably arise out of being governed in this manner, especially when these consequences are presently unfolding before us.

P.S. God is love, but more important, he is truth. When the truth is denied, God is denied, and those so doing have embraced a theology of evil.

P.P.S. Political science is a discipline that discerns acceptable courses of action from sound governing principles, constitutional considerations, and prevailing political realities. We never hear much about political science anymore, and courses on the subject have all but disappeared from our educational institutions. This is because political science is being replaced by spin science. Spin science is the art of convincing others to believe what you yourself know is not true. Political science and spin science are incompatible with each other. This is why the demise of one coincides with the rise of the other. As free and independent people, which discipline is more important to us? The answer to this question should be obvious, and being obvious, what does this say about the kind of "democracy" we live under and about the direction in which our nation is heading?

APPENDIX C3
The Shame of It All

May 2005

Governing is an honorable profession, but only if those who govern are men of honor. If they are not, it is a dirty game, and the inevitable result is tyranny. Understanding this, we should ask, how do we measure those who govern us? There is only one yardstick: do they obey and uphold the law, not just laws against criminal acts and wrongful behavior, but more importantly, the highest laws of the land as embodied within our Constitution?

A constitution is a written agreement among men. It is born of the necessity for a common defense and the need for services that individuals cannot provide for themselves. In its most fundamental form, a constitution boils down to you and me agreeing that we need these services and meeting to write a set of rules that will govern those we intend to hire to fulfill our needs. This having been done, we hire these people and, as a condition of employment, require them to swear an oath that they will faithfully follow the rules we established. This is where honor comes into the equation. If those we hire or elect are honorable men, they will follow our rules. If they are dishonorable men, they will pay lip service to our rules and work for their own interests instead of ours. It's that simple.

Honorable public officials have no interest in violating the provisions of our Constitution. Why should they? They are our employees and, as such, should only be interested in doing what we expect of them. Having taken on the mantle of being our "public servants," it is incumbent upon them to put their personal opinions and interests aside and only work for the common good according to the provisions of our Constitution. If they do not, instead of being our servants, they become our masters and, unfortunately, masters who control the mechanisms of our government and armed forces.

There is no room for equivocation here. Even if one minor provision of our Constitution is violated by those in government, the precedent is set for the violation of all provisions, and over time, our government will become what it was created to protect us from. So, it is in the United States today. Our government has become an out-of-control criminal enterprise that is so corrupt that many of those we elect to serve us, in clear and flagrant violation of their oaths of office and their pledge of allegiance to our republic, have secretly sworn allegiance to a group of filthy-rich conspirators and dictators.

Our forefathers came together two centuries ago to draft a constitution that created the United States of America. The seeds of their effort were brought here from Europe and planted in fertile soil on this continent such that we grew into the greatest nation in all of history. For the first time ever, man came together with pen in hand and wrote a set of rules that would govern those who govern them. The founders signed this document in blood and agreed that if the government they created ever stopped following *their rules*, they would rise up and remove it from power.

The government they created, the government of the United States of America, has been overthrown from within. This is not conjecture, this is not speculation, and this is not the raving of some malcontent who is out of touch with reality. We, in fact, are ruled by a group of men who believe ruling us is their birthright and, through unconstitutional legislation, have stacked the deck against us. Their way is not our way because their way is to serve themselves at our expense. They have left the shell of this once-great nation intact but only to fool Americans into thinking that nothing has changed, but everything has changed. The government of the people, by the people, and for the people have perished from the earth, and in its place is the only thing that could possibly fill such a vacuum: tyranny.

This is our shame, and this is the shame of those in government and other organizations who participated in our subjugation. These people, for the most part, were Americans who were born here and pledged allegiance to our republic. But they were greedy men who placed wealth and power above all other considerations. Their pledge of allegiance did not matter, honor did not matter, truth did not matter, history did not matter, and even God did not matter. The only thing that matters to them is money and power, and these they have garnered with great efficiency.

Think about what future historians will write about the United States of America. A great and prosperous people allowed their government to violate their most sacred laws, the laws embodied within their constitution, and as a result, a group of traitorous criminals wrongfully and illegally seized power, not all at once, but slowly over time. While this was happening, the people of this once great nation swore allegiance to a government that no longer existed and foolishly allowed these usurpers to plunder the nation of its wealth and resources while bringing war and destruction to the rest of the world. This is the history of the United States of America, and it is a history that is being written right now before God and in the wrongfully spilled blood of uncountable numbers of innocent and unknown people. This is how the rest of mankind is beginning to see us, and this is how we will be remembered until man's time on earth comes to an end.

I was once a proud American. Now I am an American who is ashamed of what our nation has become and ashamed of my fellow citizens who have no idea what has been done to us, even though the evidence of our degradation and demise is everywhere. We are a cursed and doomed people, and yet we sacrilegiously call upon God to bless our dismal state of affairs. It took several hundred years for the Roman Empire to fall. The government of the United States of America fell in a little over two hundred years, and the reason for its fall was greed and because not enough Americans cared.

Postscript

I realize that some of you live in denial and kid yourselves into thinking things are not as bad as the picture I painted. Worse than this, far too many of you actually condone and support what is being done to us. To you people, I ask the following questions:

1. How do you explain to your children that the United States of America is no longer a republic but instead a dictatorship run by demented old men? Do you hide the truth from your

children and, like the myth of Santa Claus and the Tooth Fairy, pretend something is true when it isn't?

2. How do you tell your children that when they grow up and get a job in the public service or private industry that the only way to get ahead is to tell the boss he is right even when he is wrong, and if you stand up and say what you believe to be true, even in matters of life and death, your career will be ruined?

3. How do you tell your children to work hard in school and learn all they can but upon graduating throw everything they learned into the toilet because the only thing their future bosses will require of them is blind obedience?

4. How do you explain to your children that in America, our quality of life and just about everything that makes living worthwhile has been subordinated to the almighty dollar, and that money is the only thing that really matters?

5. How do you explain to your children that a government based upon thousands of years of human development, that was the epitome of all governments, was not good enough to keep and preserve because a dictatorship is preferable to democracy? Will you be able to say that mankind has progressed or degenerated? When you tell them the truth, do you think they will be proud of the fact that yours was the generation that allowed this to happen to us?

6. When you die and meet those valiant men and women who died fighting fascism in World War II, how do you tell them that their sacrifices were in vain because Fascism is the wave of the future for the United States and every other nation in the world?

7. When you die and meet men like Thomas Jefferson, George Washington, Benjamin Franklin, Patrick Henry, John

Hancock, Theodore Roosevelt, John Kennedy, George Marshall, etc., how do you look these people in the eye and tell them that their efforts were for naught because the United States and mankind are destined to be ruled by dictators?

I do not believe you have good answers to these questions. However, if you are among those who condone and support our subjugation, don't worry about the answers to the last two questions, because when you die, it is not very likely that you will meet the people mentioned. While this is something you should be concerned about, there is one consolation: you will have many other friends to spend eternity with, namely, the amoral corporate stooges who engineered and established the New World Order will all be there to keep you company.

APPENDIX C4
Why Our Oppressors Will Win

May 2004

The founders were creating an ideal: a government that would serve them and no one else. To say the least, this was a lofty goal because its success depended upon ensuring that men of honor and integrity served in government and because it required the eternal vigilance of citizens to ensure that the fundamental ideals upon which our government was created were not violated. The enemy of the first element of success is greed. It is the basic nature of men to work for their own interests first and everyone else's second. The enemy of the second element of success is ignorance.

These two enemies the founders feared most because they knew that greed was a driving force in man, including educated and intelligent men, and ignorance was a common and pervasive quality of the electorate. As a hedge against ignorance, they gave us a senate whose members were appointed by the state legislators and an electoral college to ensure a demigod would not be elected to the presidency. Unfortunately, they never imagined that tyrants would be able to find so many of the nation's educated and intelligent men willing to sell their souls for a few pieces of silver. What the founders wrought has been destroyed. Those we elect to Congress no longer vote their conscience in the best interest of the citizens of this nation but instead vote to enhance their personal well-being, and they do this by voting to increase the profitability of corporations. A recent example of this was the passage of George W. Bush's prescription drug benefit program for seniors. This program does nothing for seniors other than make them a captive market for the drug companies while enabling the drug companies to charge whatever they wish for the drugs they manufacture. As a result, drug company profits have soared, and our seniors are paying far more for their drugs as a group than their counterparts in most other nations of the world.

President Bush's prescription drug benefit program is a document several inches thick that was developed and written solely by drug industry lobbyists who presented it to the House of Representatives one day before it came up for a vote. No senator or congressman has read this bill in its entirety. It did not pass on the first several ballots and should have failed because the time limit for voting had passed after the first few failed votes had been taken. However, those supporting this legislation convinced the Speaker of the House to give them more time to coerce and cajole dissenting members of Congress into changing their votes. Eventually, the failed bill passed, and most of those who took extraordinary measures to ensure that it would are now working as highly paid lobbyists for the companies who benefited from their efforts. As I write, the leader of this group is being paid two million dollars yearly as a drug industry lobbyist.

The present salaries of the former congressmen who forced the Medicare Prescription Drug, Improvement, and Modernization Act on this nation are being paid by the drug companies they work for. However, those salaries are really coming out of the pockets of seniors who signed up for this program. Therefore, the truth of the matter is that while the opportunists who forced this program upon the seniors of this nation, were being paid by us to look out for our interests, they were instead lining their pockets at our expense. *Sixty Minutes* recently exposed this fraud on prime-time television, but nothing will be done to rectify the situation or ensure that it never happens again because Congress has no problems with situations that allow its members to profiteer at our expense, and Americans have other things to occupy their minds.

What's wrong with America? In a word: *television!* Before the age of print, life was relatively simple. The tribal mentality dominated society and tribal leaders defined the world within which people lived. When the printed press was developed, this all changed. Ideas could be written down and disseminated to large groups of people. However, when ideas and facts are written down, they have to be consistent, coherent, and make sense. As a result, the world within which people lived reflected these qualities, and this rationality opened the door to the age of reason. The government bequeathed to us by the founders was a logical and inevitable consequence of the age of reason, and if anything can be said about the Constitution they gave us is that it is logical and make sense. This was the founders' gift to us, and because our Constitution is logical and makes sense, today it is an out-of-date anarchism that most people do not understand or care about.

We live in the age of television. The medium of print favors logic and rationality, but in contrast, the medium of television favors image and entertainment. Think of the differences between the two! In the old days, people would sit down, alone or at least incommunicado with those around them, and read a book over the course of several days. The ideas and concepts in the book came across in a logical and orderly fashion and were considered and examined slowly and in-depth. During the age of print, it was the orderliness and rationality of the printed word that shaped the world within which people lived, and anything that did not measure up to these qualities was ridiculed and held in contempt. Television changed all this.

Television is an all-encompassing form of entertainment that fills a large portion of our daily routine, and indeed many people have several televisions in their homes all on at the same time. And what kind of information do we get out of our television? Sound and video bites that teach us nothing of real value and are designed to make us feel good and be entertained. There is very little on television that demands in-depth thought or deep analysis, and even when there is, such things pass by quickly to the next feel-good item or commercial, the issue in question having been totally lost and forgotten in the flow of the show. Television asks nothing of us other than to buy the things it advertises whether we need them or not, and commercial messages rely upon selling things not by merit but by associating them with a sports hero, show business personality, or some other feel-good item.

This is also true with marketing a political candidate. In the early days of our republic, people read books. As a result, politics reflected the worldview established by the printed word, and political campaigns also reflected these qualities. Back then, candidates expounded upon issues in length and were measured by how well they made their points, not how they looked, dressed, and carried themselves. Speech writers were the most important people in a campaign. Many of our former and most revered presidents, including Abraham Lincoln, would not make it past the primaries in the campaigns of today because substance takes a back seat to appearance and marketability. The Lincoln-Douglas debates were lengthy affairs, with the longest going on for seven hours, and people sat and listened to every word. It would be impossible to hold the attention of the electorate for that long a period of time in the world of television. After all, by doing so, one might miss what Dr. Phil had to say about cheating husbands.

Today, everything about a political campaign is image and impressions. Substance and issues never come into the equation unless they are presented as feel-good items. Reason, logic, and common sense no longer are relevant or have any bearing. Instead of speechwriters, the most important people in a campaign are marketing professionals who spin webs that have nothing to do with facts and reality. Even in the political debates that are held, image and appearance are everything. The debates are short in length, and candidates are only given a limited amount of time to make their case and only two or three minutes for point and counterpoint. What they say is not important, but how they say it is, and even more important is how they look when they say it.

People no longer focus upon what is being said but instead react to who made the best presentation. Unfortunately, they vote accordingly, unless, of course, they are the kind of person who consistently votes for one party no matter what anyone says or does. This makes the decision to vote easy. My party, right or wrong, and the country can go to hell so long as my side won.

Television is a medium that has taken over our lives and now shapes the world within which we live. Ideas, concepts, logic, and reason no longer have relevance or meaning to the modern American. All we care about is feeling good—feeling good about ourselves and feeling good about the nation we live in, irrespective of reality and truth. This is why Americans living today do not want to hear about our government having been overthrown. This is a horrible thing to think, no matter how true it is, and how can it be true? Turn on your television and nothing has changed. Everything is wonderful, and there is nothing evident to be overly concerned about. Look at all the good-looking, intelligent, and successful people on television who are all oblivious to the fact that our government has been overthrown. My God, they have riches and adulation beyond our wildest dreams. How could something as horrible as a coup have taken place? They certainly do not think so and why should I? After all, they are far better off than me, and I have a right to feel as good as they do.

Americans are like lemmings. They are all moving in one direction toward a cliff, and television keeps them heading in this direction. There is an old expression that the medium is the message, but it is truly far worse than this. The medium and the media are tools our masters use, and it is through these tools that they keep us compliant, ignorant, loyal, and subjugated. This is why our oppressors will win. They know that because of television, people no longer know how to think and will believe anything you tell them so long as it is packaged in a way that makes them feel good about themselves and their country. This is what our founders feared most, and thanks to greed and television, their worst fears have been realized.

APPENDIX C5
Slavery and Democracy

February 2005

I deeply regret the tone and the thrust of an article by Ulrich Boser, which appeared on the January 24, 2005, edition of US News & World Report entitled "The Sorry Legacy of the Founders," which started out by informing us that George Washington hired a dentist to implant nine teeth into his jaw taken from the mouths of his slaves, that Sally Hemings, a slave, was the mistress of Thomas Jefferson and had at least one child by him. That Richard Henry Lee, Patrick Henry, and James Monroe also had slaves who they treated in a manner that was customary at the time. My regret over this story rises to the level of alarm when I also consider the fact that a question asked on the TV game show *Hollywood Squares* recently was something like, what did Patrick Henry, who is famous for his quote "Give me liberty, or give me death," have fifty of? The answer: slaves. Before proceeding,

Let me make this perfectly clear. I do not believe such information about our founding fathers should be suppressed. I also strongly agree that slavery was a black mark upon the history of this nation. This being so, I will accept at face value the validity of the statements made in the article. However, I do question the timing of the release of these new revelations concerning the moral turpitude of our founding fathers. Beyond this, what really upsets me is the quote by Rutgers University historian Jan Lewis, added as a conclusion to his article. This quote is as follows; "Understanding the early leaders' severe lapse in judgment over slavery, say Lewis and other historians, makes their ability to found a new and democratic nation all the more incredible." I am upset by this quote because of the realization that this is the kind of revisionist garbage that is being taught to the future leaders of this nation throughout our educational systems.

> To entrust the government with the power of determining the education which our children receive is entrusting our servant with the power to be our master.
>
> —David Nasaw

The first thing wrong with Mr. Lewis's quote is that it perpetuates the great establishment lie of omission: that the founding fathers founded a new and "democratic" nation. This is only one half of the story, and the far more important half is missing. Our founding fathers founded a new democratic republic: a democracy because of an elected leadership and a constitutional republic because that leadership was bound by a sacred oath to religiously abide by the provisions of our Constitution. This is why we pledge allegiance to a republic and not to a democracy. It is the republic that must be preserved because our rights and freedom depend upon its preservation. The republic is the only thing that limits the freedom of action of those who lead us, and thereby it is the only thing that stands between us and tyranny.

> Remember, democracy never lasts long. It soon wastes, exhausts, and murders itself. There was never a democracy yet that did not commit suicide
>
> —John Quincy Adams,

Our present leadership, drunk with power and motivated by greed, shuns the concept of a republic. Therefore, through time, they have slowly weaned Americans away from the notion of a republic and replaced it with the concept of democracy. To be sure, you will never ever see the word *republic* used by the media or politicians anymore. The word is anathema to them for two reasons: they have destroyed the one we had and because obeying the supreme laws of our nation limits their power and control over us. Concerned primarily with advancing their careers, the historians of today now follow the party line and set aside the truth and expound the myth. Like Judas, for a few pieces of silver, they have sold their souls and have become willing participants in the great "con."

The second thing wrong with Mr. Lewis's quote is that it states that the founders had a severe lapse in judgment over slavery and that this makes their ability to found a new and democratic nation all the more incredible. From this statement, one is forced to conclude that there was nothing special about the founding fathers. In fact, not only were they not very special people, they were capable of severe lapses in judgment, and the nation they founded was more of an accident than the result of ideals and tried and true principles of governing. The unsaid implication is that the government we have today is far superior to the one we first had because no one in a position of leadership today ever advocated owning slaves and abusing them. What pure unadulterated bull dung.

There was something very special about our founding fathers. They were men of intelligence and goodwill who came together and, to a man, put petty self-interest aside and attempted to create the best of all possible governments for themselves and, more importantly, for their fellow citizens, who they distrusted as much as they distrusted the government they were attempting to create. True, they were human to a fault. They had mistresses, they beat their wives, and they owned and abused slaves, but this does not make what they did incredible. What was incredible was that they put all of their petty and major faults aside and came together to create an ideal government. Not only did they accomplish this but they succeeded far beyond their wildest dreams. This is evident in the fact that the nation they created grew to be the greatest in the history of the world.

Those in power today would have us believe that the republic disappeared because, similar to the ideals of the founders, it was seriously flawed. Furthermore, it was the ascendancy of democracy in America that allowed a former race of slaves to break their chains of bondage and take their rightful place as true equals in a multiracial society. Again, nothing could be further from the truth. The founding fathers created the best of all nations for their people and, by doing so, laid the seeds for the eventual emancipation of the slaves and their rise to full equality as citizens of this nation. Evidence of this is that nowhere in the Constitution are *slaves* or *slavery* mentioned. They were intelligent enough to know that human bondage was incompatible with the document they were creating, and all that was necessary to turn things around was to substitute the word *citizen* for *property,* when talking about slaves. Abraham Lincoln's emancipation did just that, placing former slaves under the full protection of the Constitution and setting the stage for achieving full equality under the law. This result, though won at a great cost, was inevitable. No man is free unless all men are free. Our Constitution held the promise of freedom, and under it, despite the transgressions of our founding fathers, blacks have taken their rightful place in the body politic of this nation.

If anyone tells you or implies that democracy is the reason blacks hold equal status with whites today under the law, ask him if this issue were put to a vote at the end of the Civil War, would blacks be free? If at the turn of the previous century, in 1899, if a vote were taken, would blacks be free? Similarly, if a vote were taken in 1950, would blacks be free? Granted, the deeper we go into the twentieth century, the stronger the case would be for freedom, but where does that line really fall? More importantly, where would it fall today if we were a pure democracy and all Americans were free to vote their fears and prejudices? The answer to this question is obvious. If it were up to the general population of white America, blacks would still be "choppin' cotton". The Constitution was the vehicle by which blacks earned their rightful place in our society. True, they were helped by a plethora of intelligent and well-meaning whites, but the truth of the matter is that throughout our history, your average Joe American liked thinking he was superior to somebody and would have voted to keep blacks in the dreadful place that fate had bestowed upon them.

It was our Constitution that set black America free, not democracy, but the leadership of this nation would have you think otherwise because the stronger your belief in democracy is, the more freedom they have to rule us and the less freedom we have as citizens.

APPENDIX C6
The Curse of the Proud American

April 2006

As I write, most Americans are still proud to be American and think that the United States is the greatest country in the world. They also think that anyone who does not think like them is a disloyal moron who can't be trusted and should go live somewhere else. If you don't like it here, leave! Unfortunately, things are not quite that simple because a very real possibility exists that it is the "proud Americans" who are the disloyal morons.

Let's go back in American history to the turn of the century, when this nation was only 124 years old, and imagine that a coup occurred and Americans living at the time suddenly awoke one morning and found that the conspirators behind the coup had published a manifesto establishing a new government that all Americans would have to swear allegiance to. This manifesto is as follows:

- All departments and branches of the old government would remain in place and functional, but the coup conspirators would retain behind-the-scenes dictatorial power over the actions and decisions of our new government.

- The nation will go off the gold standard, and Congress will no longer coin money and regulate its value. Instead, the dollar will be backed by nothing other than good faith, and a private corporation controlled by the coup conspirators will control the money supply.

- The new government intends to dominate and control the entire world. To help finance this goal, there will be a new tax on the salaries and wages of all working Americans.

- All political parties, save two, will be rendered dysfunctional, and Americans will vote primarily for one of two candidates in the two approved parties.

- The powers of the executive branch will increase dramatically, and the president will be able to write laws, pass judgment upon laws, and ignore laws as he deems appropriate, including those within our Constitution. He will also be able to make or ignore treaties, extend or withhold human rights, including inalienable rights, and declare war when he deems appropriate, including preemptive war.

- A sitting president, once elected, will be above the law and unimpeachable for both job related and other crimes.

- State governments will no longer appoint senatorial representatives, and the new centralized national government will retain supreme authority over the states.

- Government employees, for the most part, will be paid better and receive far more employee benefits than their counterparts in private industry.

- Congress will no longer draft and write laws. Instead, they will be written by representatives from the industries affected by the laws being written.

- Congress will no longer regulate trade with foreign nations. Instead, the coup conspirators will perform this function.

- Citizens will only enjoy rights at the pleasure of the government and in no way will the consideration of citizens' rights infringe upon the prerogatives of government.

- The Supreme Court will no longer intervene with anything that government does, and the courts will not allow citizens to petition the government for the redress of grievances when these grievances concern government decisions, actions, and prerogatives.

- Citizens will no longer retain an exclusive right to their property and possessions.

- Citizens will no longer be protected from unreasonable searches and seizures.

- Citizens will no longer retain a right to privacy and can be spied upon without their knowledge whenever the government deems it appropriate.

I do not think that there is an American alive today who would not agree that if the coup occurred as described, most Americans, at the turn of the nineteenth century, would rise and do battle with its perpetrators. Furthermore, if any American living at the time sided with the coup conspirators by agreeing that such an absurd and despotic manifesto should govern this nation and its people, then that person would be considered a traitor in league with the enemy.

All of the above is a forgone conclusion, but what should also be obvious is that if you could talk to any American living at the start of the twentieth century and ask them if they thought that all the provisions of the manifesto in question would eventually become operative and functional for this nation, within the next one hundred years, they would say such a thing is impossible and conclude that you were daft for even entertaining such a ridiculous notion. Well, as ridiculous as this notion is, in case you haven't been paying attention, the absurd manifesto described above is the unwritten but functional constitution of the United States of America, and our old written Constitution, the one given to us by our founding fathers, has been rendered dysfunctional such that it is now nothing more than a historical curiosity that has no bearing on how our government functions and operates. Therefore, the government we live under today, beyond question, is illegal, unconstitutional, and rules without the consent of the governed, with the exception, of course, of all of those who are still proud to be American.

Many Americans living today, while they agree that most of the items in the manifesto are operational and undesirable, disagree that a coup has taken place and hold that we got to where we are today by a random accumulation of events similar to evolution. This being the case, while our government no longer meets or adheres to many of the ideals subscribed to by our founding fathers, it is not the result of a coup and therefore not illegal. While it is true many Americans will take solace in this line of reasoning, they couldn't be more wrong. This nation is where it is today, not by accident but instead by a purposeful design that is the brainchild of a group of international traitors and criminals known as the New World Order (NWO).

Recently, David Rockefeller, a New World Order founder and principal, went public with the following statement:

> We are grateful to the *Washington Post*, the *New York Times*, *Time* Magazine, and other great publications whose directors have attended our meetings and respected their promises of discretion for almost forty years. It would have been impossible for us to develop our plan for the world if we had been subjected to the light of publicity during those years. But now the world is more sophisticated and prepared to march towards a world government. The supranational sovereignty of an intellectual elite and world bankers is surely preferable to the national auto-determination practiced in past centuries.

From the above words, the truth is abundantly clear: a group of conspirators, with the cooperation and complicity of the mainstream media of this nation, met in secret for the past forty years to develop a plan for the world that included the gradual dissolution of our existing government and its replacement by a puppet government loyal and beholden to them. This plan, the implementation of which began slowly, has rapidly been brought to fruition by our recent presidents, and no exception to this agenda is the present usurper who occupies the White House. The truly sad reality of our situation is that all of this will have been accomplished behind our backs without the participation of our elected representatives in Congress. In other words, the plan is being implemented without our consent, unless of course, you happen to be someone who is still proud to be an American.

Well, my fellow Americans, be advised that I am not proud to pledge allegiance to a government that no longer exists, I am not proud to be a citizen of a nation where our rights are conditional, I am not proud to live under a government established by coup without my knowledge or consent, and I am not proud that this once great nation has been subjugated by the New World Order. Therefore, I am no longer proud to be an American, and furthermore, I am ashamed of my fellow Americans who still are because their ignorance gives license to what has happened to us.

> As democracy is perfected, the office of the President represents, more and more closely, the inner soul of the people. On some great and glorious day, the plain folks of the land will reach their heart's desire at last and the White House will be adorned by a downright moron.
>
> —H. L. Mencken, 1920

APPENDIX C7
What Can We Do About It?

June 2007

In 1994, Congress passed the General Agreement on Tariffs and Trade (GATT), making the United States a member of the World Trade Organization (WTO). It was then that I realized a great evil had our government within its grip and began my campaign to wake Americans up to the dangers and threats we faced. At the time, nobody, save a precious few, wanted to hear anything I had to say. America truly was fat, dumb, happy, and complacent beyond anything that could ever be imagined by our founding fathers.

One of the first things I did was write a book entitled *While We Sleep: A Story of Government without Law*. This book chronicles the shocking story of my experiences as a government employee working for the city of Fort Lauderdale. A download of this book is available at no cost on my website (alanadaschik.com). My book also informs citizens about what has happened to us, and more importantly, it identifies the future economic and political consequences of what happened. After writing my book, the next thing I did was sue the federal government in the Federal District Court of Miami over GATT and our resulting membership in the WTO. The defendants in this lawsuit were President Clinton and the United States Congress. The plaintiffs were the registered voters of this nation. Finally, I started my own website called the Constitution Forum, which is no longer online.

Thirteen years of tilting at windmills have passed, and in those thirteen years, our deficit has exploded, the value of the dollar has plummeted, our trade imbalance has worsened, corporations and manufacturing jobs are fleeing our shores, American jobs are being outsourced, our sovereignty has been stolen from us, our borders are being dissolved, and we have a tyrant for a president. I warned Americans about all but the last two of these inevitable eventualities in my book, but no one was listening or cared. Well, here we are in 2007, and Americans are finally realizing that our economy is heading into the toilet bowl. However, despite this, most people are still in denial about how and why we got to where we are even though the path we were on was preordained and clearly discernible thirteen years ago.

Most Americans still believe our present situation is some kind of accident or just happened through the incompetence of our leaders. People still haven't realized that where we are today is a direct result of a deliberate and diabolical plan by a group of international traitors and criminals who call themselves the New World Order (NWO). This group of fascist totalitarians is aided and abetted in its diabolical designs by a group of the world's most influential and richest men.

Just the other day I was having a conversation with my neighbor, and we eventually got around to discussing politics. I vented my frustrations and told him what I really believed. As anticipated, he was somewhat shocked by my revelations, and to take the wind out of my sails, he asked me if I was right about what I was saying, what could we do about it. His question was a good one. What use is there knowing what is really going on with our government if there isn't anything we can do about it? I have just told you what I have done to try to change things. The purpose of this essay is to tell you what you can do about it and how we can win back our government and freedom.

First of all, and let's get this straight right from the beginning, breaking the law or an armed insurrection is not the answer. To be sure, if in the early days of our now-defunct republic, someone had taken over our government, citizens would have been reaching for their smoothbores, and the perpetrators of the plot would end up hanging from the nearest oak tree. In this day and age, such intemperate action is insane, unnecessary, and self-defeating. It is insane because many more innocent people would die than bad guys, and there is no guarantee that what comes out of the insurrection will be any better than what we are faced with now. It is unnecessary because we still have the power of the internet and ballot box, and if we can't win in the voting booth, then we do not deserve to win.

Finally, it is self-defeating because resorting to arms will just drive people away from our cause, and this will ensure disaster.

I cannot emphasize this last point strongly enough. Any attempt at armed insurrection is doomed to failure—and worse, will galvanize most Americans against our movement. It will also be used by our oppressors as an excuse to implement more draconian measures to protect us from ourselves. We are fighting a war of ideas and ideals. This being the case, the battles we fight must be won in the minds and hearts of American citizens. This is the only path available to us to reclaim our freedom and the republic that the New World Order has stolen from us.

In any case, the first thing we must do to solve our problem is to admit we have one. If you do not think the New World Order exists and is intentionally working against our best interest, then get off your butt and start being the kind of American citizen you are supposed to be by educating yourself about the truth. I know this is difficult when the truth is such a bitter pill to swallow, but if you make the effort, the truth will set you free, and that is what this movement is all about. The internet has a wealth of information about the New World Order and what its designs and intentions are. Aaron Russo's video "America: Freedom to Fascism" is readily available for free on the internet, and you should also obtain a copy of the History Channel's video entitled *Secret Societies*. I realize there is a lot of garbage out there, but with a little effort, you will be able to separate the wheat from the chaff, and once you do, you will become part of the solution instead of being part of the problem.

Once you have deprogrammed and un-brainwashed yourself, the work has just begun. Oh, my goodness, did I say the word *work*? I hope I didn't lose too many of you by using this word, but the simple truth of the matter is that remaining and being free is hard work. How much hard work? Far more than is being done by those who are working to subjugate and enslave us. And don't forget, our adversaries are full-time professionals who are being paid by us for their efforts. The work I am talking about is educating relatives, friends, associates, and neighbors about what you have learned to be the truth: that the New World Order is a group of international criminals who have taken over our government and are working against our best interests to further their own.

The task before us is a real challenge because human nature is such that most people not only want to be fooled, they also fool themselves. This is especially true when the alternatives involve things that are repugnant and necessitate their turning off their televisions and taking action. On the other side of the coin, many Americans are beginning to feel the pinch of the New World Order, and the pain they are now experiencing is opening their eyes. For example, many are jobless or working at McDonald's, flipping hamburgers, with gasoline at $3 per gallon! Would you believe $4 per gallon? How about $5? Or perhaps you foolishly bought your first home during the so-called real estate boom and can no longer afford to live in it. Or maybe you were mugged by an illegal alien who was just given a driver's license and food stamps. Well, my friends, these occurrences are not accidents. They are the work of the New World Order, and the sooner people learn the truth, the sooner we will be able to turn things around.

If the New World Order is going to be defeated, we need numbers because numbers mean votes, and unless we have the votes, we will accomplish nothing. Who, then, should we vote for? In the past several elections, all the way back to President Kennedy, unless we voted for a third-party candidate, we were voting for our own subjugation because every Republican and Democratic candidate was a New World Order wannabe or lackey. Presidential campaigns take money, lots of it, and the best way to ensure that a campaign is fully financed is to kiss the butts of our New World Order masters. Unfortunately, up until now, this is exactly what the Republicans and Democrats have done. However, in the current race to the White House, one man stands out like a shining star from all the rest, and that man is Congressman Ron Paul from Texas.

When you decide whom to vote for, the first thing you should ask about a candidate is if he or she is a member of Skull and Bones, the Trilateral Commission, or the Council of Foreign Relations. These organizations are fronts for the New World Order, and their insiders are movers and shakers who are our enemies who work very hard to keep us dumb, docile, and subjugated. Unfortunately, most people in positions of authority presently in our government are members of one or more of these organizations, and this includes George Bush Jr. and Sr., who are both card-carrying-members of Skull and Bones. We must weed people like this out and eliminate them from public service because they put allegiance to these organizations above their oath of office and the people who pay their salaries.

Other things you should ask a presidential candidate is whether, if elected, he or she will work to repeal the Federal Reserve Act. This act created the Federal Reserve system. It is through the Federal Reserve that the New World Order controls our economy and government. It also provides them with the funding that fuels their diabolical designs to rule the entire world. Along these same lines, the federal income tax is unconstitutional, and this being the case, any candidate who is worth voting for will promise to abolish it. Our government functioned without an income tax up until 1913. The only reason one exists today is to rob Americans of the fruits of their labor and provide funds to the New World Order so they can wrongfully police the rest of the world. Finally, a candidate who intends to serve us will promise to repeal GATT, NAFTA, and all the other unconstitutional trade agreements brought to us by Bill Clinton and George Bush, which have robbed us of our independence and sovereignty.

Ron Paul is the only presidential candidate who has met each and every litmus test described above. In fact, no other presidential candidate will even address or talk about the issues raised here because by addressing them and bringing them to the light of day, there is no way that they can continue to support the status quo. Can you imagine a candidate arguing that even though our Constitution says that Congress should coin money and regulate its value, it is preferable to have a private group of bankers perform these functions? Can you imagine a candidate arguing that even though our Constitution says that Congress will regulate trade with foreign nations, it is really better for a group of foreign nationals to do this for us in the guise of the WTO? Even more ludicrous, can you imagine a candidate arguing that it is in our best interest to have Congress, the president, and our Supreme Court subordinated to the ruling panels of the WTO, which is the case under GATT?

What can we do about it? First of all, *wake up* and stop being brain-dead. Second, wake up your neighbor to the dismal truth of our situation. And finally, stop voting for people like George Bush and Bill Clinton or others like them. If no candidate in an election satisfies the litmus tests established in this essay, then don't vote. Oh no, you say, if I don't vote, I won't be able to support my pet candidate who caters to my petty issues. *Wake up!* What are your petty issues worth in comparison to our freedom, independence, and financial well-being? These are the only issues that really matter in this coming election, and besides, the simple truth of the matter is that candidates who do not pass our litmus tests are liars and con artists. How can you be sure they will even remember your pet issue after getting into office? George W. Bush lied about everything he promised to do. Wake up, bucko!

In the present national election, America is at a crossroad, and this may be the last chance we have of saving our nation and ourselves without anarchy and bloodshed. Ron Paul is a rare bird among presidential candidates. He is a man of honor and integrity who will lead this nation on the path chosen for it by our founding fathers. If we do not elect Ron Paul as our president, things will continue to get worse for us economically, socially, and environmentally. This nation is on a downhill slide engineered by the New World Order, and the only hope we have of reversing the trend is to elect Ron Paul as our president. Voting for anyone else is a vote for ruination and disaster.

APPENDIX D1
God, the Bible, and Christianity

July 2002

In normal times, religion is something personal, and for an individual to disparage or take to task the religious beliefs of another is rude and inconsiderate. However, these are not normal times. In this nation today, we see a union of political and religious forces such that politicians brag about wearing their religion on their sleeves, and religious zealots not only claim that the United States is a Christian nation but that the Bible is the basis of our laws. These people have even gone so far as to create an *alternative science* as an answer to evolution, which they insist should be given equal time within our schools.

At first glance, all this seems harmless, but a careful examination of the situation reveals these developments are not in our best interest, and such misguided efforts are an affront to science, a threat to our republic, and a perversion of Christianity. With so much at stake, not only should these issues be addressed, but as citizens, we have a duty and obligation to do so, especially when it is the religious extremists themselves who have thrown their religion into the political arena.

While this may come as a surprise to some, the Bible is not God. It is a book inspired by God, but this does not mean that every word and syllable in it was placed there in accordance with his will. The Bible was written by men who had a great reverence for God, but they were men, and being men, their writings were fallible and as much a reflection of themselves as they were of God. This truth is repugnant to fundamentalist Christians because they believe the stories of the Bible were written by God through men. Nowhere is this written in the Bible, but fundamentalists believe it because this is what they want to believe. However, the truth is that there is no way to substantiate their belief, and similar to a belief in God, its validity is a matter of faith. However, in this particular case, it is a misguided faith that is anything but harmless.

God does not change. He is a perfect being, all-knowing, and all-powerful. Therefore, there is no reason for him to change. However, if you believe the Old and New Testaments are factual accounts of God's relationship with man, then you have to concede that God changes and not in small and insignificant ways. The God of the New Testament is far different than the God of the Old. In the Old Testament, God does not promise forgiveness of sins, salvation, an afterlife, or an eternity with him in heaven. No, all the Old Testament God offers to his chosen people is a deal: obey his laws and he will bless you, do otherwise and you will suffer the consequences. This carrot and stick approach to religion is in sharp contrast with the religion of the New Testament, where there are no chosen people and salvation is a gift from God given to all those who love and accept him.

From reading the Bible, it should also be clear that in the Old Testament, God is petty, wrathful, vindictive, demanding, intimidating, unforgiving, cruel, and easily manipulated. In sharp contrast, the God of the New Testament is tolerant, loving, and forgiving. He has none of the undesirable characteristics of the Old Testament God. This being the case, God changed, and these changes are so profound that he is a completely transformed entity. In fact, one can reasonably conclude there are two Gods: a negative God of the Old Testament and a positive God of the New. Obviously, this is absurd, and being absurd, it follows that God must not have had a direct hand in writing the Old Testament because God does not indulge in absurdities. Therefore, it also follows that the Old Testament was written by men who, among other things, wrote down stories that had been passed down by word of mouth through the centuries, and God had little to do with much of what they wrote. To think otherwise makes no sense and leaves us with far too many contradictions and inconsistencies that cannot be dismissed or ignored.

The story of Noah and the flood is an excellent example of why the Old Testament is not history. Every aspect of this legend is an impossibility that defies reason and common sense. First of all, the ark is dimensioned such that it could not possibly hold the numbers of creatures necessary; never mind the food and supplies needed to survive, not only a voyage of forty days and nights, but the time required for the world to return to normal after the flood receded. Also, gathering up two of everything that lived in the world was an impossible task. Today, we are still discovering unknown species in remote areas of the world. Is it reasonable to believe that Noah had the means and resources to gather all these creatures when he didn't even know they existed? Noah had no idea New Zealand, Madagascar, Australia, North America, South America, and Antarctica were a part of the world. Are we really supposed to believe that he traveled to these places and gathered up two of all the animals that lived there? Were kangaroos, platypuses, and penguins on the ark? If not, then where did these animals come from several thousand short years after the flood drove them to extinction?

The fact that Noah and his family were the only people in the world who God deemed worth saving also defies comprehension. Surely, there must have been many other people around who loved God and led moral lives. What about all those infants and babies who were intentionally drowned? Weren't they as innocent as Noah? When the flood receded, leaving behind a world of dead people, animals, and plants, how did the animals released from the ark survive? There was nothing around to eat other than carrion, rotten foliage, and the other animals from the ark. Can you imagine what this rotting world smelled like? In any case, wouldn't the predators eat the surviving herbivores and other weaker animals? No, the story of Noah is absurd in a multitude of different ways, and this includes the specifics of the flood itself.

According to the Bible, the flood covered the entire world, including its mountains. Therefore, even the top of Mount Everest, at 29,035 feet, was underwater. The world's oceans contain approximately 310 million cubic miles of water. In order to submerge Mount Everest, approximately 3.5 times the amount of water presently in our oceans is required. Therefore, for the biblical account of the flood to have happened, this amount of new water would have to be created in our atmosphere and then allowed to fall to the ground as rain. This means a column of water 726 feet high rained down on every inch of the earth's surface each day. This amounts to 363 inches of rain per hour, nonstop, for forty days and nights. Where did all this water come from? How could our atmosphere hold this much water? Where did all the water go after the flood receded? The vast majority of creatures within the world's oceans would not survive in water diluted as much as described. Therefore, these creatures would also have died along with the land animals. Why do we find a plethora of sea creatures within our oceans just several thousand years after the flood drove those living at the time into extinction? Did Noah have huge fish tanks on his ark and gather up these creatures also? If not, how did the world's oceans become replenished with fish after the flood?

No, there is nothing about Noah and the flood that makes sense, and this includes God's purpose for flooding the world. People are born weak and prone to sin. This being the case, did God kill off all of humanity, and save Noah and his family, because people are the way he created them, or was he trying to improve his breeding stock? If the latter is the case, then he wasted his time because just a few generations later, God had to fire and brimstone Sodom and Gomorrah for many of the same reasons he brought on the flood. What kind of God behaves this way? The answer is a terrible and irrational god who has no regard for human life and believes fear and intimidation are the proper way to rule people. Fortunately, this is not the God found in the New Testament. And yet, incredibly, fundamentalist Christians want us to worship both the Old and New Testament Gods as if they are one and the same. They see no contradiction in this and are incapable of understanding that Jesus Christ came into the world to put an end to this foolishness.

As human beings, we have a strong desire to have things make sense. In keeping with this desire, we reach out to God because for most of us, living and dying without a higher purpose makes no sense. God is many things, but the one thing we can be most assured of is that he is truth. Lies, deception, and falsehoods are repugnant to him because these things are at odds with his nature. Therefore, Christians of today are faced with a dilemma. The Bible has two parts: a New Testament governed by the New Covenant, which promises redemption and salvation, and an Old Testament, which is rife with contradictions, inconsistencies, and falsehoods. What is a truth loving Christian supposed to do? Fundamentalists tell us the problem lies within our intellect, and to reconcile the situation, we should stop thinking, accept the Bible at face value as the holy word of God, and believe what we are told. They never stop to think that our intellect and free will are among God's greatest gifts, and to ignore them to find him is sacrilegious.

It is not God's intent for us to live with contradictions or falsehoods, and this brings us to the two most intentionally ignored pieces of New Testament scripture. In Hebrews 8:13, the apostle Paul says, "When He [God] said a New Covenant, He has made the first obsolete. But whatever is becoming obsolete and growing old is ready to disappear." In Matthew 26:27–28, Jesus is quoted as saying, "All of you drink this, for this is my blood of the New Covenant, which is being shed for many unto the forgiveness of sins." These two passages of the Bible are significant and profound because they tell us Jesus Christ established a brand-new religion, which would not only replace the old but would make it disappear. Therefore, there is nothing in the Old Testament that has any meaning or relevance for a Christian. How can it be otherwise when God has rendered the Old Covenant obsolete? From this, it follows that those who hang onto the Old Testament by believing there is something in its lessons and commandments that is relevant to Christians have rejected the New Covenant, have rejected the reason Jesus Christ came into the world, and by so doing, have rejected Jesus Christ. And in case you fail to see the implications of this, a person who rejects Jesus Christ is not a Christian.

The Old Covenant was simple. Obey God's laws and you will be blessed; disobey and you will be cursed. Noah and the flood are a perfect illustration of how this primitive type of religion works. The New Covenant, at first glance, also seems simple. Accept Jesus Christ as your Lord and Savior, and you will be saved. However, things are far more complicated than they appear because accepting Jesus Christ means you will follow him by making your life mirror his. Doing this requires intelligence. It doesn't take a great amount of thinking to abide by the Old Covenant because doing so is simply a matter of following a set of written laws. In contrast, to abide by the

New Covenant, you must know and understand Jesus and apply this knowledge to situations that arise in your life.

Understanding all of the above, the dilemma between Christianity and science is resolved. For those who truly are Christian, the Old Covenant, and Testament are obsolete and have disappeared. Therefore, there is no erroneous biblical history of the world to stand in the way of seeking and finding the one true God. God is truth, and science is a disciplined way of finding the truth. Therefore, instead of disproving God and working against him, science compliments God and works to reveal the majesty of his creation. Science will never prove or disprove God because its sole purpose is to tell us what, when, and how regarding the universe God made. The issues of who and why are the sole providence of religion, and rather than being mutually exclusive, the purposes of science and religion fit together like hand and glove. The problem that fundamentalist Christians have is that by holding on to the Old Testament, they have embraced a history of the world that is not only inaccurate but absurd. Then they compound this error by rejecting science and wearing this rejection like a badge of honor, never realizing that the badge of honor they are so proud of is repugnant to Christianity.

Jesus Christ came into the world in fulfillment of the Old Testament prophecy to establish a New Covenant with all of mankind. This New Covenant established a brand-new religion that replaced the old religion in its entirety. Christianity, the new religion we are talking about, is comprised of three elements:

- the forgiveness of sins
- a path to salvation
- freedom from the tyranny of religion as government

This last element is lost upon fundamentalist Christians because, like the Pharisees of Old, they think that the nature of religion is to impose a set of written rules and laws upon people. Fortunately, our founding fathers knew better, but the irony of the situation is that the founders really did create a Christian nation as fundamentalist Christians would have us believe. However, they did so for a reason

Fundamentalists are incapable of understanding. To be sure, America is a Christian nation because the men who fathered it were Christian. However, unbeknown to most, it is also a Christian nation because the founders enshrined within our Constitution one of Christianity's most profound and important principles: the separation of church and state.

God does not want us to obey him because of the law. Instead, he wants us to live good and moral lives because we love him. Written laws complicate this equation and are at odds with it. When Jesus saved the adulteress from the mob, he didn't tell them to seize and throw her in jail. Instead, he said to her, "Go and sin no more." Jesus also told us to render unto Caesar that which is Caesar's and to render unto God that which is God's. This being the case, no human being or group of human beings has the authority to enforce God's will through the power of the state. Furthermore, to codify God's law into man's law is repugnant to God. This is what the New Covenant is about; this is what the United States of America is about. These truths are lost upon fundamentalist Christians. They truly are the new Pharisees, and their misguided efforts to resurrect the Old Covenant in a wrongful attempt to create God's heaven here on earth will only do the opposite, not only for those of us who truly are Christian but for every freedom-loving American as well.

Postscript

When people read the Bible, they do so under the assumption that they are reading the holy word of God. From this point forward, no matter what they read, it has to be true irrespective of how unreasonable, illogical, or absurd it is. This is what they believe: never stopping to think that what they are doing is an affront to God. What God worth his salt wants people to come to him through ignorance? Yet this is what most people do because they have been told this is what God expects of them.

APPENDIX D2
Tithing and Christianity

April 1996

To be a Christian, one must believe that Jesus Christ is God and that the Holy Bible is his inspired word. This second requisite is necessary because, without the Bible, we have no way of knowing anything about God or his intentions. The Bible is God's handbook that tells us what to believe and how to behave in order to find favor with him. Therefore, for Christians, the Bible is the final word on truth, and intentional distortions of that truth are a sacrilege. A minister or priest is the recognized leader of his congregation and as such holds ultimate responsibility for the integrity of God's word. Unfortunately, to promote the financial well-being of their churches, many ministers have distorted God's word and created a false impression of Christian responsibility.

The Bible contains two major divisions: the Old Testament and the New Testament. The Old Testament, called the Preparation because it lays the groundwork for the coming of Jesus Christ, is concerned with the Old Covenant. A *covenant* is a formal agreement between two or more parties. In the Old Testament, God entered into a covenant with the people of Israel such that if they obeyed his commandments, he would bless them and provide them with a homeland. A majority of these covenants are called Levitical laws because they come from the book of Leviticus. They dealt with all aspects of Jewish daily life including food preparation, dressing, sexual relations, grooming, business, interpersonal relations, planting, harvesting, healing, worshipping, sacrificing, fasting, support of the church, etc. Most of these God-ordained Levitical laws, although still observed by Orthodox Jews, are obsolete for Christians, save one: support of the church through tithing.

Like all Old Testament law, the one concerning tithing was explicit. It first appeared in Genesis 28:22 when Jacob promised God that "Of all that thou dost give to me I will surely give a tenth to thee." It was reaffirmed by God himself in Leviticus 27:30–32, when God told Moses, "Thus all the tithe of the land, of the seed of the land or of the fruit of the tree, is the Lords; it is holy to the Lord. And for every tenth part of herd or flock, whatever passes under rod, the tenth one shall be holy to the Lord." Tithing, therefore, was an important but small part of the Levitical laws adhered to by the people of Israel in the Old Testament.

The New Testament, which commences upon the birth of Jesus Christ approximately four hundred years after the close of the Old Testament, was a new beginning for mankind. Jesus Christ was born to save the world, and to do so, he established a new relationship between God and man. This New Covenant was foretold by God within the Old Testament in Jeremiah 31:31–33, where he says, "Behold, days are coming when I will make a New Covenant with the house of Israel and the house of Judah, not like the covenant which I made with their fathers in the day I took them by the hand to bring them out of the land of Egypt, My covenant which they broke, although I was a husband to them, but this is the covenant which I will make with the house of Israel after those days, I will put my law within them and on their heart I will write it; and I will be their God, and they shall be My People."

God specifically spoke of a New Covenant that will be "not like" the Old Covenant. This point is clearly made by the apostle Paul in Hebrews 8:13, which reads, "When He [God] said a New Covenant, He has made the first obsolete. But whatever is becoming obsolete and growing old is ready to disappear." God never intended to include part of the Old Covenant within the New Covenant because one is entirely different from the other. The Old Covenant was behavior oriented, and finding favor with God was a matter of religiously following an extensive set of laws and commandments. In the New Covenant, salvation is a gift from God and is dependent upon accepting Jesus Christ as your personal Lord and savior. This point is succinctly made in 2 Ephesians 2:8: "For by grace you have been saved through faith; and that not of yourselves, it is the gift of God; not as a result of works that no one should boast," and in John 3:16: "For God so loved the world, that He gave His only begotten son, that whoever believes in Him should not perish, but have eternal life."

There is nothing in the New Testament that remotely suggests that a Christian should give 10 percent of their earnings to the church, similar to Jews in the Old Testament. The sole mention of tithing in the New Testament appears in Hebrews 7:5–6 and is in reference to tithing as required in the Old Testament. On the contrary, the New Testament is clear about the financial responsibility of Christians toward the church. In 2 Corinthians 9:7, the Apostle Paul says, "Every man according as he purposeth in his heart, so let him give; not grudgingly or of necessity; for God loveth a cheerful giver." Therefore, a minister or priest who urges tithing as a Christian responsibility does so in contradiction to the Apostle Paul and is contrary to the New Covenant established by Jesus Christ when he said at the last supper, "All of you drink this, for this is my blood of the New Covenant, which is being shed for many unto the forgiveness of sins" (Matt. 26:27–28).

The last quotation in the above paragraph is taken from the King James version of the Bible, which is the most respected translation of the Bible available. Curiously, if one reads this same passage from the New American Standard Bible, a newer translation that is subscribed to and recommended by many fundamentalist Christian ministers, one cannot help but notice that "blood of the New Covenant" has been changed to read "blood of the covenant." The dropping of the word *new* in the New American Standard Bible is significant because it changes the intent of Christ's message and paves the way for the acceptance of passé Levitical laws into Christian theology.

Irrespective of scripture, the act of donating 10 percent of all income to the church, as practiced by Old Testament Jews, is not comparable to donating 10 percent today. When the early Jews gave 10 percent of their earnings to the church, they were giving to their government, which was the church. Therefore, the tithes given were not just for religious purposes but also funded non-religious services that are now typically provided by our federal, state, and local governments. To illustrate this point, consider the situation where a married couple in America has a taxable income of $50,000 yearly.

Today, this couple would pay approximately 17 percent of their earnings to the federal government in taxes. If this same couple chose to tithe, they would be paying a combined total of 27 percent to church and state, as compared to the 10 percent paid by their Old Testament counterparts.

At this point, it is reasonable to wonder, if tithing is not a part of our Christian heritage, how have so many people come to believe that it is a Christian responsibility? The answer to this question is simple: a significant number of today's ministers realize that a belief in tithing increases church revenue. Therefore, they do nothing to rectify these misconceptions but instead help perpetuate them. For example, there exists a pamphlet written by Kenneth S. Keyes of real estate fame, who founded the Keyes Company. This pamphlet, entitled "In Partnership with God: A Business Man's Testimony Regarding Christian Stewardship," was published by the Keyes Foundation and is actively distributed in a large number of churches throughout this country and the world. Although this pamphlet is deceptive in regard to statements made about Christian stewardship, no leading Christian minister has come forward to denounce it.

It is not possible to reprint "In Partnership with God" here in its entirety, but it is important to discuss some key points made by Mr. Keyes. Mr. Keyes begins his essay by pointing out that we owe everything to God: our lives, possessions, abilities, and souls. Mr. Keyes then concludes that God also has first claim on our money, because our income is derived from the abilities He gave us. While this may be true, Mr. Keyes fails to understand that under the New Covenant, God has placed no claim on our earnings but has left support of the church a matter of individual choice and conscience. Mr. Keyes then claims that God must be first in our pocketbooks if he is to be first in our lives and states that Jesus emphasized this truth when he said, "Where your treasure is there will your heart be also" (Matt. 6:21). However, Mr. Keyes does not quote the two verses immediately preceding Matthew 6:21, which give an entirely different meaning to this verse. These passages read, "Do not lay up for yourselves treasures upon Earth, where moth and rust destroy and where thieves break in and steal. But lay up for yourselves treasures in heaven, where neither moth nor rust destroys and where thieves do not break in or steal; for where your treasure is, there will your heart be also."

Mr. Keyes continues his essay by telling us about our obligation to tithe and about how tithing "brings blessings." The problem is that all his justifications concerning these obligations and blessings are taken from the Old Testament and are no longer valid or binding for Christians. He offers no justification at all from the New Testament because there is none. Mr. Keyes then goes on to give testimony from others about the blessings they have received from tithing and proposes that because God is entitled to the first 10 percent of our income, our giving only begins after he has received his first tenth. This is a subtle way of saying that if you really are a good Christian, you should give more than the 10 percent tithe. There is no New Testament substantiation for this statement, and it is contrary to New Testament scripture.

In describing how to tithe, Mr. Keyes again distorts the intent and meaning of scripture. He advises that we should separate 10 percent of our salary each payday from the money that we spend on ourselves. To justify this procedure, Mr. Keyes quotes part of 1 Corinthians 16:2 as follows: "Upon the first day of the week let every one of you lay by him in store as God has prospered him." However, reading 1 Corinthians 16:1–2 reveals a slightly different meaning for the passage than the one claimed by Mr. Keyes: "Now concerning the collection for the saints, as I directed the churches of Galatia, so do you also. On the first day of every week let each one of you put aside and save, as he may prosper, that no collections be made when I come." It is clear from reading this passage that while the apostle Paul did endorse setting aside a portion of weekly earnings for the church, he did not endorse donating a specified amount. Furthermore, Paul also recommended a respite from collections for the duration of his visit to Corinth, which is in direct opposition to the concept of tithing.

Mr. Keyes concludes his essay with a summary, where he makes the following statements:

1. Tithing is a God-ordained plan by which believers recognize His claim on their time, resources, and earnings.

Tithing is not God's plan. It is an Old Testament Levitical law that has been replaced in the New Testament with the New Covenant. God makes no claim on our time, energy, ability, and money in the New Testament.

2. Tithing is a means of showing our love and appreciation to God for His goodness toward us.

    There are many ways of expressing our love and appreciation to God that, unlike tithing, are in keeping with New Testament scripture.

3. Tithing was endorsed by Jesus Christ.

    This statement is not true. Jesus Christ came into the world in fulfillment of Old Testament prophesy and to establish a New Covenant with mankind that replaced the Levitical Laws of the Old Testament, including tithing.

4. Tithing will enhance our lives as Christians.

5. Tithing often is financially rewarding.

6. Tithing is a way of obeying God's commandment: "Thou shalt love the Lord thy God with all thy heart, with all thy soul, and with all thy mind."

    There is no basis or justification for these statements in the New Testament, and they are contrary to New Testament scripture.

Karl Marx wrote, "The ends justify the means." This philosophy has allowed communist leaders to impose a multitude of sins and atrocities on their subject peoples, all in the guise of building a better society. In this country, we recognize the rule of law among individuals and nations and subscribe to the philosophy that it is not so important whether you win or lose, but how you play the game that counts. In other words, we believe in truth, honesty, honor, and fair play, which is part of our Christian heritage. It is true that our churches need money to operate and grow. As Christians, it is important for all of us, according to our own conscience and ability, to financially support our church. But is it right for church leaders to distort scripture and misrepresent God's intentions toward us for the purpose of increasing church revenues? Do the ends justify the means? The answers to these two questions should be obvious to us all.

APPENDIX D3
The Politics of Christianity

January 2002

To call yourself a Christian, it is necessary to accept Jesus Christ as your Lord and savior. This is the litmus test for Christians, and to deny the divinity of Christ is to deny Christianity. Beyond this, being a Christian means that you mirror God in your thoughts, actions, and daily life. God, above all things, is truth. There is nothing false or hidden about God. God also embodies three spirits, which we call the Father, the Son, and the Holy Ghost. Mirroring this trinity are the three fundamental aspects of God's truth: love, tolerance, and forgiveness.

There you have it. True Christians accept Jesus Christ as their Lord and savior but also strive to be a reflection of God in mind, body, and soul. First and foremost, Christians never lie. Lies are anathema to God and a reflection of Satan. Christians also love God and all other people as they do themselves. Because they love others, they are tolerant of them and show other people respect even if they are not Christian. Finally, they forgive others for their transgressions.

In the Florida *Daytona Beach News-Journal*, it was reported that 78 percent of all born-again Christians voted for George W. Bush as president of the United States. This vote is alarming for several reasons, but the most compelling one is that these born-again Christians have chosen a man to be their leader and the leader of this nation who reflects none of the values that define being Christian.

The stock and trade of President Bush is that he is a liar. He used subterfuge and lies to lead this nation into war and subterfuge and lies to defeat his opponent in the recent presidential election. This alone disqualifies President Bush from the ranks of Christianity. But beyond this, his lies are bringing death, destruction, and mayhem to millions of innocent people throughout the world. A man who does such things is not a Christian but instead is doing Satan's work.

Furthermore, as far as love, tolerance, and forgiveness are concerned, you do not love people by killing them, and you are not tolerant and forgiving if you subscribe to the non-Christian notion that if someone is not with you, they are against you. Such a doctrine is not only un-Christian, it is un-American as well.

All of the above being true, why did so many born-again Christians vote to keep President Bush in the White House? Simply put: because he supports their political agenda, and that agenda is to make this nation reflect Christian values. In consideration of what Christian values are, this should be a good thing, but left unsaid is that the fundamentalist Christians want to codify their perception of Christian values in civil law. There's the rub. Anyone who subscribes to the notion that Christian values should be codified into civil law is both un-Christian and un-American.

God wants people to come to him freely, willingly, and without compulsion. This being true, codifying God's laws—if you foolishly wish to call them that—into man's law offends God and is repugnant to him. And as much as it may surprise you, this includes abortion and murder. Proof of this is when Jesus said, "Render unto Caesar what is Caesar's and render unto God what is God's." During his time in this world, Jesus never once spoke out against the brutality of Roman rule or the dismal institution of slavery, even though many of his followers wanted and expected him to. Why? Because man's law is irrelevant to God and works at odds with everything that God stands for.

In conclusion, 78 percent of born-again Christians supported President Bush for reelection even though he is anything but Christian because of a shared political agenda that is anything but Christian. Truly, a Christian political activist is an oxymoron because the moment one turns to man's law to do God's work, that person offends God and has turned away from him.

Civil law is a set of rules enforced by the barrel of a gun. We tolerate the abomination of civil law because we all fall short of the Christian ideal. However, Christian ideals should never be the basis of civil law because civil law applies not only to Christians but to everyone. Those who strive to make civil law reflect Christian values are not being Christian because what they really are trying to do is make others conform to their way of thinking through the power of the state. Logic and reason alone should be the basis of civil law. To hold otherwise is un-Christian and un-American.

APPENDIX D4
The Jewish State Debate

March 2014

On February 23, 2014, the Associated Press issued a news article written by Dan Perry entitled "Israeli Demand sparks 'Jewish State' Debate." Essentially, the thrust of the article was that many Jews believe and demand that Israel declare itself to be a Jewish state by law because Judaism is not just a religion, not just a nationality, and not just an identity because it is all three of these things simultaneously. However, this position raises many complicated philosophical and practical issues. For example, should a religion be a state, and conversely, should a state have a religion? On the practical side of the coin, what does declaring Israel to be a Jewish state say to the Palestinian people about their status in Israel, especially the ones who happen to be its citizens?

While the subject article delves into the examination of these issues in some detail, it fails to include an examination of this matter from an American's point of view, and it also tiptoes around issues such as fairness from a Palestinian's point of view. This essay is an attempt to rectify these shortcomings.

The United States is a nation created by people seeking a better life and who fled the Old World to escape religious persecution. For this reason, it is a nation where church and state are separate. The founders understood that a constitution is a contract between citizens created exclusive of God while religion is a relationship between God and people. Therefore, the basis of law in America is reason and justice to the exclusion of religious dogma. Jesus endorsed these governing principles when he said render unto Caesar that which is Caesar's and render unto God that which is God's. He said this not only to avoid being charged with treason by the Romans but also because Christ wanted people to come to him willingly and without compulsion, not because of some man-made law.

The simple truth of the matter is that a hallmark of a religious state is tyranny. This is true because government officials rule with God's blessing instead of the consent of those they govern. The old adage, "Power corrupts and absolute power corrupts absolutely," is operative here. What is more absolute than rulers who rule on behalf of God? To see the truth in this, we only have to look at the Spanish Inquisition, where people were tortured and put to death because they offended those in positions of authority. The fact that people in Europe fled their homelands to seek freedom of religion in the New World is further validation that the religious states of the Old World were the embodiment of tyranny and oppression.

Therefore, Americans should be wary of religious states. Furthermore, we should be opposed to new ones being established, especially when it involves usurping the territory of a weaker and unwilling group of people. Unfortunately, Israel falls into this latter category. Granted, the Holocaust and the end of WWII created a situation where Jews deserved special considerations, but how do we justify forcing the Palestinians to pay this price? Indeed, how just is it to force them to continue to pay this price?

The subject article pointed out that many Palestinians oppose Israeli demands for them to embrace the concept of Israel being a Jewish state because it would mean Palestinian refugees would have to give up their dreams of returning to their "lost properties." This is a curious choice of words because it implies that the Palestinians played some role in losing them, which is not the case at all. The truth is that the Jews were mandated part of Palestine by the United Nations following the close of WWII. In keeping with this United Nations mandate, the Palestinians were forced from their homes and the land they had occupied for centuries. Complicating this equation is that Israel, through the years, has expanded its occupation of Palestinian lands through war and annexation.

The nation of Israel, throughout its existence, has claimed a "right of return" to Israel for Jews throughout the world. If this is a fundamental and recognized right for a Jew, then in all fairness, it should also be a fundamental and recognized right for a Palestinian. The point is that if Israel declares itself to be a Jewish state, then the Palestinians indeed will have been denied their right of return, ensuring that they will be second-class citizens forever. In other words, if Israel declares itself to be a Jewish state, in order for a Palestinian to be equal to a Jew in their eyes and the eyes of everyone else in the world, he will have to fight for this right. What this means is that unless Palestine defeats Israel or Israel wipes out the Palestinians, the wars of terror in the Middle East and throughout the world will go on forever.

APPENDIX D5
The Creation Con Job

June 2003

Most people are under the impression that there is a debate raging within this nation between evolution and creation science, and indeed there is. However, for the most part, this debate is one-sided, and the side doing the debating are those who subscribe to what is alleged to be creation science. I use the word *alleged* because creation science has nothing to do with science, and in truth, it is nothing more than religious dogma masquerading as science. This being the case, the notion there is really something of substance to debate is a key and essential element of the creationist con job.

Science, fundamentally, is a disciplined search for knowledge. The keyword in this sentence is *disciplined*, and the first litmus test for being disciplined is a lack of bias. It is here where the creationists fall flat on their faces. A scientist seeks to explain the world within which we live. He does so by observing phenomena and coming up with the most plausible explanation or theory for what he sees. But he doesn't stop there. Next, he devises methodologies for testing his theory. If his theory fails these tests, he develops a new theory, and the process begins again. If the new theory passes muster, he publishes his work for others to test and validate. Finally, when a general consensus is reached within the scientific community that a theory is correct, only then is it accepted as being true.

Similarly, a creation scientist starts out with a theory: that God created the world according to scripture. However, this is not a theory in the true sense of the word because the theory itself is tainted with bias. When a scientist creates a theory, he has no ownership of it, and it is understood at the outset that if the theory proves to be incorrect, it will be rejected. A creation scientist has no intention of ever rejecting God or scripture, so his so-called theory will not be proven wrong under any circumstances. Indeed, the creationist does everything possible to ensure that this is the case. This is accomplished by dismissing all evidence contrary to his theory and grasping upon anything that can possibly support it. In truth, very little does, and most of this evidence is obtained by stretching logic and reason to their breaking points. This same twisted reason and logic is used to attack and discredit evidence that is contrary to a creationist's preconceived notions.

There are two kinds of scientists: those who believe in God and those who don't. To sustain the illusion of debate, creation scientists would have us believe that most scientists who subscribe to evolution are atheists, and being atheists, they are biased by their intent to disprove God. Nothing could be further from the truth. The vast majority of scientists who subscribe to evolution are religious men who sincerely believe in God. This being the case, they are also men who would willingly and gladly embrace creationism if creationism was the best explanation for what they find in the world. It is not, and being good scientists, they conclude accordingly while maintaining their faith in God.

Creation scientists would have us believe that evolution is only a theory and has not been proven. The truth of the matter is that evolutionary theory, by its very nature, will never be proven. However, like other scientific theories, it can be validated, and creation scientists, of course, conveniently ignore and deny this. When Charles Darwin first published *On the Origin of Species*, he based his work on the evidence available at the time. Since then, uncountable new discoveries have been made that reinforce and support his theory. Do creation scientists acknowledge this continually growing pile of evidence? No, of course not! They ignore it and point to what has not yet been discovered, knowing full well that there will always be a gap in the fossil record to help them assail the obvious truth.

Creation science is not science. It is a distortion of science used by religious fundamentalists to lend an air of legitimacy to their claims. The danger in this is that by doing so, they are undermining science and the scientific approach to obtaining knowledge. This is their real goal. Intelligent and thinking human beings are a threat to the power and control that the religious right has over people.

Anything that is a threat to the power and control that the religious right has over people is also a threat to their political power as well. And that's what creation science is all about: political power.

APPENDIX D6
Creation versus Evolution

March 2005

Presently, there exist two explanations of how living things came into being: creation science, which is Bible-inspired, and evolution, which was inspired by the physical evidence found throughout the world. Until recent times, creation science did not exist. Science was left to scientists, and the biblical account of creation was held in reverence by those who so desired, irrespective of what scientists claimed or believed. However, this status quo presented a dilemma to fundamentalist Christians. If the Bible is a historical document as they believe, then evolution must be an error-laden theory that is not an accurate description of how life formed, and worse, this wrongful secular view of the world is being taught to our children throughout the nation as being an established fact.

If one professes to believe in the biblical story of creation as being historically accurate— and more importantly, believe it is a God-inspired account of how he created the world—then anyone who believes otherwise is at best misguided and, at worst, someone in league with the devil and an enemy of God. In either case, to fundamentalists, there are no areas of gray, and as far as creation of the world is concerned, things are either white or black: those who are with God and those who are not. Of course, those who are not, the evolutionists, are automatically assumed to be adversaries, and the fact that many of them are sincere Christians is totally ignored. To fundamentalists, all evolutionists are atheists who are on the opposite side of the fence from them. Unfortunately, this unfair, lopsided, and inaccurate view of the situation is reinforced by our mainstream media and used as political fodder by those who lead us for the purpose of garnering votes and because our government no longer has an interest in educating citizens so they are able to discern fact from fiction.

The truth of the matter is that while some scientists are atheists, many of them are not and most have no problem integrating evolution with their Christianity. In fact, to a Christian who happens to be a scientist, science, including the science of evolution, is a discipline that continually reveals the magnificence of God's handiwork and thus brings such scientists closer to God. Such a notion is repugnant to fundamentalist Christians because accepting the truth means that the biblical account of creation is a myth. This being the case, the entire Old Testament is thrown into question. Fundamentalist Christians, by definition, believe the Bible is historical truth, and even God's own truth, the truth being revealed by scientists, must be rejected for the sake of the god they really worship, the god not of the Bible, but their god, which is the Bible

By believing that the Bible and God are inseparable, fundamentalists are able to achieve what they really desire in life: a resource that enables them to posture that they are God-chosen individuals with the knowledge and moral authority to tell everyone else what to think, what to believe, and how to act. At this point, we should step back and ask which makes the most sense: creation science or evolution? Before proceeding, it should be understood that evolution is not a science. Instead, it is a theory first proposed by Charles Darwin many years ago. The driving force behind Darwin's theory is called natural selection, which is also known as the doctrine of survival of the fittest. As mutations occur, beneficial ones increase the survival chances of those having the mutation, and eventually, it becomes the norm throughout the population. However, natural selection is not a science either. Instead, it is a description of the driving force behind evolution. Where then, does science come into the picture? Science is the tools and methodologies used by naturalists and biologists to substantiate and validate what they find in nature. For example, carbon dating of rocks and fossils is a scientific method used to determine when in time something lived. Knowing when something lived is critical to establishing the evolutionary nature of life because, through it, one can discover the orderly development of a species and even the development of new ones.

Now let's just take a big step back and wait a minute here! Creationists claim that science has never demonstrated that one species ever evolved into another. While this is what creationists claim, nothing could be further from the truth, and this is where creationists demonstrate their lack of understanding of the science of evolution. Species are nothing more than a logical, but artificial, categorization of various living things into groups. It is a convenient way for scientists to look at the animal kingdom but so doing only has validity from an academic point of view. In the beginning, all species were one, but due to differing circumstances, they evolved differently.

Throughout the evolutionary process, isolated animals remained the same species, or more correctly, stayed in the same category of species for long periods of time because early on, mutational differences between them were not significant. However, after eons, the differences became too great to ignore, and then man, not nature, declared these animals to be separate and distinct species. The best example of this phenomenon is the evolution of dinosaurs into birds. Clearly, birds are not dinosaurs, but also just as clear is the fact that they once were, and we have found a plethora of transitional animals that establish this to be the case.

Here again, we are getting ahead of ourselves, and to settle the issue of creation versus evolution, we must step back and ask, what evidence is available to make a definitive determination in the matter? The answer to this question is the fossil record. Let's assume for a moment that creation science is true. For this to be the case, what would we expect to find in the fossil record? The answer to this question should be clear. On the surface of our planet, we will find everything that is alive today, and as we dig down into the past, more and more extinct species are found, adding to the total number living at that point in our planet's history. Eventually, we reach a point where all living things disappear, and just above that level is where we will find every animal that ever lived all mixed together in one huge biological soup. In other words, we reach the "big bang" point of creation—the point where everything living today was created along with everything else that ever lived. Below this point, there is nothing, and at this point, all creatures that ever lived suddenly appear. To be sure, if a unique creation occurred such as claimed by creation scientists, then the fossil record would be as described.

To put it mildly, the picture described above is absurd for a number of reasons, the first of which is that this is definitely not what the fossil record shows. We live on the surface of planet earth, but the surface of our planet is continually growing, and it grows by the accumulation of material on top of the existing surface. This means that as we dig down into the surface of our planet, we are digging back into time, and when we do this, we do not find that the number of species continually increases and eventually proceeds to a point where all species that ever lived are there. Instead, throughout the entire fossil record, we find that species continually come and go, and as we dig down to life's early beginnings, we find that all species converge into one and then disappear. This is the true picture of the fossil record of our planet, and even an individual with little training can easily verify this to be the case. To deny this truth is to deny reality, and this is exactly what proponents of creation science do. They deny the physical evidence that is readily available for all to see and latch onto a description of the fossil record that does not exist in nature. Their sole reason for taking this giant leap into fantasy is because this is what they choose to believe.

The second reason that all the species of the world could not exist at the same point in time is that there is not enough physical room or natural resources on our planet for this to be even a remote possibility. Every living thing requires a certain amount of physical space to survive, and each individual group of animals requires more and more space in proportion to their numbers. If you examine all species of animals that ever lived, calculate their population levels on the planet when they were here, and make a determination of how much physical space and other resources each population of animals requires, then it becomes obvious that one puny planet earth will not cut it for all these animals. To put this another way, if all the animals that ever lived were on the planet at the same time in its history, then in short order, they would denude the world of plants, and the entire surface of the planet would be covered with manure. Furthermore, the air would be so polluted by the stench of feces and dead animals that those surviving would willingly join their more fortunate brethren who are already dead. It is just not possible for everything that ever lived to be alive at the same time, and this absurdity is at the very core of creationist belief.

Finally, all the world's animals could not possibly exist on the surface of our planet at the same time because certain populations of animals are not capable of living alongside certain other populations of animals. Case in point: large mammals and dinosaurs! Meat-eating dinosaurs were ferocious predators. The mammals that existed during their reign were small and inconsequential because any large mammal would not survive in a world populated by the likes of T-Rex. Can you imagine how long a herd of present-day elephants would survive when predators several times their size roamed the land and could run much faster than they could? Elephants cannot hide under rocks or in caves like smaller mammals. Obviously, if elephants had lived during the age of the dinosaurs, they would not have lasted long at all. Therefore, it is ridiculous to believe that all the animals that ever existed occupied and thrived upon our planet all at the same time. We consider the lion to be the king of beasts. In a world full of dinosaurs, lions would be the king of feasts for these huge and ferocious predators. To hold otherwise is absurd, but this is what creation scientists would have us believe.

We live in an exciting and dynamic world that is ever-changing through time in wondrous and miraculous ways. In contrast, the world that creation scientists propose is anything but. Instead, it is a dying world that started out in a glorious way, but through time, nothing new is created, and what is there dies off and becomes extinct. The world envisioned by creationists is in a continual state of decay. Think of how absurd this view of the world really is. All of life miraculously appeared in a flash, and this grand event is never to be repeated again, not even for the lowest of creatures. Is this an intelligent way for a deity to run a universe, or is it the mark of one who is shortsighted and has no love for his creation? To be sure, it is comforting to think that we were created by something superior to ourselves. This may indeed be the case, but the idea that creation was a one-time event is absurd in consideration of the fossil record. Nothing that a creation scientist postures can change this. They try to sound intelligent with all their jargon and scientific talk, but the truth of the matter is that what they are saying is ridiculous and the work of fools.

A very real problem we have with the fossil record is that it is so incomplete, and this gives creationists their greatest weapon against it, but only for people like themselves who are predisposed to being gullible. Over the history of the world, millions of different species of animals have lived and died, but most of these will never be found. This is a given, but this given does not alter the fact that throughout the fossil record, animals appear, persist for a while, and then disappear. Furthermore, while all the missing links will never be found, transitional species abound, and to deny their existence is absurd. Despite this, creationists deny that any links exist, never stopping to think that even if no links are ever found, the fossil record is such that it never will support their views. Perhaps there is another undiscovered explanation for what we find in the fossil record. This certainly is a possibility, but irrespective of what the right answer is, it is definitely not creationism because the fossil record eliminates it from even being a remote possibility.

On the other side of the coin, evolution is the only explanation we presently have for what we find in nature that makes sense. Yes, there are flaws and shortcomings in our knowledge of what really transpired, but this does not give anyone license to dump a theory that is essentially correct for one that is totally absurd. Only a person who wants to believe in absurdity would do this.

There are many things about evolution that we may never explain. How did eyes and vision develop? How did the first single cell come into being? Indeed, how did life itself begin? But because we may never be able to answer these questions does not mean we should throw out the baby (the fossil record) with the bathwater and take an illogical quantum leap to the totally untenable theory that a creator created the world by waving his magic wand and poof— everything that ever lived popped into being. All the missing links will not be found, and all the questions we have will not be answered, but the fossil record is there, is undeniable, and as time goes on, more and more evidences are continually being discovered that confirms the fact that life evolves. And if life evolves, eventually, when an accumulation of changes becomes significant, bingo—a new species will come into being.

All the newly discovered evidence supporting evolution will never be enough for a creationist because they truly are not interested in evidence and care nothing for proof. Their minds are made up, and logic and evidence mean nothing to them because of the axe they have to grind, the axe being that the creation myth of the Bible is history. Creationists and their supporters, presently, are demanding equal time in the science classes of our schools, and incredibly, this is what some politicians, including President George W. Bush, want to give them. Many people believe in creationism and are honest and sincere in their beliefs. However, those who are making money from the "creation revolution" through books and lectures are, for the most part, nothing more than con artists preying upon an uninformed and gullible public.

People want to believe that the Bible is the inspired word of God, and this includes the Old Testament. It is this heartfelt desire that makes these people easy fodder for the "creation con job" because they want to believe so strongly in what they are told. Unfortunately, for the rest of us, these confused and misguided people are a voting block that Republicans are all too willing to exploit. The tragedy for the rest of us is that the union of misguided citizens with con artists and self-serving politicians is gaining ground such that superstition may one day be taught on par with science in the classrooms of this nation. When this happens, we truly will be raising a generation of children who do not know how to think and will believe anything they are told no matter how absurd it is. In other words, our schools will be producing perfect citizens for the grand designs of the New World Order.

Authors Statement

The United States of America became the greatest nation in history because of its Christian beginnings combined with a reverence for logic, reason, science, and the arts. Nowhere is this more exemplified than in the likes of Thomas Jefferson, Benjamin Franklin, Thomas Edison, Alexander Graham Bell, the Wright

Brothers, etc. This being the case, it is truly mind-boggling that we have fallen so far so fast. As a nation, not only do we no longer have any respect for logic, reason, and science, we now have a great many citizens who give credence to an obviously flawed and ridiculous theory like intelligent design. Not only is intelligent design not intelligent, it is an absurd and ridiculous travesty perpetuated by those who have no idea what they are talking about. What is most disturbing about all of this is that these charlatans and those who fall under their spell could care less about the implications of their doings. In their minds, God and the Bible have been proven, and this is all that matters even though this isn't true.

APPENDIX D7
Abortion and the Republicans

July 2008

The United States of America used to be a nation with a bedrock principle of the separation of church and state. The founders enshrined this principle in our Constitution because early Americans, especially those who fled Europe to escape religious persecution, abhorred the thought of a federal government that mixed governing and religion. Despite the fact that they were for the most part pious and religious men, the founders believed that when men come together to write laws to govern men, religious belief should be put aside, and logic and reason should be the basis of civil and criminal law.

A constitution is an agreement between men as to what kind of government and laws they will live under. Religious dogma is a set of rules and values that a person believes will enable him or her to find favor with God. The two do not mix together very well, and when one group of people becomes organized enough to establish their religious dogma as the law of the land, then many other people are forced to live their lives in a manner not in keeping with their own beliefs. This situation constitutes tyranny. The founders understood this, and so did most Americans throughout our history. However, things have changed. We now live in a nation where politicians proudly proclaim that religion plays a role in how they vote. President George W. Bush's faith-based initiative funneled billions of dollars of borrowed money yearly to various religious groups, and a political party has been formed, calling itself the Constitution Party whose bylaws, incredibly, specify that being a Christian is a condition of membership.

What happened? What happened is *Roe v. Wade*, where the Supreme Court ruled that women have the right to make decisions that affect their own bodies and that no one, not even the state, should interfere with a woman's decision in this regard. In other words, what happened is that *Roe v. Wade* legalized abortion.

Religious fundamentalism is a mode of thought subscribed to by people who think that their beliefs about God and religion are the only true and acceptable ones, and that to believe otherwise brings you into disfavor with God. Therefore, religious fundamentalists, more than any other group of people, are prone to legislating their religious beliefs. In the past, the First Amendment created what Thomas Jefferson described as a wall of separation between church and state, and this wall served to keep the tendencies of religious fundamentalists in check. However, the *Roe v. Wade* decision turned out to be the crack in this wall that fundamentalists had been waiting for. Abortion is the termination of human life, and to a fundamentalist and many other people, this constitutes murder.

Abortion is murder, or so many people believe, and because it is murder, it is the obligation and duty of every God-fearing Christian to rise and wrest control of our government from the godless sinners who have taken over and steered it away from its Christian roots against the will of our founding fathers. This is the mantra of the Christian political movement in the United States today, and unfortunately for the rest of us, the Republican Party has heard this mantra and embraced it as their own. Indeed, every Republican presidential candidate running today, with the exception of Rudy Giuliani, is pro-life, and Republican presidents have been stacking the deck in our Supreme Court so that *Roe v. Wade* will eventually be reversed. This being the case, as Americans, we should step back and discern what is really going on and ask if this is best for America and its people.

A legitimate government governs by the consent of the governed, and its constitution is nothing more than a formal agreement among citizens as to how they wish to be governed. Therefore, in a pluralistic society, religion should play no role in determining what is in its constitution and how its government governs. For example, assume that your religion forbids you to eat meat on Friday. On the other hand, my religion prohibits eating meat on Wednesdays. If your religion is the majority and establishes a law that no meat can be eaten on Friday, then by law, I am forced to respect and practice your religious belief while you can legally ignore mine. This is not fair and is the very essence of tyranny. This example illustrates the case for the separation of church and state, and this is why the founders, who valued freedom and liberty so highly, enshrined this governing principle within our Constitution. In a just and tolerant society, people should be able to live by their own beliefs without interference or coercion from government.

The fifth commandment admonishes us not to kill, and indeed, murder is a heinous crime that is outlawed throughout the land. However, it is not outlawed in deference to the fifth commandment as religious fundamentalists would have us believe. Instead, murder is against the law because you and I agree not to murder each other, and more importantly, we further agree that our government should have the authority to apprehend and punish anyone who murders. This has nothing to do with God and the Bible. True, murder is also an offense against God, but nowhere in the Bible does God authorize us to be his avenger. Vengeance is mine, sayeth the Lord, and to avenge murder with murder or any other kind of punishment is an affront to God. On the other hand, as men, we agree that our government should punish those who kill as a deterrent to murder. An added benefit of doing this is that we personally avoid the wrath of God by having the state violate God's fifth commandment instead of us.

There you have it. The fundamentalists, in their quest for political power, have it all wrong. The basis of law in America is not the Bible or Christianity as they posture and would have us believe. Instead, as the founding fathers believed, reason and common sense should be the basis of our laws. To codify God's law into man's is not only bad government, it is bad religion because it turns issues that are a matter of conscience into ones that are enforced by the state through the barrel of a gun. America is not a *godless nation* because our government has removed religious practice and belief from public life; it is a godless nation because those who lead us have turned away from God as human beings. The surest manifestation of this is the deceptive farce our government has become. Lying and deceit are routine practices among those we elect to serve, and such things are the mark of Satan, not God. Another clear example of

241

godlessness in government is the plethora of misguided congressmen who think they have the moral authority to decide matters of faith and conscience for everyone else. Not only is this un-American, it is un-Christian as well.

Let's summarize where we are. It is wrong to kill for two reasons: because God says so and because of the golden rule. You and I do not wish to be killed, so we agree that killing should be against the law. However, to outlaw murder and punish those who kill because of the fifth commandment offends God and is repugnant to him. God wants us to come to him of our own free will, and the very essence of tyranny is when one religious group becomes dominant and legislates how other people should live their lives. Jesus Christ would never approve of doing such things. He has far more respect and love for humankind than that.

Understanding all of the above, we have arrived at the central point of this essay: abortion, beyond question, is the termination of human life, but is it murder and should it be outlawed as such? This is not an easy question to answer, and its complexity is what is being exploited by religious fundamentalists to wrongfully breach our wall between church and state. The problem focuses upon the difference between human life and a human being. Fundamentalists do not make any distinctions in this regard. There is no doubt that abortion is an abomination to God, and that those who have an abortion have sinned before him. However, for all the reasons previously discussed, this does not give a legislator license to ban abortion. Abortion should be outlawed only if doing so makes sense from a humanistic and rational point of view.

A fetus is a human life, but it is not a human being. It is only a potential human being. Surely, from a logical and scientific point of view, a fertilized egg is not the same thing as you or me. Early on, it cannot think, talk, move, breathe, eat, or do anything that we associate with being a viable living person. Granted, as time goes on the fetus takes on more and more attributes of a human being, but it really does not fully become one until it is removed from the womb and begins its walk-through life as an independent person. This being the case, it is very easy to understand why some people would hold that the termination of a pregnancy is not murder even though many other people believe otherwise. The facts are clear in this matter. Early on in a pregnancy, several hundred cells in the womb, even though they have the potential of growing into a human being, scientifically, they are not much different from any other tumor or cancerous growth. Therefore, their removal is not murder. These are the facts, and no amount of pompous posturing or references to the Bible can change these facts.

Man is created in the image of God. The Christian God is three entities: the Father, the Son, and the Holy Spirit. A human being, similar to God, is also three things: mind, body, and soul. If you take away any of these three things, a person no longer exists. Therefore, the destruction of a body without a mind cannot be and is not murder. We substantiate this truth every time life support is withdrawn from a brain-dead individual so as to allow them to die naturally. Using this same line of reasoning, the destruction of a fetus without a functioning brain cannot be murder either, even though the cells that are terminated, if left alone, would eventually develop a functioning brain. The potential to have a brain is not the same as having one, and it is wrong to convict someone of murder for stopping something that may eventually happen but hasn't yet.

Similarly, if the soul is a necessary component of a human being, as Christians believe, then from a Christian point of view, the termination of a living organism with no soul is not murder. Therefore, as Christians, the question that must be answered before we are justified in declaring that the destruction of a fetus is murder is at what point in the development of a fetus does God provide a fetus with a soul? No one knows the answer to this question, and nowhere is this addressed in the Bible. A soul may be present at conception, but it is just as reasonable to believe that a soul enters the body at first breath. Fundamentalists choose to believe God gives a fetus a soul at conception, but there is no biblical or scientific basis for their belief, and what they believe is simply a matter of personal choice.

Therefore, it should be clear that a good Christian can believe that abortion, while being morally wrong, is not murder and should not be against the law for this reason. Fundamentalists, on the other hand, without any rational or biblical support for what they believe, choose to believe that abortion is murder and, far worse, are self-righteously and wrongfully trying to force their beliefs upon everyone else through the power of the state. They have made a personal choice as to what they believe and having made this choice, they want to deny the right to make this choice to everyone else. This is tyranny! The fundamentalists call themselves pro-life. What they really are is pro at making everyone else abide by their religious beliefs and having the state throw people in jail who do not.

Irrespective of religious or moral issues, *Roe v. Wade* was a realistic and practical ruling by our Supreme Court. First of all, it recognized the difference between a fetus and a human being. By doing so, it acknowledged that it was a matter of individual choice as to whether or not the termination of a pregnancy constituted murder. Some people believe it does, while many others do not. Once this difference was acknowledged, the practical aspects of the situation came into the equation. Women were going to have abortions whether they were legal or not, and the carnage and misery associated with illegal abortions was a reprehensible blot on society. Furthermore, the courts recognized that forcing a woman to bring unwanted children into the world was not good for the mother, the child, or society in general.

Therefore, because women were going to have abortions whether they were legal or not, because illegal abortions were dangerous and nefarious affairs, because forcing a woman to raise a child she does not want is morally wrong, because forcing a child to live in a home where it is not wanted is harmful to the child, and because classifying the termination of a pregnancy as murder is an opinion unsupportable by reason or science, the Supreme Court ruled that government should stay out of the womb, and the decision as to whether or not to terminate a pregnancy was a woman's alone.

This ruling, if you pardon the expression, reflected the wisdom of Solomon and was in keeping with our principles of freedom and individual rights, but this was not good enough for the religious right. Abortion is murder because they say it is, and because it is murder, tearing down the walls of the separation of church and state and forcing their personal beliefs on everyone else through the power of the state is not only justified but God's will. They think they know

God, and they think they know God's will, and by God, if you are going to violate God's will as they know it, then in God's name they will use the power of the state to throw you in jail. Nothing is more reprehensible than this kind of thinking.

One of God's greatest gifts is our free will, and how we exercise our free will is his basis for judging us. Therefore, it is wrong for one man to force another to act in accordance with God's will through the barrel of a gun. This kind of power and authority resides with the state alone, and for anyone or any group of people to use the power of the state to enforce God's will is wrong. Jesus lived during a time when slavery was an accepted practice, and people were being thrown to the lions for sport and amusement. He never once spoke out against these practices. Why? Because how you died and the particular circumstances of your life are unimportant to him. Jesus only cared about what was in your heart and your relationship with God. Above all other things, Jesus taught tolerance and love. When the crowd was about to stone the adulteress, he admonished them and sent them away. He didn't tell them to throw down their stones and take her to prison. He also didn't tell the adulteress that God would punish her for her sins. Instead, he forgave her and told her to go and sin no more.

It should be clear at this point that believing that abortion is murder has no basis in reason, scientific fact, or religion. It should also be clear that those who choose to believe that abortion is murder are hard at work to ensure that their beliefs are forced upon everyone else through the power of the state. In the past, our Constitution and Supreme Court protected us from this kind of religious tyranny, but unfortunately for this nation and its people, the Republicans, for the sake of garnering votes, are not only catering to the religious right but have joined forces with them to reverse *Roe v. Wade*.

The Republicans should know better. As the namesake party of our republic, more than any other group of people, they should be protecting our rights under the Constitution. But no, they have chosen the low road, not the high. Being in power is more important to them than our rights and our Constitution. To please the religious right and garner their votes, they have embraced this un-American, un-Christian, and wrongful way of thinking about abortion and by so doing have forsaken their conservative values, forsaken our Constitution, and forsaken the people they are sworn to serve.

APPENDIX D8
Gay Marriage

May 2002

As if life in America today is not bad enough, of all things, we are now being subjected to a war between the religious right and gays over whether or not the institution of marriage for gays and lesbians should be recognized under the laws of this nation. Unfortunately, for those of us who prefer to walk in the middle of the road because this issue is now appearing as a constitutional amendment in many elections throughout the nation, we are forced to choose between one side or the other. As fate would have it, because of the gender differences between the two kinds of marriage and the fact that there are more heterosexuals around than lesbians and homosexuals combined, in California, Florida, and Arizona, the religious right won at the ballot box, and this perpetuated a strong backlash from the gay and lesbian communities. The battle lines are drawn, people are flocking to the barricades, and voices of reason are being shouted down by both sides. What's a citizen to do? What would Jesus do?

These are difficult questions to answer because the issue boils down to semantics. No one, except the very far right, argues that gays and lesbians should not have equal rights under the law and should not be allowed to enter into what is known as civil unions. The problem is that gays want a civil union to be called a marriage under the law. In opposition, the religious right believes that the term *marriage*, under the law, should be reserved exclusively for heterosexual unions. To gays, the issue is one of civil rights and equal treatment under the law, and to the religious right, the issue is one of protecting the institution of marriage. This is where the worm turns. By voting to restrict the use of the word *marriage* to heterosexual relationships, Americans believe they are not being anti-gay but instead are protecting an institution that is the backbone of our society.

Before proceeding, it is necessary to clear the air. From my perspective, proponents of both sides of this issue are placing far too much importance on what they believe to be true. If everything available under the law to heterosexuals is also available to gays, and the only exception to this is the name we assign to their particular kind of union, then with the exception of this restriction, they are being treated equally under the law. However, forcing the issue by not allowing gays the right to call their unions a marriage is significant and boils down to the discredited separate but equal argument used by southerners to keep blacks in place during the first part of this past century. You're equal, but you are not equal enough to use the word *marriage* to describe your relationships, and we are going to use the law to see that you don't.

On the other side of the coin, if the law permits gays to call their union a marriage, contrary to the posturing of Christian ministers and clergy, it is no threat to the institution of marriage. The words used to describe things can never be a threat to the thing being described because there is no causal relationship whatsoever between a thing and its name. The connection between something and its name is in our minds only, and it is absurd to hold that if gays are allowed to call their unions a marriage, then heterosexual couples will not want to get married anymore. This argument implies that gay unions are so contemptuous that they will spoil the name marriage such that heterosexuals will not only refuse to use it but will shun the institution itself. This is absurd!

What would Jesus say? Jesus would hold that homosexual and lesbian acts are sinful. Having settled this, it is important to realize what Jesus would say is not pertinent to the issue at hand. The pertinent question is, what would Jesus do? Jesus taught tolerance in all things, and in keeping with this, it is reasonable to conclude that he would not condone or sanction a group of narrow-minded individuals changing a constitution so as to deny a particular group of his children the right to use whatever name they wish for their unions. Furthermore, Jesus would condemn the unmitigated gall of people who use the power of the state to tell other people how to live their lives even if the people in question are living in sin. Morality is not an acceptable basis for law, and codifying morality into law offends God. Furthermore, doing this is not only un-American, it is un-Christian as well. When will Fundamentalist Christians learn that Jesus endorsed the separation of church and state when he said, render unto Caesar what is Caesar's and to render unto God what is God's? Morality is the province of God, and civil law, which is enforced through the barrel of a gun, has no place in the kingdom of God. We live moral lives because we love God, not because some cretin with a gun says we should.

A constitution is a document that establishes government, delineates how it will function, and enumerates the various rights and privileges of citizens, which government should not infringe upon. In no way, shape, or form is a constitution supposed to tell citizens how to behave or what they should and should not do. To include such provisions in a constitution is a perversion of the document and sets a dangerous precedent, whereby the majority is able to tyrannize the minority. Furthermore, no constitution worth the paper it is written on will permit legislators to enact laws such that one group of people have the right to use a particular word under the law while another does not. To think otherwise is absurd. How can such a hypocritical state of affairs be justified from a legal or rational point of view? Doing so legislates that one group of people is superior to a different group of people, and the thing that establishes superiority is superiority in numbers. How would heterosexuals feel if gays became the majority and turned the tables by voting to reserve the word *marriage* exclusively for same-sex unions? The bottom line is that tyranny should never be tolerated under the law, even if the tyranny is against gays, because whether you realize it or not, tyranny against gays is tyranny against all of us.

No government or group of people has a right to force their conceptions of morality on others. If you believe that homosexuality and lesbianism are sins, you have a right to not engage in these activities. However, you do not have a right to tell others to live like you, and even more importantly, you do not have the right to ask our government to do this for you. Obviously, the circumstances are such in America today that this wrongful state of affairs has been established, not just under the law, but within state constitutions as well. You can rest assured that God condemns these actions because they usurp his authority and because his plan is to have us live free of tyranny and compulsion. As Christians, our lot in life is to love each other and be tolerant. And yes, this extends to gays and lesbians. Like us, they are God's children, and to demonize them is wrong and sinful.

APPENDIX E1
I'm Just a Dumb Arab

December 2004

My name is Ahmed and I am nineteen years old. I was raised and used to live in the village of Bhareem, a short drive East of Baghdad. I am just a dumb Arab, not dumb because I am not smart, but dumb because I have no education and know little of the world beyond where I used to live. That has all changed, but I am now getting ahead of my story.

Saddam Hussein was president of Iraq when I was growing up. I knew little of him, but most people in my village thought he was a bad man. However, one man named Jamel, who lived nearby thought he was a good president. Jamel did not get along with my family or our neighbors. Most people were afraid of Jamel and thought he was crazy, but my father did not fear him and once had strong words with him. Because of this, Jamel hated my father and swore he would get even with him. We avoided Jamel as best we could and went on with our lives.

One day, the village elders told us that the Americans were coming to destroy Saddam Hussein and take over our country. At first, I did not believe this. How could this be true? Americans do not take over other countries, and what did they need Iraq for? Some people said the Americans wanted to avenge Saddam's attack on Kuwait, and others thought they wanted to steal our oil. Either way, I did not care. I had no use for Saddam Hussein, and the oil beneath our feet does nothing to ease the emptiness in my belly or feed the animals I tend in the fields.

One day, an officer from Saddam's army came into our town to recruit young men to fight against the Americans. He told us that the Americans were coming soon and would begin their offensive by bombing Baghdad in an air raid called Shock and Awe. I asked this officer why the Americans wanted to shock and awe the Iraqi people.

He said that by bombing us, they hoped we would be afraid so they could have their way with us. They wanted to take everything we had, rape our women, and turn us into slaves. I did not believe this man, and when I saw my chance, I hid in the fields until he left.

Three days later, the bombs started falling on Baghdad, and I could not believe the news. Could the Iraqi army officer have been telling the truth? At this point, I was very confused and afraid. How could the Americans be attacking my country? Two days after the bombing started, my family learned that my cousin Ishmal and his parents, who lived in Baghdad, were killed by an American bomb. I loved my cousin, and his death turned my confusion into anger. When the Americans came, I would fight them any way I could.

A day or so later, some Iraqi troops came back into our village. This time, they gave guns to the men and told us that we must slow the American advance on Baghdad. Saddam and his army needed time to prepare their defenses, and we would buy them that time. Despite my feelings about Saddam, I accepted a weapon knowing that as a citizen of Iraq, it was my duty to defend my nation and its people despite the hopelessness of the situation I was in.

Several of us took up positions outside our village and waited for the Americans to arrive. We didn't have to wait long. At first, all we could see was the dust of their vehicles on the road, but soon their monstrous machines came into view. Frightened out of our wits, we began to fire in the direction of the Americans, and suddenly there was a tremendous noise. That is the last thing I remember of the Iraq I knew.

When I awoke, my hands were tied behind my back, and I had a sack over my head. I soon realized that I was not alone, and I was in a room with several other prisoners. I lay on the ground for hours on end and was sure that I would soon be killed. After what seemed like an eternity, two men brought me to my feet and dragged me into an interrogation room. My hood was removed, and I gazed into the face of an American for the first time in my life. In the course of my interrogation, I learned that a man from my village had told them that I was an al-Qaeda operative and that the only way I could save myself was to tell them everything I knew. Apparently, Jamel had finally made good his boast.

My interrogation went on for several days. I was threatened, beaten, and humiliated, but of course, I could tell the Americans nothing because I knew nothing. One day, I was tied, hooded, and loaded into a truck. I was sure this was the end, and my fate was to be a pile of bones buried under the desert sands. However, despite my fears, I was taken from the trunk and loaded into what turned out to be an airplane. I had never been in an airplane before and wished they would remove my hood so I could see what flying through the air was like. My wishes were in vain, and after many hours, we finally landed and I learned I was in Guantanamo Bay, Cuba.

I have now been in Guantanamo Bay for four years, and the only thing that keeps me going is my hatred for Americans. I have endured the worst kind of inhumane treatment, and now know that Americans are no better than animals. I have no idea if anyone from my family is still alive and, in four years, have not heard anything about them. In order to survive, I have learned to play up to my captors and do so while thinking I would like nothing better than to slit their throats while they sleep. However, I know that if I behave, someday I may be released, and when that time comes, I will take my revenge. My only wish is to kill as many Americans as I can before I die, and I know that Allah will reward me greatly if I do. Each day I turn to Mecca, fall down on my knees, and pray that soon the whole world will know that the only good American is a dead American.

Authors Comment

The story above is a fabrication and not true. However, while the facts are contrived, the situation described, or something similar, has been experienced by untold numbers of young Arabs throughout the Middle East. And we self-servingly call these young men and women terrorists, even though in a different time and place, they would be called patriots and freedom fighters. The tragedies being experienced by these unfortunate people are a direct result of the way our war on terrorism is being fought and prosecuted. But no matter, if we win our war, no one, save a few relatives and friends, will mourn the passing of these innocents, and we will be able to celebrate a great victory over the "forces of evil."

As an American and Christian, I do not feel like most of my fellow citizens. I do not believe that "shocking and awing" a downtrodden and defenseless people is the way to fight terrorism or avenge 9/11. I also grieve and abhor the fact that my government has brought murder, mayhem, and terrorism to defenseless and innocent people just because they were the easiest target available.

We are told the cost is worth it because we are bringing democracy to Iraq, but we fail to ask ourselves what good democracy is to a dead person. We are told we must win the war we started because if we do not, the terrorists will rule the day, and we never ask ourselves, what good can come out of winning a war against terrorism if we become terrorists to do it? We also never ask how we can defeat terrorism when, by fighting a conventional war against it, we create more terrorists than we destroy. We are told we must continue the war so those who have died will not have died in vain and never ask how more deaths in an unjust and wrongful war can bring honor to those who have already died. As Americans, have we truly come to believe that might makes right and winning an unjust war will make fighting one honorable?

I am an American. I love my nation and its people, and yes, I place our safety and well being ahead of all others. However, in my eyes, what we are doing to the world is not in our best interest and is against everything we hold dear as Americans. We have become what we hate the most—oppressive tyrants trying to mold the world to our liking, not to make Americans and America safer, but to make others just like us so we think we are safer. I am ashamed of what our government is doing to the rest of the world, and I am ashamed that so many Americans think what we are doing is in our best interest. These notions are not just wrong; they are ill-conceived, perverted, bankrupt, and criminal. May God have mercy on this nation and the people in it that support a government that is now pursuing a course that is not just un-American but the epitome of evil.

APPENDIX E2
Lest We Forget

January 2006

It is difficult to remember important things these days because the media outlets of this nation, similar to those within the Soviet Union under Communism, bend so far over to be politically correct that they actually distort the news and create erroneous impressions in the minds of Americans. Nowhere is this truer than when discussing the seeds of our invasion of Iraq. This adherence to political correctness has progressed to such a degree that one is justified in wondering if the government and the media have entered into an unholy alliance to deceive the American people and keep them as ignorant as possible about important governmental issues.

Of late, it has become common knowledge that we are not winning the war in Iraq. Therefore, starting this war was a grave mistake, and someone or something is responsible for this mistake. If someone is responsible, then justice demands that we should hold that person accountable. If something is responsible, then steps should be taken to ensure that whatever happened never happens again. According to our government and everything we hear from the mainstream media today, "someone" is not responsible, but instead "something" is, and that something is euphemistically called faulty intelligence.

The label "faulty intelligence" is misleading and deceptive because the information available about Iraq prior to our invasion was not faulty. Any reasonably intelligent and unbiased individual surveying this information would conclude that Iraq had no weapons of mass destruction and had no capability of developing any in the foreseeable future. Furthermore, it was also known throughout the intelligence community that Saddam Hussein was not supporting terrorists or supplying them with military equipment. In other words, the intelligence we possessed about Iraq prior to our invasion was sufficient to conclude that an invasion was unwarranted and ill-advised.

Why did we invade? We invaded Iraq because President George W. Bush wrongfully thought that by so doing, he was defending this nation and its people. While these intentions are honorable, the truth of the matter is that the only thing faulty about the intelligence President Bush used to justify his invasion was the way he used and presented it to Congress to get their approval for an invasion. In other words, President Bush and his cronies "cooked the books" on intelligence. As a result, they deliberately lied to Congress, deliberately lied to the American people, and deliberately lied to the rest of the world. It was these lies that brought this nation to war, and the reason President Bush lied was because he thought lying for a good cause was the right thing to do.

Therein is the tragedy of George W. Bush. He was wrong because he lied about such an important issue, and he was wrong because he thought that a president should defend this nation and its people through lies. From this, it should be clear that President Bush is an amoral and grievously flawed human being who thinks one can accomplish good by doing evil. Like a Communist, he subscribes to the notion that the ends justify the means. He wants to save and protect America, and he thinks his honorable intentions give him the license and moral authority to condone or commit any action no matter how despicable or immoral.

We see validation of the above in President Bush's nefarious invasion of Iraq, his despicable condoning of torturing prisoners of war, and in his unconscionable destruction of the human rights granted to us by God and protected by our Constitution. The tragedy of George W. Bush, which is now *our* tragedy, is his inability to realize that his beliefs and actions are destroying America. Because George Bush is destroying the values and principles upon which this nation is based. Therefore, he is our worst enemy, an enemy far more sinister and despicable than Osama Bin Laden.

Our wrongful invasion of Iraq for contrived and surreptitious reasons was a criminal act that will not be absolved by simply withdrawing our troops from that nation. Far too many innocent people, on both sides of the conflict, have died because of the misdeeds of our president and his cronies. Upon withdrawing from Iraq, a thorough and complete investigation of this entire affair, followed by appropriate constitutional and criminal proceedings, is warranted. Anything less will not restore the honor we have lost nor cleanse the blood that now stains the hands of all of us.

To those of you who say such action is absurd and unwarranted, I ask you, if bringing the nation to war on lies and thereby causing the unnecessary, unjustifiable, and wrongful death of thousands upon thousands of innocent people, including those of our finest young men and women in the military, is not an impeachable offense and a prosecutable criminal act? What acts committed by a sitting president are impeachable and prosecutable? I sincerely hope you respond to this question because I am at a loss to think of any.

And while you are thinking about an answer to the above question, also consider this. If we do not impeach and hold George Bush accountable under our criminal justice system, what deterrence is in place to dissuade some other mentally challenged individual provided to us as presidential fodder by global financial interests from doing the same or similar things? Isn't a government with checks and balances supposed to cleanse itself of bad apples or at least set the precedent that such behavior from a sitting president is unacceptable and will not escape legal censure and condemnation? Apparently, the government we have is no longer capable of doing the right thing or taking steps to rectify its mistakes. This being the case, we are on a slippery slope, and we have nothing to stop or slow our slide into depravity.

APPENDIX E3
A New Year's Perspective

January 2005

We stare at our televisions in horror and disbelief at the destruction and death caused by the recent tsunamis in the Indian Ocean and rightfully so. When over one-hundred thousand people die in a natural disaster, only the most hardened and uncaring would not be moved by such a tragedy. Indeed, the outpouring of sympathy and assistance from the rest of the world is testimony that people care and will go to great lengths to help each other in times of need.

We also stare at our televisions and watch our war unfolding in Iraq. Over one hundred thousand people have died there also, but what is our reaction to this tragedy? Certainly not horror and disbelief! We are used to death by war and view these deaths as justified and necessary despite the fact that most of those killed were just as innocent and just as blameless as those whose lives were snuffed out by the forces of nature.

We truly are strange animals. We feel great sorrow when our kind dies by accident and are indifferent when people die because of ignorance and stupidity. We view the twisted and broken bodies of those killed by tidal waves and fault God for letting such a tragedy happen. We then look to Iraq and ask God to bless our war even though it results in the same twisted and broken bodies. Being the hypocrites we are, we never stop to think that by petitioning God to bless our hypocrisy, we make a fool of Him.

APPENDIX E4
Torture Is Nice

February 2010

During the last Republican presidential debate, Republicans were asked, if a nuclear device had been detonated somewhere in the United States and more attacks were planned, would you use torture to get information, which may prevent future attacks? In other words, the moderator wanted to know if torture was an acceptable option when it came to the possibility of saving the lives of Americans. This is an interesting question because in past wars, despite the carnage and toll on human life, Americans overwhelmingly held that torture was wrong under any circumstances. However, today, as was made evident by congressman Tom Tancredo's much applauded reply, many Americans now condone torture if it will save American lives. What has changed?

Several things! First and foremost, 9/11 happened, and three thousand Americans were killed in less than an hour's time on prime-time television with the entire nation watching. Second, the technology to make small nuclear devices is now available to third-world nations, increasing the possibility of one falling into the hands of a terrorist organization. Finally, our government has already made the decision to use torture to protect Americans, and many people hold that if our government does it, it must be okay. In other words, there are two elements at play that have made torture acceptable to Americans: fear and the fact that our government has already resorted to torturing suspected terrorists. To be sure, it is the fear of a nuclear terrorist attack that is being nurtured and stroked by our government to justify its use of torture. Furthermore, it is also being used to justify preemptive war and the trashing of the inalienable rights of people, both foreign and domestic.

Congressman Tom Tancredo summed it up best when he said, "It is almost unbelievable to listen to this: a nuclear device has gone off, more are planned, and we are wondering if waterboarding [torture] is a bad thing to do. Under these circumstances, anything we can think of doing, including torture, is permissible. We are the last, best hope of Western Civilization. When we go under, western civilization goes under. We better respond in a way that makes them [terrorists] fearful of us, otherwise, we guarantee something like this will happen." Upon concluding these statements, the applause was deafening. However, the great irony of the situation, apparently lost upon Congressman Tancredo and those applauding, was that by resorting to torture, even under the circumstances described, Western civilization has already gone under, and instead of being its last hope, we have become its murderer.

Although the hypothetical question asked during the Republican debate is appropriate to the times, there are grave implications associated with its asking, which must be considered. If citizens condone evil (i.e., torture) on the part of our government to save American lives, even in a hypothetical manner, then Pandora's box has been opened, and the evil we only accepted hypothetically, becomes real because our government will act upon the license we gave it. The thinking of government officials proceeds as follows: if citizens condone the use of torture to protect them from a nuclear attack, and if terrorists had a nuclear weapon, they would certainly use it to attack us. Then it logically follows that citizens condone torturing terrorists or people who we think are terrorists. This is where we inevitably end up! Torture has become a legitimate tool of government, and this is no longer hypothetical. Not so, you say! Then why are we torturing people in Iraq as a part of our war on terror? The truly regrettable and despicable aspect of this line of reasoning and its inevitable course of action is that we have become what we despise most, and to posture that this transformation leaves us as the last hope of Western civilization is ludicrous. No person or group of people who torture is civilized, and this is true no matter how we rationalize our decision to use torture.

Congressman Tancredo's views in this matter not only speak for right-wing conservatives, but most fundamentalist Christians as well, and this being the case, a fair question to ask is, what would Jesus say? If Jesus were here today and we asked him if we should torture other people to prevent a nuclear attack on the United States, do you as a Christian really think in your wildest dreams that Jesus would say, "Sure, that is the best course of action and our Father in heaven would approve"? I am sure that if you are really honest with yourself, you would have to admit that the response Jesus would most likely give is that it is wrong to fight evil with evil, and if you do, you will be condemned. This being the case, why do the so-called right-wing conservatives and their fundamentalist Christian allies condone torture? They do so because fear is a powerful motivator, and it is fear that clouds their thinking and makes them choose the low road instead of the high.

Author's Statement

I am a Christian. Death is not a comfortable thought, but I do not fear death because by believing in Jesus Christ, I have been promised eternal life. I am also an American. Being American, whatever our government does is done in my name. As a Christian and an American, I deeply resent the fact that fear-mongering is now a legitimate tool of my government and is being used to justify acts that are illegal, immoral, and evil.

APPENDIX E5
War as a Terrorism Tool

September 2009

During World War II, the Nazis, in retribution for the death of one of their soldiers or officers by resistance operatives, would arbitrarily murder twenty or so citizens of the offending town or village, irrespective of whether or not these people were guilty of any action against the Nazis or not. Their thinking was that it was the civilian population who hid and harbored members of the resistance. Therefore, it was the civilian population that should bear the consequences of resistance to wartime actions. The Geneva convention has condemned such action as being barbaric and beyond the bounds of civilized warfare.

On September 11, 2001, terrorists destroyed the World Trade Center (WTC) in New York City. In response, the United States invaded the nation of Iraq even though it was known at the time that Iraq played no role in the WTC disaster and had no ties to any terrorist organization or group. Similarly, with the backing and complicity of the United States, in response to the actions of Hezbollah, Israel has chosen to rain death and destruction upon the civilian population of Lebanon, the nation where Hezbollah unfortunately resides.

It is clear that both the United States and Israel want to send a clear message to terrorists that there will be serious consequences for their nefarious and deplorable actions. The problem is that in both situations cited above, because of how this message is being sent, it is innocent civilians, men, women, and children by the hundreds and thousands, who are bearing the consequences of our actions. In other words, to fight terrorism, the United States and Israel have, without conscience or regard for human life, deliberately brought death and destruction to innocent civilian populations. This being the case, how much different are we from the Nazis we condemned in 1945, and how much different are we from the terrorists we despise? I guess nothing has changed in thousands of years of human development; we fight wars to end wars, and we terrorize innocent people to fight terrorism.

If a group of homegrown terrorists in Brooklyn fired rockets into the borough of Manhattan, would the appropriate response be for the United States to indiscriminately bomb targets in Brooklyn? Of course not, such action would be considered insane and criminal. Well, it is just as criminal and ludicrous to attack Iraq and Lebanon as has been done by the United States and Israel. Terrorism is a terrible thing because it makes victims of innocent people. How many innocent people are victims of how Israel and the United States fight the war on terror? If numbers count, then the terrorists are small potatoes compared to us.

APPENDIX F1
Our Environment

August 2000

I am an environmentalist and use this label with reluctance because these days, being one is not politically correct, and to the average American, environmentalists are, at best, somewhat out of touch with reality and, at worst, left-wing socialist nut jobs. To be sure, the political right views environmental issues as red herrings that are being used to impose a socialistic agenda on a free and independent America. Unfortunately, nothing could be further from the truth. Many environmental concerns are not only legitimate but are serious issues that we ignore at our peril.

Our problem, or more appropriately, the situation that keeps us from realizing the nature of our problem, is that we are victims of our past. For man's entire existence on planet earth, he has been free to do as he pleases without regard to the consequences. Humankind could indiscriminately use what was found in nature, transform it into anything desired without noticeable consequence, and discard anything without concern for the impact that this would have on our environment.

As recently as fifty years ago, industrial corporate stock certificates pictured factories with billowing smokestacks because a smoking chimney was a sign of wealth and prosperity. The accepted panacea of the day for poisonous waste was, "Dilution is the solution to pollution." In other words, whatever we wanted to dispose of could be dumped into a river or lake where it would disappear into the environment and no longer be a problem.

We have come a long way from those days, but unfortunately, we have not come far enough. Many people are now sensitized to the need to keep our environment clean, and certainly, there are now many laws in existence to ensure this is the case, but these laws are a Band-Aid on a severed artery. They make us feel better and enable us to think we are doing something to solve the problem, but we are not. The truth of the matter is that we still behave like the world will supply us with an endless flow of raw materials and that it has the capability to absorb an endless flow of waste and pollutants. Only a fool thinks this is the case, but while we pay lip service to environmental concerns, we continue to think and act like fools.

Our problem is that we do too much. We take too much out of the ground, and we discard too much into the environment. Therefore, the key to understanding the root cause of our problem is to ask why. The answer to this question is obvious: we do too much because there are too many of us. The root cause of all our environmental problems is not our doings but the fact that we have overpopulated our planet. This being the case, it now must be asked, how serious is the problem? The answer to this question is a matter of intense debate around the globe, but from where I sit, we are in serious trouble, and all that is necessary to see how bad things are is to open our eyes and look at the record. For example,

Population growth—The population of the world is presently 6.2 billion human beings, and for the past fifty years, it has increased more rapidly than ever before in history. At the time of Christ, the world population was about 300 million people. By 2050, the world population is expected to increase another astounding 50 percent and is expected to level off at about 9 billion people.

Mass extinctions—Mankind is presently causing and witnessing the greatest mass extinction event that has ever occurred in the history of life on our planet. If established trends continue, one-half of all the species that presently exist will be gone in the next several decades. This rate of destruction of life is even greater than the mass extinction caused by a giant meteor collision that occurred 65 million years ago and wiped out the dinosaurs. Our present mass extinction is being fueled by human activity that destroys the habitats of plant and animal life.

Rainforest destruction—Rainforests, today, are rapidly disappearing in all areas of the world, and their depletion, without considering anything else, rivals that of the disappearance of the dinosaurs 65 million years ago. Every year, Brazil chops down an area of forest the size of the state of Nebraska. In addition to the disappearance of the Amazon basin rainforest, many other forests are being cut down as well. In Indonesia, Zaire, Papua-New Guinea, Malaysia, Burma, the Philippines, Peru, Colombia, Bolivia, and Venezuela, rainforests are disappearing at an alarming rate, and there is no end in sight to the devastation. The primary reason for rainforest demise is their deliberate destruction to make way for farms that will only be used for several years. After that, the exposed soil is depleted of nutrients and will no longer support crops or other plant life and animal life. The farmers responsible for this crime against nature then move on to do the same thing deeper in the rainforest.

Global warming—Global warming, while still a controversial topic, is being recognized by more and more scientists as a problem that must be dealt with. The evidence in this regard is real, and with each passing day, it becomes clearer and more compelling. Glaciers throughout the world are receding, the Arctic and Antarctic ice packs are disintegrating, global sea levels are rising, world average temperatures are increasing, storms such as hurricanes and cyclones are becoming more numerous and severe, climates are changing, and animals and plant life are shifting their ranges in response to shifts in climate.

Ice cap melting—Ice sheets of our planet are melting at an ever-increasing rate due to global warming and the overall increase in atmospheric temperatures worldwide. Ice sheets spanning thousands of miles in Greenland and Western Antarctica, are presently losing approximately120 cubic-miles of ice yearly. This melting of continental ice has resulted in a worldwide rise in sea levels of 11 millimeters since 1992. While this does not seem like much, the trend is alarming because the melting is happening at an ever-increasing rate. Scientists presently predict a sea level rise of 11 to 18 inches by the year 2100. If these predictions come to pass, rising oceans will wreak havoc on coastal regions of the world where most people live.

Acid rain—Acid rain is caused by airborne pollutants that acidify falling rain with highly destructive results. Among these is the dying off of trees in the world's forests and reduced agricultural production. Scientists first discovered acid rain in 1852, when the English chemist Robert Agnus invented the term. Acid rain, itself, cannot be seen, but its effects are clearly evident. The prime contributors to acid rain are automobile emissions and coal-burning power plants. Almost all industrial activity makes a contribution. Different regions of the world experience different levels of acid rain, however, so many contributing gasses are now being produced that the problem is global and no area of the planet escapes this onslaught.

Solid waste disposal—Human activity produces solid waste, and far too often, this waste is hazardous and dangerous to living things, including man. The levels of hazardous waste are continuing to grow throughout the world, and this is especially true in developing countries. The more advanced a society is, the more hazardous the waste it produces, so as third-world countries industrialize, the hazardous waste they produce increases accordingly. Hazardous waste is cumulative in the environment. Once dumped, it stays where it is for many years, and the world's ecosystems are still being affected by waste discarded many years ago. Adding to this problem is the hazardous waste presently being produced and all that will be produced in future years. Included in this waste are spent fuel rods from nuclear power plants, which will remain lethal for thousands upon thousands of years.

Water pollution—Fourteen billion pounds of solid waste and nineteen trillion gallons of liquid waste are dumped in the oceans of the world each year. The oil spill of the *Exxon Valdez* is a horrible example of this kind of pollution, but what people do not realize is that the total amount of old spilled by the *Exxon Valdez* was only 5 percent of the total amount of oil spilled that year. Ocean pollution affects every nation around the world because water movement disperses pollution to every corner of the globe. Presently, in the center of the Pacific Ocean, there is a huge area where ocean currents concentrate solid waste, and this area looks like a garbage dump. Industrialization is the prime source of water pollution, and as nations become more industrialized, water pollution increases and has a greater impact on fish stocks and the ability of the oceans to support life.

Dead zones—A dead zone is an area in the world's oceans where oxygen depletion causes the death of all living creatures unable to escape from the zone. The size and number of oxygen deprived dead zones throughout the planet have increased steadily since the 1970s, and now they number about 150. Dead zones are a threat to the world's fisheries and to humans who depend on those fisheries for sustenance. They are caused by excesses of nitrogen, which flows into coastal waters from farm runoff, sewage, and emissions from vehicles and factories. In what scientists call a nitrogen cascade, the chemicals pass untreated into our oceans and trigger a proliferation of plankton. In turn, this depletes oxygen in the water. Fish are able to flee from these areas, but slow-moving bottom dwellers like clams, lobsters, and oysters are less able to escape and die. Dead zones can range from less than a square mile in size, but the largest one is now 45 thousand square miles and growing. (Author's note: the size of this immense dead zone, as of today, is 70,000 miles, a 55 percent increase in 15 years' time.)

Red tide—For the past several decades, red tide breakouts have been increasing in number and size all around the globe. Red tide is an explosion of one-celled organisms that form a bloom toxic to fish, mammals, and shellfish. Exposure to red tide has sent humans into coughing fits, and blooms in Florida are known to have killed dolphins and manatees. The cause of red tide blooms, which can come in a multitude of colors, is not known with definitive certainty, but research has shown that sewage and agricultural runoff exacerbate the problem.

Fish stock depletion—Mankind depends upon the oceans to produce a significant amount of the food it eats. Since the 1950s, fish stocks throughout the world have been significantly decreasing, and more and more varieties are being classified as being overexploited or depleted. Currently, only 3 percent of marine stocks are classified as being underexploited while 21 percent are moderately exploited, which means that present fish stocks could support a modest increase in fishing and harvest levels. However, 52 percent are being fished at their maximum biological productivity, and this means they are fully exploited such that increased fishing would reduce future harvest levels. The remaining 24 percent are classified as being overexploited (16 percent), depleted (7 percent), or recovering from depletion (1 percent). Of the top 10 food species of fish, 7 of them are presently fully exploited or overexploited.

Is the human race truly in peril? In light of all of the above, I fail to understand how anyone can conclude that we do not have a problem, especially when one considers the fact that the world's population is expected to increase by 50 percent in the next fifty years, but the situation is far worse than this. All biological systems, irrespective of whether or not we are talking about a lake, a person, a river, a plant, an area of the planet, or the entire planet, carry on life processes that include ingesting material, using it in some manner, and ejecting unwanted byproducts. Biological systems, by their nature, are resilient and have the ability to ingest varying amounts of pollutants or poisons without harm. However, each biological system has a finite capacity in this regard. There are three stages of pollution evident in biological entities: the green or healthy stage, the yellow or cautionary stage, and the red or lethal stage.

In the green stage of pollution, pollutants are introduced into a biological system and are broken down into harmless chemicals and/or expelled by the system's natural cleansing processes. The overriding characteristic of this stage is that pollutants are introduced at a rate where there is no net buildup within the system. The cleansing processes function fast enough to handle the influx of unwanted material.

In the yellow stage of pollution, pollutants are introduced into a biological system at such a rate that the cleansing processes cannot cope with the influx and a backlog of unwanted material begins to accumulate. The overriding characteristic of this stage is that if the rate of ingestion is slowed or stopped, the biological system, of its own accord, will return to the green stage, and no irreversible damage has occurred. However, if the influx continues, then this will drive the biological system into the red stage of pollution.

In the red stage of pollution, the yellow stage has persisted for so long that the resulting buildup of pollutants destroys or alters the biological system's natural cleansing processes. The overriding characteristic of this stage is that permanent damage has been done to the system that is irreversible unless someone or something external to the system takes action. The red pollution stage is critical for a biological system because, without outside intervention, death is assured.

If a person ingests poison, the correct antidote will cure him. If a lake becomes choked with algae and all life in it dies, the algae can be removed, the water treated, and living things reintroduced. These actions will restore the lake to its original vitality. If man acts in a timely manner and takes the proper corrective action, he can save almost all troubled biological systems from destruction. However, what if the biological system we are talking about is the world's oceans, its atmosphere, or the entire planet itself? What will man be able to do to save himself when the entire planet enters the red pollution zone?

No intelligent person with a smattering of knowledge about what is going on in the world today believes that our planet is presently in the green pollution zone. On the other side of the coin, very few people believe our planet is in the red or lethal pollution zone. Therefore, it should be clear that most people would agree that we are in the yellow pollution stage; the real issue is, how close are we to the red stage? I think the answer to this question is that we are too close for comfort and that we should be doing everything possible to reverse the direction we are heading. Furthermore, I also believe that if the population of the world doubles in the next fifty years, as predicted, we are doomed. This being the case, what can we do to save ourselves? It may already be too late to do that, but the only hope we have is to radically change how we think and how we behave. Let's pretend for a moment that this nation has constructed a spaceship to colonize a planet in a distant galaxy, which will take several human lifetimes to reach. The number of people sent on this mission would be limited by the physical space available and the spacecraft's biological ability to sustain its population of interplanetary pilgrims. For survival's sake, the population level of our starship would have to be carefully controlled, and the right to procreate indiscriminately would be suspended. Additional children would only be allowed to replace existing travelers who died. Obviously, these restrictions would be willingly accepted by those brave enough to make such a dangerous journey. If not, those who could not live by such rules would not be allowed to go.

The above scenario is hypothetical, but having landed a man on the moon, the possibility of man colonizing other planets is not something that an educated person of today would judge to be impossible. This being the case, it is self-evident that the number of people on the starship would have to be kept under control so as not to overwhelm the craft's environmental and life-support systems. If this is so easy to understand and accept in regard to our starship, why is it so hard to understand that we are now at a point on this planet where restrictions on procreation are necessary to ensure our survival? We live on an object we call earth, and planet earth, in truth, is nothing more than a spaceship we travel on, not to a far-off planet, but to a questionable and uncertain future.

The huge rock we live on has everything we need to survive, including mechanisms for dealing with pollution. However, there is a finite amount of everything that is here and a limit to how much pollution our world can process. This means that to survive, we have to limit how many of us are on board the rock. Technology and the more efficient utilization of resources may be able to increase the sustainable population limit to some degree, but technology also has its limits, and even if we do everything in the most efficient manner possible, a limit to how many people can live here will always be there. The undeniable truth is that if we allow too many of us to live on the rock, it will lose its capability of supporting us, and we will die. To think this is not the case and that technology will always bail us out is absurd. The real issue, then, is not whether or not the world has a finite capacity to support the doings of man but at what level of population will we reach the point of no return.

Presently, the world's population is six billion people. Industrialized nations use the most resources and produce the most pollution. The United States, with 3 percent of the world's population, presently consumes about 20 percent of its resources. This consumption results in a similar percentage contribution to the pollution of our planet. The world is presently in the yellow pollution stage, and the question is, what stage of pollution will we be in if the other 97 percent of humanity is raised to our standard of living? Is there anyone in their right mind that would hold that this wouldn't put us over the edge?

Scientists have calculated that to be safely in the green pollution zone, with all people enjoying the same standard of living as we have in the United States, the world population should be no more than three billion people. Presently, we are at two times that number and climbing rapidly. How deep into the yellow pollution zone does being three times over a sustainable level of population put us? Indeed, in consideration of these numbers, isn't it more reasonable to wonder if a population level of six billion people has placed us well into the red pollution zone? After all, aren't we already witnessing most other forms of life on our planet dying off? Like a *canary in the mine*, doesn't this tell us something?

Beyond any doubt, we are in the yellow or cautionary pollution zone and moving deeper into it. This being the case, it is imperative that we take action now before it is too late. Indeed, if we are truly rational creatures as we so pride ourselves in being, then the prudent thing to have done was to address the problem when we first passed from the green pollution zone into the yellow one. Granted, no one knows when this occurred, so we did nothing when it happened. However, we now know beyond any doubt that we are over the line. To argue that there is no need for alarm, or that we can forgo addressing the problem until we get a little closer to the red zone, is absurd. But this is what the naysayers would have us do. They argue that there is no need for concern, not all scientists agree with these more "radical assessments," and the best thing to do now is nothing.

In other words, they hold that if we ignore the problem, there is no problem and it will go away.

Recall if you will our starship and the interplanetary pilgrims aboard it. Would any of them be listened to by the others if they argued that they should allow more births because the yellow pollution zone was not really something that they should be concerned about? Of course not! If someone onboard the ship held that it was wise to allow pollutants to continually build up on the starship, they would be judged to be insane. Furthermore, if someone aboard the starship actually became pregnant when they weren't supposed to, that pregnancy would be terminated irrespective of the person's wishes. Doesn't this make sense, and wouldn't this be the way things would be if our starship was a reality? Please understand that I am only making a point here. I do not believe that this draconian action is necessary to save this planet. However, what is necessary is to realize we have a problem and to educate people about what must be done to solve the problem.

We did not act when we entered the yellow pollution zone, not because we shouldn't have, but because no one realized what was happening. We now know what is happening, and this being the case, there are no sound reasons for not taking action. To argue otherwise is lunacy and a death warrant.

APPENDIX F2
Homo sapiens: A FaileD Species

November 2003

Human beings are capable of great and wondrous things. However, we also have a capacity for the vilest and most despicable actions. People are familiar with many of these, but unknown to most of us is that our worst attribute is we are not able to ensure our continued survival as a species. As responsible human beings, we are supposed to pass a better world onto our progeny. Not only will this generation fail in this regard, but the world we will pass on to our children is poised upon the greatest manmade disaster in all history; the collapse of our environment. Most people will take issue with this conclusion, and herein is the crux of the problem. Instead of using logic and reason as an approach to our situation, greed, gullibility, and wishful thinking take over and blind us to the truth. Greed comes into play as the motivating factor for those who wish to continue to plunder the world of its resources. Gullibility factors in when we believe these people when they tell us we have nothing to worry about. The first two attributes fit hand and glove with people who foolishly choose to believe we live in an unchanging world that will go on forever.

In order to become enlightened, or more correctly, in order to become alarmed—the first thing that must be understood is that we live in a finite world with a finite amount of resources that have a limited ability to support and nurture life. True, each year, tons of material are added to our planet from the dust of meteors and comets, but this amount of new material is insignificant in the grand scheme of things. For all intents and purposes, what is here now is all we have, and this will never change. Understanding this, the first and most fundamental truth about our existence on planet earth becomes evident. If the world we live in is finite and its ability to support and nurture life is limited, then a population level or limit exists, which should never be exceeded. Most of us are not capable of understanding this, so I will say it again in a different way: an inescapable truth of the human condition is that we live in a finite world, which places a limit on how many of us can safely live here at any given point in time.

If there is a limit on how many people our planet can nurture and support, how do we determine what it is? This question is difficult to answer for three reasons. First, it is not easy to determine the parameters we should use to make a calculation of this nature. Secondly, the number of people who can safely live here depends upon the average lifestyle of those living here, and finally, this number also depends upon the levels of technology being used. More sophisticated lifestyles place greater demands on our environment while advanced levels of technology allow more people to live on a given piece of real estate. However, these reservations are not insurmountable, and while the elusive number we are looking for cannot be calculated with absolute certainty, we are able to make a useful determination—or more correctly, a determination that will be useful if we care enough to use it.

Let's recap where we are. We live in a finite world with a limited ability to support human activity, and this limit can be determined with an acceptable degree of accuracy. Where does this leave us? The answer to this question should be obvious, but unfortunately, it escapes most people. If we wish to live on this planet in a manner to which we are accustomed, then we must take steps to keep population levels below the calculated maximum. Saying this is one thing, but doing it is quite another because most people are vehemently opposed to having the government make such a significant intrusion into their lives. There are a number of reasons for this. First of all, most religions hold that procreation is the providence of God and government does not have any say in the matter. Secondly, the right to procreate is considered sacred, and no government should tell people how many children they should have. Finally, in denial of what is intuitively obvious, many people believe that our planet will always be able to accommodate more people, and to limit population levels based upon a scientific calculation is absurd.

It is now evident how difficult solving our problem is. Our social, economic, and religious realities are such that the thought of population control is repugnant. Therefore, despite the dire consequences, instead of addressing the problem, we con each other into believing that our self-destructive thinking is justified. Lost in this mental shell game is the fact that most of us foolishly ignore that we live in a finite world that limits how many of us can live here. Even when this is not lost in the shuffle, we dismiss the whole affair by believing this is something the next generation should worry about. This is where we really go wrong, not because we may have time left, but because thinking this way spells eventual disaster for us all. In any case, the glaring truth we foolishly ignore is that we no longer need scientists to tell how many people can safely live here because the world itself is telling us that we no longer enjoy the luxury of unbridled procreation. The signs of trouble are clearly evident all around us and to not heed them is insane. Yet it is this mass insanity that holds us firmly in its grip.

Following World War II, many scientists realized that population levels were outstripping our planet's ability to support life as we live it. Indeed, in 1968, Paul R. Ehrlich published his book *The Population Bomb*, which warned us that a catastrophe of biblical proportions was looming. Concurrent with the publication of his book, Mr. Ehrlich and several associates formed an organization called Zero Population Growth. The purpose of this organization was to make its title a reality. Forty years of doing nothing has transpired since Mr. Ehrlich pointed out that we have a pressing problem, and for forty years, Mr. Ehrlich, his book, and his organization have been ignored because most of us think that Mr. Ehrlich and his ilk are nothing more than over reactionary people crying wolf about things which are of no real concern to us. What is going on?

Of late, Al Gore, our former vice president, produced a documentary called *An Inconvenient Truth*. In this documentary, we are warned that global warming due to human activity has been recognized by scientists for the past fifty years and is now rapidly reaching a critical point that can only be ignored at our peril. And even when a man of Mr. Gore's stature cries out that a problem exists, people still refuse to listen. The world's glaciers are in rapid retreat, our polar ice caps are melting at an ever-increasing rate, ocean levels are rising, super violent hurricanes and storms are becoming more and more common, and people still refuse to listen. And the reason they refuse to listen is because most world leaders, buttressed by an army of well-paid scientists, are telling people there is no pressing reason to be concerned. What is going on?

Mr. Ehrlich knows what is going on. We are way over the line in regard to how many people can safely live on this planet. Al Gore, who surely knows this to be true, will not even mention overpopulation as being the primary cause of global warming. No, Mr. Gore knows better. If he alludes to the fact that there may be too many of us around, the inevitable backlash will hurt his chances of ever reducing the amount of greenhouse gasses entering our atmosphere, so Mr. Gore confines himself to talking about greenhouse gas reduction and not population control. As vice president, Mr. Gore never told us that he passionately believed that the production of greenhouse gasses by human activity was a threat to mankind. Why didn't he? Why was Al Gore silent about something he passionately believed when the position he held offered him the best opportunity of doing something about it? What is going on?

Glaciers are receding, the polar ice caps are melting, animals are becoming extinct in droves, the rainforests of the world are disappearing, acid rain is destroying our forests, the world's oceans are becoming more polluted, fish stocks are being depleted, dead zones are growing at the mouths of the world's rivers, and we still refuse to acknowledge what is happening right before our eyes. We know we live in a finite world with limits on how many of us can live here. We know that someday it is inevitable that we will have to take steps to limit our numbers. We know that delaying action in this regard makes it far more difficult to solve our problems. We know that delaying too long may make it impossible to solve our problems. We know all of the things mentioned above are happening now, and in light of this knowledge, we still refuse to listen and continue to believe we can go on forever with no concern for the truth that stares us squarely in the face. What is going on?

In 1913, Congress was cajoled, duped, and bribed into passing the Federal Reserve Act, creating the unconstitutional Federal

Reserve Bank. By so doing, America's fate was sealed by a group of conspirators who were now positioned to own and control everything. The hold they had on our government made these men wealthy beyond their wildest dreams and enabled them to create a New World Order. However, no matter how wealthy and powerful these men become, the truth about them and their kind will never change. They are demented, greedy men who place making money above all other considerations. Think not? Then consider the fact that in their lust for power and money, they deliberately compromised and corrupted the greatest government ever devised by mankind. Money and their thirst for it dominate every aspect of their lives and the rule of law is only an inconvenience to them. Anything that stands in their way of making money is repugnant, and this includes human and environmental concerns. They believe their wealth will insulate them from what concerns the rest of us, including the kind of air we breathe, the cleanliness of the water we drink, and our ability to survive as a species on this planet.

What is going on? Our government is controlled by the New World Order and the corporate moguls who run it. These men are not humanists, they are not philosophers, they are not statesmen, they are not scholars, they are not scientists, they are not environmentalists, and they are not honest and responsible people. Instead, they are greedy, self-serving businessmen who, like their forefathers in 1913, place making money above all other considerations. Their drive to globalization was spurred in part so they could avoid the environmental policies adopted by this nation. Our founding fathers feared the ignorant and impressionable masses. These men do not. Instead, unknowing and unthinking people are their biggest assets. This is what is going on! The New World Order is using its power and money to ensure that people do not become concerned about what is clearly happening to us. They do this because they know informed citizens are a hindrance to their continued rape and plunder of our planet. They also know that a stable and sustainable population is incompatible with the monetary system they forced upon us in 1913, a monetary system that requires continually expanding growth, continually expanding markets, and the continued rape of our environment at an ever-increasing rate to remain viable.

What is going on is that in the guise of the New World Order, we are being led by a cabal of greed-driven men who play upon our ignorance and gullibility to keep us in the dark about the fact that our biggest threat is not world terrorism, illegal drugs, or even global warming, but instead our exploding population. In order to survive on this puny, overburdened planet, we need to mount a war against overpopulation, but our New World Order masters will have none of this. Instead, they keep us ignorant while they selfishly work to become richer, never stopping to be concerned about what they are doing to the planet that sustains us. Hogwash you say! Then I say open your eyes because the evidence is all around us. To reiterate, we know that:

- we live in a finite world with a limit on how many of us can live here
- we will have to take steps to limit our numbers
- delaying action makes it far more difficult to solve our problems
- delaying too long may make our problems impossible to solve
- the warning signs of environmental collapse are all around us

In light of this knowledge, most governments including ours ignore what we know and behave as if none of this is true. Governments exist to serve the needs of man, and our first and most important need is survival. We have reached a point in history where only an idiot would conclude that our exploding population is not a threat to our survival, and yet this is exactly what most people believe because our New World Order masters keep it this way.

What are the facts they want us to ignore? Presently, the world population stands at approximately six billion people. Scientists have determined that a sustainable world population is only about three billion people. In other words, there are about three billion people here that shouldn't be. Even more alarming is that world population is still growing rapidly and is expected to increase by half again over the next fifty years to about nine billion people. Complicating this situation and grievously compounding it is that the third world is becoming industrialized at an ever-increasing pace. This means that all our efforts at conservation and living green will do nothing to alleviate the problems we face. Whatever gains we make in this regard will be completely overwhelmed by industrial growth in Asia and other undeveloped areas of the world.

Herein we find the duplicity of the New World Order. They encourage us to live green while they engage in a mad rush to ravage and plunder the remaining undeveloped areas of the world. Add to this the fact that over the next fifty years, there will be three billion more people in the world to sustain, and you should begin to see the hopelessness of our situation. Our problems are dire, critical, terminal, and imminent, yet most people still think our government will save us and do the right thing in a timely manner. And while we foolishly think this, the plundering of our oppressors continues with a vengeance.

In conclusion, the New World Order is led by a group of morally bankrupt criminals who place power and money above all other considerations. Toward this end, in 1913, they saddled the people of this nation with a tax on our income and a monetary system destined to rob us of everything we own. An inherent feature of this monetary system is that its viability is dependent upon the ever-increasing plunder of the world's resources and the unbridled rape of our environment. As a result, today, we are reaching the end of the rope on everything. Our economy, our monetary system, our environment, our atmosphere, our oceans, and the world's ecological systems are failing, and these failures are the direct result of the leadership and policies of our New World Order masters. To deflect the blame from where it rightfully belongs and to keep the con going as long as possible, these men prey upon our ignorance and gullibility. They deliberately keep us in the dark so we can't see what is happening right before our eyes. This is why God is no longer on our side, and this is why we are a species destined to fail.

Postscript

Years ago, miners used to bring a caged canary into the mines with them. They knew that as long as the canary lived, so would they, and when the canary died, they made tracks and got out of there. Today, we watch as the natural world dies off around us. However, unlike the miners, we have nowhere to run. So, what do we do? Instead of addressing the root cause of our problems, which is that the world we live in is overpopulated, we go on and continue to delude ourselves into thinking that more Band-Aids will solve our problems and that the future is rosy and bright—what unmitigated hogwash, what unmitigated delusion, and what unmitigated stupidity. This is our legacy. Humankind is a failed species because of greed and because we are incapable of seeing real danger when it stares us in the face.

ABOUT THE AUTHOR

Alan R. Adaschik was born in New London, Connecticut, on June 27, 1943. He was raised in Brooklyn, New York, and attended Franklin K. Lane High School. Upon graduation, Al was accepted as an engineering student at the University of Michigan in its naval ROTC program. Upon completing college, Al qualified for Navy flight training and received his wings as a jet fighter pilot in June of 1966. After completing his tour of duty, he left the service and earned an MBA from Long Island University.

Al has worked as a flight test conductor for the Grumman Aerospace Corporation, a financial analyst for the Singer Company, a senior financial analyst for Pratt & Whitney, and a financial administrator for the city of Fort Lauderdale. He retired from this position after twenty years of service in 2001. Upon moving to Florida in 1976, Al and his first wife, Pam, opened and managed a school of gymnastics called the Gym Inc. The Gym was the home of the Tumblebees, the girl's gymnastic team, and the Stingers, the boy's gymnastics team. The Tumblebees, under the tutelage of Pam and head coach Tim Rand, became the most successful gymnastics team in the Southeast United States, winning many honors and awards at both the state and regional levels of competition.

Eventually, Al, in partnership with Dann Smith, began franchising Tumblebee mini-gyms in malls and shopping centers throughout South Florida. Nine locations were developed, and Dann and Al had visions of going nationwide with their concept. However, an undercapitalized situation, coupled with the launching of an ill-fated "gym-on-wheels" venture, drove the Tumblebees into insolvency.

When hired by the city of Fort Lauderdale, Al was on a fast track to become department head of the city's Utilities Department. His career came to a standstill three years after being hired when he learned that the Utilities Department was dumping raw sewage into the river that ran through the heart of town. After failing to rectify this situation by himself and not willing to accept this state of affairs, Al enlisted the help of two friends. Their involvement brought the matter to a satisfactory conclusion.

Despite the difficulties Al experienced with his superiors subsequent to the pollution incident, his contributions did not go unrecognized. On March 1, 1988, the Riverside Park Residents' Association honored him with a plaque that read, "In profound appreciation of your many contributions to our community, we acknowledge your dedication, wisdom, generosity, and reliability which have been a foundation of our neighborhood's progress and which have made Riverside Park a better place to live." On November 2, 2001, the day he retired, the mayor and city commission officially decreed the day to be Al Adaschik Day. This honor was offered in appreciation for his dedication, professionalism, and the leadership he had exhibited throughout his career as a public servant.

In 1994, Congress passed the General Agreement on Tariffs and Trade (GATT), which made the United States a member of the World Trade Organization (WTO). According to the Sun Sentinel News, GATT was passed by "pushing sovereignty issues aside." This revelation motivated Al to obtain a copy of the GATT accord. This document revealed that our membership in the WTO was unconstitutional. Acting as his own attorney for the voting citizens of this nation, Al sued our government over the constitutionality of GATT. The court ruled his lawsuit was without merit for technical reasons, and Al did not pursue the matter further.

Subsequent to Al's lawsuit, he wrote a book, available free online, entitled *While We Sleep: A Story of Government without Law*. This book begins with a description of his idyllic childhood, goes on to describe how he stopped the city from dumping raw sewage into Fort Lauderdale's New River, details his efforts to jumpstart his stalled career, and concludes with a narrative of his efforts to undo the harm done to this nation by the passage of GATT.

Al also developed and hosted a website called the Constitution Forum. As host of this website, he authored a plethora of political tracts and articles, many of which are included in the appendix of this book. Al is now retired and lives in Green Mountain, North Carolina.

www.ingramcontent.com/pod-product-compliance
Lightning Source LLC
Chambersburg PA
CBHW021612120626
46545CB00001B/190